IN A LEAGUE OF THEIR OWN!

The Dick, Kerr Ladies

Football's best kept secret

GAIL J. NEWSHAM

Published by Gail J Newsham
Publishing partner: Paragon Publishing

ISBN 978-1-78222-183-8

Book design, layout and production management by Into Print
www.intoprint.net
+44 (0)1604 832149
Printed and bound in UK and USA by Lightning Source

CONTENTS

ACKNOWLEDGEMENTS

Many times over the years I have heard the statement that the Dick, Kerr Ladies story is in the Public Domain. In my experience this is usually said when others seek to gain without giving due credit. Here are two other statements to consider; Facts that have been published as a result of individual research are considered the Intellectual Property of the author. Proper attribution to the author should still be given, even if the work is in the public domain, to avoid plagiarism. Little was known about the Dick, Kerr Ladies until my book was published in 1994 and being the first person to attempt to document the history of the team, I found myself in the unique position of being given a scrap book that actually belonged to Alfred Frankland in 1917 and laterly Kath Latham, covering her time as manager of the team from 1957 to the 1960's. Joan Whalley gave me her scrap book which accurately documents the years from 1937-1952 and Jean Lane's diary record of her years with the team from 1950 until it folded in 1965 was an equally important piece of the jigsaw. Without this exclusive and otherwise unavailable archive information I feel sure it would be virtually impossible to compile such a comprehensive record of the team.

The birth of the internet in 1993 made my work more widely available and many have written about this trailblazing team since 1994, but strangely nothing new appears to have been discovered since my original work. If other research had been done, surely the facts contained in this new publication would have been discovered before now? This has been my inspiration for revising and updating this edition. I want to give the Dick, Kerr Ladies a voice and compile the most factually accurate account of their journey and set the record straight once and for all. Following the success of London 2012 there have been many accolades to some of our elite players as being the best this country has ever produced. As talented as they undoubtedly are, this is not strictly true. There are some pretty amazing women whose contribution to football has been buried for far too long. They also deserve their place in the spotlight and this is my final attempt to do that for them. Without doubt the Dick, Kerr Ladies helped lay the foundations for women's football today. Their contribution should never be diminished so get ready to re-write the record books.

I could not have completed this enormous task however without some invaluable help from the following people. Edna Sibbert told of the origins of the team and other family history, when she exclusively revealed to me the part her mother Grace had played in its formation. Colin Jose sent newspaper reports covering some of the USA tour. Bert Stanley gave me access to his mother Alice's diaries from the 1920s. Tony Frankland donated a photograph album passed down from his grandfather. He told me he had previously offered it to the WFA, but they weren't interested! I also spent hour after hour in the reference library at the Harris Museum in Preston uncovering the early years. Winnie Bourque shared memories of her Mom, Alice Mills life in Preston and USA, and other relatives of the early members of the team helped put the whole story together. I recorded my personal interviews with the players I met - Lydia Ackers, Joan Whalley, Alice Barlow, Nancy Thomson, Kath Latham, Jean Lane, Elsie Yates, Joan Burke, Frances Appleby and Eva Gardner. Their comments should not be presumed to be my opinions. I also recorded interviews with Alec Bolton, the son of Lizzy Ashcroft and John Brown who shared stories from when he worked with Lily Parr. I wish to assert my moral rights to be acknowledged as the owner of all of these recordings. My immense gratitude goes to the very special Lenore McNulty, who faithfully transcribed many of those interviews and saved me an immeasurable amount of time. I am grateful for her love, endless patience, support and advice. Other sources of reference were: Ali Melling, The Munitionettes; The Dick, Kerr Story, by John Price and research by Patrick Brennan helped pinpoint the arrival of Alice Woods to the team and shed more light on the Ladies Football Association. My most sincere thanks goes to the legendary Sir Tom Finney and his family. Words could never express how much I appreciate their support. Special thanks to my dear friend Howard Gore for his advice and superb proof reading skills. Last but by no means least, special love to my sister Pat (LFP); her love and support is unconditional. Remembering too my Mum and Dad (Sadie and Joe); their love still surrounds me every day. Without all of their help a truly amazing account of a unique women's football team would never have been told.

The majority of images are from the extensive personal archive collection of the author unless otherwise stated. Apologies for any omissions in this respect and will be pleased to make appropriate acknowledgement in any future edition.

FOREWORD

In 1937, I was serving my plumber's apprenticeship at a firm which was next door to the fruit shop owned by Alfred Frankland, the manager of the Dick, Kerr Ladies Football Club. It was thought at the time that women's football was something new, but of course this was wrong, as they had already been playing for twenty years when I first heard of them.

I did take an interest in the team and kept in touch with their progress, and I knew even in those days that they travelled all over the country playing the game and that they were very successful. I remember being invited to referee at several of their matches and being presented to the girls. There wasn't very much women's football played in those days and to actually see them play was quite remarkable. Some of them were very good players and they always had big crowds at their matches. I knew that the Football Association did not look very kindly upon them, and it was thought that we, as professional players, should not encourage the women's games. I personally couldn't see that they were doing any harm, especially when they were helping so many people by raising such a lot of money for charity.

But that's all behind them now. The FA are promoting women's football and the future looks very good indeed. Perhaps this is due in some way to the grit and determination of those factory girls from Preston, who played on after the FA ban and helped to lay the foundations for the women's game today. Their incredible playing record speaks for itself and their formidable reputation is well deserved. Given the rich history of football in Preston, we can all be proud that The Dick, Kerr Ladies went on to become the most successful women's football team in the world. This book is a fitting tribute to all they achieved.

Sir Tom Finney

CHAPTER ONE
THE REUNION

I grew up in Preston just a stone's throw from the Dick, Kerr works on Strand road. For more years than I can recall this factory was at the heart of the town and provided jobs for thousands of families for generations. Even to this day many people have relatives who worked there and they all have their own stories to tell and as long ago as I can remember, I do recall hearing tales of a football team called the Dick, Kerr Ladies. My Dad also told me he had seen them play and what a good team they were. I couldn't quite understand how they were allowed to play though because when I was growing up football was exclusively for boys. Girls playing football simply wasn't allowed and we had to be content with either hockey or netball and I hated them both with a passion.

As a young lass growing up in the early 1960's, I was always out playing football with the lads either in the street or on the local parks and being the only girl in either team, I heard comments from passers-by suggesting that perhaps I too should be playing for the Dick, Kerr Ladies. They were quite well known and always portrayed as a very skilful side and I remember thinking how unusual it was for there to even be a ladies team and how lucky they were to have the opportunity to play in a proper match. Although I had never seen them, I envied them nontheless.

In the late 1960's women's football began to flourish again and the North West Women's Football League was formed in 1970. I began my football career in the early 1970's with Peter Craig Ladies before moving on to Preston Rangers. I was a steady and reliable left back and utterly dedicated to my sport. We were a good team and had success along the way playing in two WFA Cup semi finals. We were also League and Cup double winners in the mid 1980's.

Although I didn't know then, the photograph of Preston Rangers (below) was taken on Ashton Park on the area known as Lively Polly Corner where the Dick, Kerr Ladies used to play and train. We would often do our training there too. How uncanny is that! I have many happy memories of those times but we had little, if any support from the Lancashire FA and this was sometimes very frustrating. The old fashioned attitudes towards women's football were very evident and everything we did was all self-administered and self-funded. In spite of this I think it is safe to say that we did succeed

Preston Rangers 1982.

Back row: Chris Shepherd, Gail Newsham, Bev Hills, Oonagh Matthews, Carole Carr, Sally Pilkington, Louise Coleman, Sheree Livesey, Jim Clitheroe.

Front row: Jayne Mottram, Michelle Haylett, Lynn Arstall, Wendy Skerritt, Alison Farnworth, Sandra Graham, Julie Hindle, Tina Clitheroe

and for many years I also served on the League Management Committee in various officer positions and I was later presented with a special award for services to women's football.

In 1986 I was responsible for setting up The Lancashire Trophy, a two day residential International Women's Soccer Tournament which at the height of its success was regarded among the best in Europe. During its lifetime teams from Austria, Switzerland, Germany, Sweden, Eire, Scotland and England all competed to be the winners of the Lancashire Trophy.

Football was played all day Saturday and Sunday and the winners received their medals at a gala presentation evening when we entertained them with a star cabaret and disco. Over the years we had guest appearances from Geraldine Rees, the first female jockey to complete the Grand National racecourse on her horse 'Cheers'. Shirley Strong, the toast of British women's athletics after she won a silver medal in the 100 metre hurdles at the 1984 Olympic Games in Los Angeles. Sheila Ferguson, former lead singer with The Three Degrees, who entertained us with her superb talent on four occasions. And top class comedienne Mia Carla who was always a big favourite with the audience. It was a fabulous weekend with a wonderful atmosphere which captured the true spirit of what this very special tournament had come to represent. Winning it was a bonus, being part of it is what really mattered.

Gail Newsham and Sheila Ferguson 1988

To this day I am incredibly proud of what was achieved at The Lancashire Trophy and the warmth in which it is still remembered. Here is a letter I received from Martin Reagan after he came to visit us one year which still brings a lump to my throat. Martin was the former manager of the England Women's National team and he also soldiered with my Dad during WW2.

Dear Gail,

A brief note to thank you for your courtesy, kindness, and hospitality during my visit to your tournament. I know you had so much to do and many matters to attend to, and your attention was greatly appreciated.

The surroundings and the atmosphere of your tournament were excellent

and you deserved to succeed. Football played in those conditions, and in that way, is a great credit to the game, and is an example for others to follow. You brought a lot of pleasure to a great number of people over the weekend and I hope that you think that all your efforts were worth while. It was a great pleasure to meet up with you again and to renew friendships with others.
Kind regards,
Yours sincerely,
Martin Reagan

In the Spring of 1991, I had my first ever meeting with a former player from the Dick, Kerr Ladies. Brenda Eastwood was guest of honour at a local women's football tournament presenting medals to the winning teams. Formerly Brenda Keen, she had always dreamed of playing football for the Dick, Kerr Ladies but this seemed highly unlikely to happen. She was born with a serious heart defect and her parents had the constant fear that she would die. However after years of medical supervision she was given a clean bill of health when she was 19 years old and she never looked back. She wrote to the manager of the team asking if she could be given a trial and against all the odds, Brenda made her debut in goal in the first post war fixture played at Glossop on Good Friday 1946 in front of 5,000 spectators.

As a result of meeting Brenda I had the idea of trying to organise a reunion of the Dick, Kerr Ladies to meet up again at our tournament during Preston Guild year 1992. The competition had been included on the official list of events and this was the first time a women's football tournament had been recognised in the official Guild calendar. Given the history of women's football in the town and the prestige of our event having Guild status, I wanted to do something extra special at The Lancashire Trophy. As the Guild occurs only once every twenty years I thought that in all probability the 1992 celebrations were likely to be the last opportunity they would have to be together at such a special time in Preston's history.

The origins of Preston Guild began in medieval times. In 1179 King Henry II granted a charter to the town and this privilege was renewed in further charters granted by later Kings and Queens of England. The Preston Guild Merchant was initially set up to protect traders from outside competition. Anyone who wanted to trade in Preston had to be a member of the Guild Merchant or suffer the consequences. Members of the Guild would meet to discuss official business but these meetings were generally infrequent and came to be regarded as a reunion and joyous gathering. It therefore evolved to become an occasion of civic celebration and great festivity. Since then Preston has celebrated this historic charter with all kinds of trade fairs, pageants, processions, carnivals, concerts and street parties all over the town. Ex-Prestonians living in all four corners of the world still return home for these unique week-long celebrations. What better time to try to stage a reunion of the world famous Dick, Kerr Ladies?

I asked Brenda if she knew the whereabouts of any other members of the team so that we could get the ball rolling. She had a telephone number for Joan Burke. That was a good start so I called to explain what I was trying to do and arranged to meet and have a chat with her about it. Joan Burke (Tich), began playing for the team in 1939 when she was just 14 years old. She lived on Marsh Lane and was kicking a ball about more or less as soon as she could walk and she used to run rings around her brothers. In fact all the lads in the area wanted her on their team! When she was very young she was spotted playing football on a nearby bit of spare land known as Coulthards pad by Alice Kell, the first player to captain the Dick, Kerr Ladies back in 1917. Alice had watched Joan's skills develop over the years and thought she would be an ideal player for her former team when she was old enough. Tich showed me some old photographs from her playing days and I could hardly believe the size of the crowds on the touchline. She told me this was the norm, they always had thousands watching them. I had no idea that so many people actually went to watch women's football. They certainly didn't in my day. If we had the manager and two subs on the touchline we were lucky and I couldn't quite get my head around it. Tich loaned me the photograph and I contacted the local press to see if they could help me locate more players. It turned out to be very successful.

As a result of the publicity I went to see Frances Appleby who first played for the team in 1946. She had a couple of old newspaper clippings from *The Daily Herald* of that year and I was amazed by the length of the match reports she had carefully preserved. I had no idea they had received such extensive media attention. This was a light bulb moment for me. Thousands turning up to see them play and generous columns of newspaper coverage? It didn't take long to realise that this was a big story, bigger than perhaps anyone could ever imagine, yet there was nothing officially documented about these women and their achievements. Something needed to be done sharpish or there was a danger their history would be lost forever. The next lady I visited was 78 year old Edna Clayton. Edna had played for Dick, Kerr's in the early 1930s. Sadly, she had suffered a slight stroke some years earlier which affected her memory and she could remember only snippets of her days with the team. But she took me to meet Lydia Ackers who was 88 years old and living in a residential home for elderly gentlefolk. Lydia was a bright old lady who was eager to share her memories of those far off days. She had a twinkle in her eye as she recalled her time playing football in the 1920s. *"We were famous you see, and everybody wanted to see us"*, she said.

Several more former players got in touch and in total I was able to locate seventeen of them. They were eagerly anticipating what lay ahead and plans for their very special day came together extremely well. I am proud to say that on Sunday, 2 August 1992, at The Preston Guild Lancashire Trophy, the Dick, Kerr Ladies were reunited for the first time in almost forty years. Some of them came along during the day to watch the football and they were thrilled to be part of the women's game again. It was wonderful to see the reactions from the younger players too when they realised that the Dick, Kerr Ladies had arrived. They were eager to meet them, have their photographs taken with them and get their autographs. The Press covered the story of their reunion and the BBC came along to film the occasion. In spite of the length of time since they had last kicked a ball together, The Dick, Kerr Ladies turned back the clock to show they were still big news. The reaction to the mere mention of their name after all those years was a credit to them and the respect and admiration given to football's elder stateswomen was a joy to behold. But tongue in cheek they said that *they* had played the best football when they were at their peak! In those days of course they played with heavy leather balls which would absorb water when it was raining and consequently required a lot of force behind the kick to lift it. Joan Whalley said, *"These balls they use today are wonderful. I managed to get the chance to kick one earlier and I thought it was marvellous. I wish they would have had those when I was playing"*.

No one had seen or heard of Joan Whalley for years. There were rumours that she had *'dropped out'* from society and become something of a recluse but they knew little of her life or whereabouts. She really was quite a shy lady who would rather avoid the limelight and it had taken a lot of gentle persuasion to get her to agree to come along and join us. I was concerned that had she been aware of the film crew she might have stayed away, so we decided the best plan would be to keep it secret until she arrived. By then it would be too late for her to escape.

We entertained them with a VIP champagne reception and a Civic flavour was added to the occasion by the Mayor, who came along to offer an official welcome to everyone on behalf of Wyre Borough Council. It was wonderful to see them greet one another with hugs, kisses and tears of joy and as they reminisced about 'the good old days', the years in between just seemed to melt away. They were youngsters again reliving old times and the champagne was flowing as they celebrated their long overdue reunion. What a wonderful night it was for '*my ladies*' and the event would change the remainder of their lives.

Together for the very first time in all those years were:- Joan Whalley, Dorothy Whalley, Edna Clayton, Joan Burke, Frances Appleby, Marjorie Foulkes, Audrey Coupe, Muriel Heaney, June Gregson, Jean Lane, Brenda Keen, Barbara Prescott, Sheila Parker and Barbara Widdows. Joan (Tich) Burke said: "*Suddenly, as I walked in the door, all I heard was, 'Oh Tich is here', then I was surrounded by everybody because we hadn't seen one another for such a long time. Years had gone by but it was just as though we'd never been apart. We just seemed to click into one again, and that was it*".

The Reunion 1992

Back row seated: Barbara Prescott, Frances Appleby, Marjorie Foulkes, Edna Clayton, Jean Lane, Joan Whalley, Dorothy Whalley, Audrey Coupe Front row: Barbara Widdows, June Gregson, Brenda Eastwood, Muriel Heaney

Interviewed by the BBC Joan Whalley said, "*It's been well over 30 years since I saw any of these girls and I have thoroughly enjoyed seeing them and meeting old friends over again. None of us have been in contact but over the last few minutes it's been like travelling back in time. It's a wonderful feeling.*

You get very lonely when you get older, you miss all the girls and you miss the comradeship. It's a wonderful thing really when you are all in a team". Frances Appleby said, *"It's lovely to see everyone again, I've looked forward to this night for weeks and weeks".* June Gregson was reunited with her best friend Barbara Prescott. Both girls would sit together on the bus when travelling to and from matches. June fought back tears as she said, *"Coming back and seeing all these people here today is absolutely fantastic and I miss it".*

It's impossible to put into words just how special this experience was for all of us and I was choked with emotion as I saw just how much the night had meant to them. I was so proud of *'my ladies'* and it was indeed a great honour to meet them and be the one responsible for bringing them back together. We can all be guilty of looking at older people and forgetting they were ever young. But not on this night; we all had the common bond of being football players, we were as one.

Expectation and excitement had been gathering momentum in the main function room as everyone anticipated their arrival. An evening like this had never happened before and when the moment finally came, the present day players gave the Dick, Kerr Ladies a standing ovation and erupted into deafening cheers, whistles and applause as these legends from the greatest era of the women's game came in to take their seats. It was a fitting tribute to all they had achieved so long ago. The World Famous Dick, Kerr Ladies were back together! Muriel Heany said, *"As we walked in, they were all clapping and cheering, it was brilliant, it took our breath away. Never in our wildest dreams could we have expected anything like it. The girls were all saying things like, 'Oh, it's the Dick, Kerr Ladies, look it really is Dick, Kerr's. What it was it like when you played?' It was lovely to receive a reception like that"*

When all the formalities were over we gave a surprise presentation to honour them and commemorate their reunion in Guild year. They each received a copper engraving of a Preston scene with the inscription, *'PRESENTED TO DICK, KERR LADIES, PRESTON GUILD 1992'.* I introduced them to the audience individually and brought them on to the stage one by one. Each was given a rapturous welcome and they seemed deeply moved by the warmth of the reception. At 78 years of age, Edna Clayton was the oldest member of the team present on the night. I informed everyone of this as Edna came up to receive her award. An extra loud cheer was given to her and Edna raised her arm in acknowledgement as she gracefully accepted the applause. I purposely kept the introduction of Joan Whalley until the end to enable the rest of the Dick, Kerr Ladies to join in applauding her on to the stage. I knew they all had a deep respect for her and I wanted her to see just how much regard everyone had for her. In women's football she was a legend in her own lifetime. It was a wonderful moment for her as she received the applause of her peers, and the whole room erupted with cheers and whistles for this truly remarkable woman, which she modestly accepted while wondering what all the fuss was about. Her quiet, secluded and lonely existence would never be quite the same again.

After the trophies had been presented to the winners and all the formalities done, it had become something of a tradition for one of the girls to hijack the microphone and give us a song. There was something rather special about the Lancashire Trophy that brought people together, and this particular part of the whole weekend was always warmly anticipated. Maria Harper from Merseyside was the lady in question. She played for Knowsley United, (now Liverpool Ladies). Maria was a very talented and gifted football player and a popular young woman full of that wonderful scouse wit, who was not afraid of the limelight, and her singing voice wasn't all that bad either! This year, Maria dedicated her song to the Dick, Kerr Ladies. The song she chose was, *'Those were the Days'*. It really was quite a moving experience as the whole room joined in with her to pay their own tribute to these very special ladies. *"Those were the days my friend, we thought they'd never end, those were the days, oh yes those were the days"*.

It truly was an unforgettable occasion which far exceeded anything I could ever have hoped for and I was sure the night would stay etched in their hearts with many special moments for each to treasure. They swapped addresses and pledged not to lose touch again. These ladies from the greatest era of the women's game were back together and the name with which they were all so proud would continue to live on. Frances Appleby said they felt as though they had been treated like royalty but it was nothing more than they deserved. They are women's football royalty!

The whole event though was soon to be tinged with sadness. Less than forty eight hours after such a fantastic evening, Edna Clayton passed away. She had been ill for some time and it was touch and go whether she would be well enough to make it to the reunion, but thankfully she found the strength to be with us. Everyone was deeply shocked and saddened at the suddenness of her passing and none of us could quite take it in. I had felt a bond with Edna, a feeling of belonging that usually only comes with knowing a person for many years and it seemed too soon to be saying goodbye. We had only just begun to get to know one another. But when you put things into perspective, I don't suppose the timing could have been more perfect. Death is inevitable for all of us and I guess we all hope we can leave this earth with some kind of dignity. Thankfully Edna was granted that and the last days of her life were spent celebrating the success of The Dick, Kerr Ladies. We can perhaps take some comfort in the knowledge that before she died she had the recognition of her part in this world famous team and for that at least, we can all be grateful.

As a result of the reunion, Frances Appleby and Joan Whalley were able to renew their old friendship and began writing to each other every week. When they were younger they lived just a few streets away from one another. Thankfully they had the opportunity to catch up on past years, share their memories and hopes for the future. Brenda Eastwood took charge of keeping them all in touch and their next meeting was another great success. They invited me along and it was wonderful to sit and listen to them reminiscing about the days when they were the toast of women's football and it was plain to see how happy they were to be back together again. Behind the scenes they had secretly organised a surprise for me and I was completely gobsmacked when *they* presented *me* with a trophy. The engraving read, *'TO GAIL, PRESTON GUILD 1992, COMMEMORATING THE REUNION OF DICK, KERR'S LADIES FC".* Words seemed inadequate at that moment as I tried to search for something that would appropriately express my gratitude. I felt a deep sense of pride for bringing them back together but I wanted them to know just how much they had all come to mean to me and I knew that The Dick, Kerr Ladies would be part of my life for the rest of my days. And that trophy still takes pride of place in my home and in my heart!

This book is a testament to them and is dedicated to each and every one of those remarkable women who, throughout their incredible 48 year history, have left us with such a glittering legacy. They have shown just how much can be achieved even when all the odds are stacked against you. No matter how much opposition and prejudice they encountered, their

My Trophy

16

spirit could never be broken. Joan Burke said, *"I don't think you can learn to play football, it's born in you, and even today if there's a tin or anything that comes in front of me, I'll kick it. I can't help it".* Joan Whalley said, *"But for this book, all the old members of the Dick, Kerr Ladies would go to their graves forgotten forever, but this will keep us all alive in the pages of history".*

Hopefully it will and future generations will know of their incredible success story. Let The Dick, Kerr Ladies take their rightful place in the Sporting Hall of Fame and receive some of the long overdue recognition their fantastic achievements deserve. Women's football should now have a greater sense of its own history. Let us all help take football's best kept secret from those dark forgotten corridors and make The Dick, Kerr Ladies, and all its players, the household names their unequalled success demands! They are our sporting heroines and they should be given the same accolades that we readily give to our top sportswomen today. They have waited far too long for their own place in the spotlight. This is their story.

CHAPTER TWO

KICKING OFF

Around the turn of the last century, women's attitudes to their place in the world were beginning to change. They were 'coming out of the kitchen' and wanted to contribute more to the society in which they lived and were damanding the right for their voice to be heard. Women wanted to work, they wanted to vote and they wanted to play. They were no longer prepared to accept that they were any less capable than the rest of the male population. Many women thought that the Victorian values of simply being expected to marry and have children were no longer acceptable. They were finding a much bigger agenda. The Suffragette movement was proof that women wanted to determine their own lives as they fought for the right to vote. In 1915 Emily Davidson stepped out in front of the King's horse at the Derby and tragically died from her injuries. Emily Pankhurst was later arrested after a protest rally at Buckingham Palace where she had chained herself to the railings. Clearly the wind of change had begun to blow and a womans place in the so-called 'pecking order' was about to change forever.

The outbreak of war in 1914 demonstrated that these changes were not only needed but were a necessity. The 1914-18 war was regarded as the war to end all wars and the loss of human life was unimaginable. The battlefield had to be fed with a constant supply of weapons, ammunition, food and medical supplies, and the demand for them increased as the war continued. But as Lord Kitchener's image reminded men ***"YOUR COUNTRY NEEDS YOU"***, the country also needed women too. They were the nation's hidden army, and they began to take up their places in the work force as fast as the men were leaving for the battle fields.

Women were no strangers to working in factories, but during the war the amount of manual labour undertaken by them was greatly increased as more and more were needed to help keep the war machine alive. Being thrown together at such a terrible time and all fighting for the same cause, a new comradeship between them was being born and teamwork was the order of the day.

Women worked in munitions during both World Wars but many people are not aware of the kind of work they did, or just how tough the conditions were. From operating the most complicated machinery, to work in farming, there were women in every position. They could even be seen lugging hundredweight (100 cwt) sacks of coal from the mines on their backs. A small concession to them being the 'weaker sex' was the introduction of this 100 cwt sack instead of the usual 200 cwt. (100 cwt = 112 lbs which is 8 stone). In fact any job that needed to be done to keep the country going and help us win the war, there is no doubt that women played a vital role in achieving that aim.

Those women working in munitions became known as the *Munitionettes*. They were exposed to dirty and dangerous conditions involving the use of toxic chemicals and heavy machinery. They were expected to work extremely long hours and regularly put their lives on the line. The most visible side effect of munitions work was to be seen by those women who had the task of filling shells with TNT. This highly explosive chemical caused the hair and skin of the workers to turn yellow and this was a visible sign of toxic jaundice. Hence, they earned the nickname, *Canaries*. The first deaths from toxic jaundice caused by TNT, were reported in 1915 and at least 349 known cases of serious TNT poisoning were registered during the war. There was no treatment for it; doctors simply stood by and waited to see if the patient recovered. Added to that was the constant danger that the TNT might explode unexpectedly. If this did happen, the women would suffer facial injuries resulting in the loss of eyes and fingers and sadly some of them did die from their wounds.

Clearly, the Munitionettes didn't have an easy time of it, but having said that, many women were empowerd by the war. They may have lost husbands, sons and brothers, but despite their devastating loss, they gained a new self confidence from being thrown into male spheres, proving they could more than hold their own, in equal if not superior terms.

But with thousands of munitions girls being drafted into towns it became obvious that after work activities needed to be arranged to help keep them occupied. The Government appointed women welfare supervisors and sent them into the factories to oversee the moral and physical well being of the girls. They were also responsible for encouraging the development of sporting activities and among the many recreational activities arranged for them was football, and football became the official sport of the munitons girls. Almost every factory across the United Kingdom involved in war work, had a ladies football team. Many may have only played against other departments within their own factories, but teams were recorded from one end of the country to the other.

But even through those most difficult times, ladies playing football was not completley unheard of and maybe this is where the inspiration came from. The first recorded ladies football match actually took place in March

1895 at Nightingale Lane, Crouch End Athletic Ground in North London. Middle class feminist Nettie Honeyball, founded The British Ladies Football Club and organised a game between the north and south. Nettie was quoted in *The Daily Graphic*, *"I founded the association late last year, with the fixed resolve of proving to the world that women are not the 'ornamental and useless' creatures men have pictured. I must confess, my convictions on all matters where the sexes are so widely divided are all on the side of emancipation, and I look forward to the time when ladies may sit in Parliament and have a voice in the direction of affairs, especially those which concern them most".* She saw no reason why women should not be allowed to particiapte in more physical sports and as such, advertised to find enough girls to play *"a manly game and show that it could be womanly as well".* They practiced twice a week on a pitch close to the Alexandra Palace Racecourse.

However Nettie was not the only forward thinking member on the board as Lady Florence Dixie had consented to become President of the club. Lady Dixie and her twin brother James Douglas, were the youngest children of Archibald, the 7th Marquis of Queensberry. She was a war correspondent for the London Morning Post and covered the Zulu wars. She was also a novelist, travel writer, and an excellent horsewoman who championed the cross saddle position for female riders, (when interviewed for the *Women's Penny Paper,* the reporter concluded that she was *'made of heroic stuff that knows not what defeat means')*

The result of the ladies match was a 7-1 victory for the North and although the football skills of both teams left a lot to be desired, they showed a great deal of enthusiasm for the game even though they were reported to have forgotten the rules and didn't even change ends at half time. A reporter in *The Sketch* was quite scathing when he said, *"Let not the British Ladies misconstrue the enormous attendance into a sign of public approval. They had attended purley out of curiosity. Now that novelty has worn off it would not attract tens (of people) where on Saturday it attracted thousands. It must be clear to everybody that girls are totally unfitted for the rough work of the football field. As a means of exercise in a back garden it is not to be commended; as a public entertainment it is to be deplored".* A female correspondent writing in the *Manchester Guardian* also said of the match, *"When the novelty has worn off, I do not think that women's football will attract the crowds".* Despite the harsh criticism other matches were arranged by Lady Dixie during 1895, which were mainly played in her native Scotland.

But it was in Preston, Lancashire, where the most successful team in the history of women's football was born. Formed at Dick, Kerr and Co Ltd, these very ordinary working class girls would quite literally, take the country by storm.

The Dick, Kerr Factory

The firm of Dick, Kerr and Co Ltd was named after its two Scottish founders, William Bruce Dick, and John Kerr. In the mid 1890's John Kerr became involved with a group of businessmen with plans to set up a tramway rolling stock and electrical works in Preston. They bought a disused factory and the company was registered in 1898. This formed the nucleus of the traction works at Preston and the company became the leading British firm for the traction industry and were responsible for the electrification of railway from Liverpool to Southport in 1904. The factory turned its attention to the production of ammunition during the first world war.

The country was desperately short of ammunition when war broke out in 1914. The Admiralty and War Office approached Dick, Kerr and Co Ltd to undertake the manufacture of shells for both armed services. Works manager James Conner, was given the task of converting the company into a munitions factory for which he received an MBE. When re-organisation began practically the whole of the works' equipment was unsuitable for the production of ammunition and had to be replaced. The first batch of shells were bonded on 3 March 1915. This was the start of an output of missiles that reached some 30,000 a week and during the war period, a total of 3,300,000 of all calibres including both light explosive and shrapnel were produced.

Machine Shop making Shell Components

Preston had been a Garrison Town since the completion of Fulwood Barracks in 1848 and this was where countless young men enlisted for battle during the First World War. Local lass Molly Graham, was a child growing up near the barracks during that time and she shared some war-time memories which give a tiny insight into life for the community during those difficult days.

"We lived off Deepdale Road, and I remember me and my Grandmother watching the soldiers leaving for war. They were on trams going up and down to the train station from 7 o'clock in the morning till 12 o'clock at night, you'd wonder where they all came from, there must have been thousands of them. They were only young lads and were all dressed in khaki. They were in high spirits and singing their hearts out and every tram was so packed they even had to stand up. My Grandmother frightened me when she said,"You know love, a lot of those lads will never come home again".

It has to be said that the vast majority of young men were swept along on a sea of patriotism all eager to fight the Germans. They thought going to War would be a big adventure that would probably be over by Christmas. It seemed a perfect opportunity to travel and escape the harsh conditions they had endured working in the cotton mills.

Here is an example of a typical soldier from Preston. 12453 LCPL Joe Newsham, 7th Battalion Loyal North Lancashire Regiment, killed during the Battle of the Somme on 23 July 1916. Molly may have even seen him pass by on one of the many trams she saw. There is no known grave for this young man but his name is inscribed on the Thiepval Memorial as a tribute to the many fallen. He was my great uncle. My Dad was named after him and he was always incredibly proud of his namesake.

Molly continues with her recollections

Lance Corporal Joe Newsham

"I remember when I was a kid, we used to collect money for the wounded soldiers at Moor Park Hospital. We'd buy packets of Woodbines for them and they'd cry when we gave them the cigarettes, they seemed really sad. They wore blue uniforms with red ties so that they could be distinguished from other soldiers up at the barracks. After they'd been home a while, I know some of them didn't want to go back to France knowing what they had to face at the front. I know of one occasion when my Dad's two mates refused to go back and the Red Caps (Military Police) came and took them. My Dad went to war but he didn't like leaving us four children. It was hard. It was tough for the women who were left behind too but us kids didn't really understand, we didn't bother about the war. We weren't frightened until the sirens sounded and then we would hide under the table. They didn't bomb Lancashire so much but my friends sister worked at White Lund (munitions factory) in Lancaster and she got blown up by a shell. A lot of Lancashire women got hurt".

"I went to school with the daughter of Pte Young who was awarded the Victoria Cross. They made such a big fuss to honour his bravery and gave him a Civic reception with the Mayor at the Town Hall. I think everybody in Preston must have been there when he got his medal. He was very badly wounded, he didn't live long after that".

Born in Glasgow in 1876, William Young was awarded the VC for bravery whilst serving with the 8th Battalion, The East Lancashire Regiment. He returned to the trenches more or less as soon as he had left hospital following treatment on his eyes after being gassed. He saw his sergeant fall injured in

23

front of the wire and volunteered to bring him back. Acting without orders and oblivious to the dangers of enemy fire, he climbed over the top of the trench and went to save his sergeant. He managed to get him as far as the parapet when he was hit by two bullets, one shattering his jaw, the other entereing his chest. His commrades tried to get him back to safety but he refused to move until his sergeant was safe. With the help of another soldier, he brought his wounded sergeant back to safety and then walked to the medical station to have his wounds attended to.

He was married with eight children and like most men who perform heroic tasks, he was extremely modest about his achievement. Even his wife knew nothing of it, *"I could never draw from my husband any account of how he won his VC"*, she said. Pte Young was brought back to England for treatment and was given a civic reception in Preston. A fund of £560 was raised for the benefit of his family. Sadly he didn't live long enough to enjoy the honour and never actually received his award personally from the King. He died at the Cambridge Military Hospital in August 1916, whilst undergoing an operation on his jaw. He was buried in Preston and received one of the most magnificent funerals ever remembered by the people of the town.

As we have already established, during the 1914-1918 war, ladies football teams were being formed up and down the country as a means of raising much needed funds for charitable causes, but the north of England saw the sport flourish more quickly than in other parts of the land. But the ladies of Dick, Kerr and Co Ltd in Preston, were about to make a bigger impact on the game than they could ever have dared to imagine.

Their incredible journey had its humble beginnings in, of all places, the factory yard! During tea breaks and lunch times the girls would often join in with the lads while they were having a kick about. A regular member of these friendly games was Grace Sibbert. She was an outspoken young woman who was always game for a laugh. It was October 1917 and the lads football team were going through a bad run having lost several of their recent games. They were beaten quite heavily that weekend and were taking some flack from Grace and her friends in the works canteen. *"Call yourselves a football team? We could do better than you lot!"* The lads didn't like having their noses rubbed in it so they challenged the girls to prove their skills in a proper match. Grace accepted the challenge immediately saying, *"Come on girls, let's have a go, it'll be a laugh"*. They accepted the challenge and the arrangements were duly made for the game to be played on on a field in the Penwortham area of Preston. Although there is no record of the result it was obviously a very enjoyable pursuit for the girls as they were soon to continue with their newly formed football team.

The first ever photograph of the unofficial Dick, Kerr Ladies following their match with the lads shows several of the girls who went on to play in the original team. Grace is pictured on the front row with the ball on her lap. She was allowed to keep the match ball as a 'thank you' for getting the team started. She was delighted with the gesture and made sure it was with her on the team photo.

First ever picture of the girls, 1917

Back row: Mrs Cross, unknown, Florrie Rance, unknown, G Whittle, unknown, Annie Crozier?

Middle: unknown, E Clayton unknown,

Front: unknown, Grace Sibbert, unknown, Alice Standing

Grace was born in 1891. Her father was a greengrocer but liked to spend a lot of his time in the pub and he was very unpleasant when under the influence. On the eve of her wedding day, Grace and her Mum had been busy preparing food for the reception. After the pub had closed, he came home in a drunken rage and threw almost everything on the fire. She was heartbroken and couldn't believe he could be so cruel. She hated him for it and cried herself to sleep. Of course he was full of remorse the next morning and the wedding went ahead as planned with the guests being none the wiser. She married John James Sibbert (Jimmy) on 29 November 1913.

Jimmy joined the Loyal North Lancashire Regiment and fought on the Somme in France during the war. The Battle of the Somme was one of the great offensives of the First World War. It began on 1st July 1916 and continued until the end of November. The British and French Armies attacked the German positions on a front of 25 miles. The total British losses in this great battle were almost 500,000 men. Jimmy was captured and taken prisoner and suffered at the hands of the Germans. Grace meanwhile had been drafted to work at Dick, Kerr's in munitions as part of the war effort. She also worked as a photographers model to help make ends meet. She prayed for Jimmy's safe return and when he was finally released she travelled to London to welcome him home but he would never talk about his ordeal in the prison camp. Unable to have children of their own, they adopted two young girls, Edna and Myra, who had been placed in the local work house. As a single parent, Edna's biological mother was forced to give her up for adoption because the scandal of being an unmarried mother had brought shame on the family. Thanks to the Sibberts, Edna was given the chance of a very good life. Jimmy died in 1955. Grace passed away in 1963.

Not long after the October match with the lads at the factory, the Matron of the local Moor Park Military Hospital approached the Dick, Kerr factory to ask if the girls would help raise much needed funds for the wounded soldiers over the Christmas period. The Moor Park Hospital had been established to treat service personnel wounded during the First World War and was originally no more than an Agricultural Pavilion. It was extended several times to eventually include an operating theatre and remained in use until 1919. The Matron suggested a charity concert as a possible venture for the fund raiser. The welfare of employees and their dependants already in the Forces had not escaped the concerns of either the directors at the factory or the workers. A relief fund had already been set up to aid their families. Subscriptions were given weekly by the workforce and the firm added a similar amount to the total. Over £20,000 was distributed in relief and many familes benefited. The reputation of the company was enhanced because of its charitable donations and as the only major munitions manufacterer in the town, they were an obvious choice in the approach by those at the Moor Park Hospital. The request from the Matron was met with great enthusiasm by the girls who were delighted to be able to help. Alice Kell said, *"The Matron asked if we would help with concerts, but we decided on football instead".* There where so many girls at the factory who were keen to play in the football team that trials needed to be held to choose the best players. Alice said, *"The team was chosen from about 200 members of the ladies sports club."* Unfortunately ill health prevented Grace from taking any further part in the football team when she was struck down with tuberculosis and the family eventually moved to the countryside.

It was Alfred Frankland who was soon to take charge of the team. Born in 1882, he was the youngest of 10 children living at the family home in Freckleton, just outside Preston. He worked at Dick, Kerr's as a draughtsman in No 6 Department Office and may well have been a member of the sports and social club which might explain his involvement. From his office window, he would often watch the girls playing football with the lads in the factory yard and he obviously saw a great potential waiting to be nurtured. He sought permission to arrange the match from Mr Conner the works manager. Mr Conner needed little persuasion to support the idea and Alfred Frankland became the team's mentor. He possessed excellent organisational skills and had an obvious flair for marketing and the Dick, Kerr Ladies were about to become his 'dream ticket.'

The neighbouring Arundel Coulthard Foundry on Marsh Lane accepted the challenge to play in the charity football match and arrangements were made for the game to be played at Deepdale, the home of Preston North End. At a meeting held on 6 November 1917, the minutes from the North End Board read as follows:

Resolution 3: Resolved that the Board allow the female munition workers match with Dick, Kerr's v Arundel Coulthard & Co to be played on Christmas Day.
Resolution 4: Resolved that a charge of £5.00 be made for the use of the ground on Christmas Day - the money so received to be given to charity.
Resolution 5: That the match on Christmas Day be advertised on Preston North End's posters, with the munition workers to pay a proportion of the cost.

At the next meeting on 13 November 1917, the Board must have been in a more generous mood as they decided to waiver the £5.00 charge for use of the ground. The match was given quite a high profile and was advertised in the local paper as being a 'Great Holiday Attraction'.

Christmas Day 1917 saw the start of a remarkable venture into the sporting arena for these very ordinary working class girls from Preston. They had prepared well for the game and were taking things very seriously in the run up to the match but in the dressing room before the big occasion nerves were getting the better of some of them. It was all such a daunting experience and they could hardly take in that they were actually about to play football in a proper stadium. They were nervous and excited at the same time and didn't know what to expect before they ran down the players tunnel. Alice Kell had been given the job of team captain and tried to calm them down with some words of encouragement, *"Come on girls we can do it, just remember we're doing it for the soldiers."* With hearts pounding twenty to the dozen, they ran down the tunnel into the arena and could hardly believe their eyes as 10,000 spectators were there to greet them. This was the start of what was to become the most phenomenal success story in the history of women's sport.

Coulthard's played in red and white stripes and Dick, Kerr Ladies played in black and white stripes with the addition of neat close fitting hats to match but the wearing of corsets was barred! The game was refereed by Mr John Lewis of Blackburn and the 'kick off' was performed by a Miss Hollins. The match report in *the Daily Post* reads:

After their Christmas dinner the crowd were in the right humour for enjoying this distinctly war-time novelty. There was a tendancy amongst the players at the start to giggle, but they soon settled down to the game in earnest. Dick, Kerr's were not long in showing that they suffered less than their opponents from stage fright, and they had a better all round idea of the game. Woman for woman they were also speedier, and had a larger share of that quality, which in football slang is known as 'heftiness'. Quite a number of their shots at goal would not have disgraced the regular professional except in direction, and even professionals have been known on occasion to be a trifle wide of the target. Their forward work, indeed was often surprisingly good, one or two of the ladies displaying quite admirable ball control, whilst combination was by no means a negligable quality. Coulthards were strongest in defence, the backs battling against long odds, never giving in, and the goalkeeper doing remarkably well, but the forwards who were understood to have sadly disappointed their friends, were clearly affected with nerves. All the conventions were duly honoured. The teams on making their appearance (after being photographed) indulged in 'shooting in', and the rival captains, before tossing the coin for choice of ends, shook hands in the approved manner. At first the spectators were inclined to treat the game with a little too much levity, and they found amusement in almost everything from the pace, which until they got used to it, has the same effect as a slow moving Kinema-picture, to the "how dare you" expression of a player when she was pushed by an

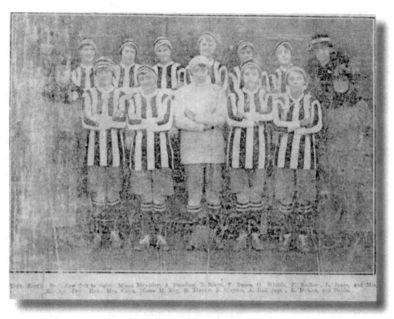

The Dick, Kerr Ladies

Back row players: Alice Standing, E Nixon, Florrie Rance, G Whittle, Florrie Redford, Lily Jones

Front row: M Kay, B Traynor, E Clayton, Alice Kell (capt), E Birkins

opponent. But when they saw that the ladies meant business, and were 'playing the game' they readily took up the correct attitude and impartially cheered and encouraged each side. Within five minutes Dick, Kerr's had scored through Miss Whittle, and before half time they added further goals by Miss Birkins, a fine shot from 15 yards out, just under the bar, and Miss Rance. Coulthards who were quite out of the picture in the first half 'bucked up' after the interval, and quite deserved a goal, but it was denied them, much to the disappointment of the spectators. They had a rare opportunity from a penalty in the last few minutes, but the ball was kicked straight at the keeper. On the other hand, Dick, Kerr's added to their score, Miss Rance running through and netting whilst the backs were 'arguing' about some alleged offence, a natural touch which greatly delighted the onlookers. Mr John Lewis plied the whistle with discretion, whilst keeping within the four corners of the law, though he was clearly in a dilemma, probably for the first time in his official career, when one of the players was 'winded' by the ball.

More positive comments about the game were also found an article in Mr Franklands scrap book:

Coulthards Ladies

Back row players: N Charnley, M Coates, C Waring, J Rangley, L Rayton, A Billington

Front row: B F Proudfoot, L Atkinson, A Sumner, L Forshaw (capt), T Fitzgerald

PRESTON GIRL MUNITION WORKERS AT FOOTBALL

About 10,000 people witnessed the match, easily the biggest crowd that has been seen this year at the historic enclosure. The majority no doubt went with the object of being amused, but all agreed at the end that the quality of football shown was much better than they had expected. One or two individual performances indeed were surprisingly good, particularly in regard to what the expert describes as "ball control". These outstanding players showed that they had made considerable progress in the dribbling art, and they could put a good deal of power into their kicks, whilst their attempts at shooting at goal were by no means to be despised.

The result was a 4-0 victory for the Dick, Kerr Ladies as they notched up the first of many famous victories, and raised in excess of £600 for the wounded soldiers at the Moor Park Military Hopital. (According to www.thisismoney.co.uk, the £600 raised in 1917 would today compare to a value of £38,364) Everyone was incredibly proud of what was achieved that day and hardly slept a wink all night. This was only the beginning. They could hardly believe the wonderful life changing event they had just experienced and were thrilled at the huge amount of money their efforts had raised for the wounded soldiers. But equally important was their victory and all agreed they wanted to continue to play football if they could. Mr Frankland was more than happy to oblige with the running of the team and so the Dick, Kerr Ladies Football Club was officially established.

Following their initial success, further games were organised with the intention of raising money for servicemen and their families affected by the war. Such was the scale of those who perished on the bloody battlefields of war torn Europe that few families were left untouched by the conflict. Several of the girls in the team had also lost brothers and they too were trying to come to terms with the devastation of their own loss. The demand placed upon charitable organisations at this time was at saturation point and the new wave of ladies playing football for charity was met with great enthusiasm. Ladies football was without doubt a growing spectator sport. Naturally the novelty aspect probably played a big part initially, but the skill and dedication shown by these girls was enough to ensure the respect of the public and the Dick, Kerr ladies were fast becoming a household name. They found themselves in much demand and were enjoying their new found celebrity status. Signing autographs and posing for the camera soon became the norm for these ordinary Lancashire lassies. They also received a great deal of support and encouragement from the management at Dick, Kerr & Co Ltd and their fame also ensured a higher profile for the company.

Alice Kell was an excellent choice as the first ever captain of the team. Born in Southport in 1899, as a young girl she played football with her brothers and this is no doubt where she developed her skills. Her father was a ticket enquiry clerk on the railways and when his job brought him to Preston, her parents Joe and Clara set up home on Marsh Lane. She had two sisters, Ethel and May, and four brothers, Sid, Reg, Alf and Tom. Brother Tom was born in 1890 but he was tragically killed during the first world war after enlisting with the Preston Pals. The family were devastated and life was never quite the same again. Reg and Sid were very good footballers and played for two Lancashire teams, Morecambe and Lancaster. Her family was always very proud of her and thought she was a wonderful football player. Alice became an integral member of the team, not only for her ability on the football field, but her diplomacy and natural leadership qualities made her the ideal choice as the team's figurehead.

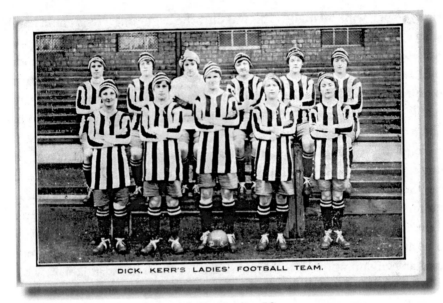

DICK, KERR'S LADIES' FOOTBALL TEAM.

Dick, Kerr Ladies FC

Back row: unknown, E Birkins, E Clayton, B Traynor. Alice Kell, M Kay

Front: Alice Standing,Florrie Redford, Florrie Rance, E Nixon, Lily Jones

But it wasn't all plain sailing. There were of course others on the horizon who were totally opposed to the whole concept of women playing football. The hangover from late Victorian values of women being involved in any sporting activity was still very much apparent. Sport had remained a generally closed world for working class women and girls. Many thought a woman's only role in sport was to merely stand on the sidelines, watch and applaud. Others believed that the female frame simply wasn't built for such a rough game and playing football could damage their health. As ridiculous as it sounds, there was a belief that sport was unnatural for women and strenuous games, especially during puberty and menstrual periods, would drain energy from vital organs, damage their bodies and seriously affect their fertility. Molly Walker who played for the Dick, Kerr Ladies during those years was a real victim of these absurd opinions and treated as an outcast by her boyfriend's family because of their disapproval of her wearing shorts and showing her legs.

It is important however to clarify the support and co-operation given to ladies football at that time from the male bastion of soccer. That initial support was no doubt based upon the patriotic nature of their fund rasing activities and the Preston North End Board were extremely supportive to the

Dick, Kerr Ladies. We must remember that this was early 1918, the world was fighting a bloody war and women's rights were not high on anyone's agenda. Indeed it wasn't until the General Election later that year that women over the age of thirty were allowed to vote for the very first time and it wasn't until 1928 that it was lowered to twentyone to bring them in line with men.

It is clear that ladies football had quickly been recognised as a means of making money for charity and further obvious from the North End Board meetings that they saw the ladies matches held at Deepdale to be profitable for them too. The large crowds attending the Dick, Kerr matches generated additional revenue at the ground and it would appear to be a mutually beneficial arrangement for Deepdale to be the 'home' venue for the Dick, Kerr Ladies. Extracts from the Preston North End Board meetings read:

5 February 1918 - Resolved that we allow Dick, Kerr and Co Ltd the use of our ground for two ladies football matches on 23 February and Easter Monday on the following terms: We take charge of the gate and pay over to Dick, Kerr and Co 80% of the net gate. That is after all expenses incidental to the match are paid. 26 February 1918 - That the day of the ladies football match be altered from Easter Monday to Good Friday and use of the ground be allowed also on 9 March. Both matches on similar terms to the match played on 23 February.

Making her debut in a 2-0 victory over Barrow YWCA on 9 March 1918, was 15 year old Annie Crozier. Annie worked as a weaver at Brockholes Cotton Mill and went along to a meeting when she heard they were looking for more players. Annie later went on to become the team's physio.

On Good Friday, 29 March 1918, the Dick, Kerr's team took on Bolton Ladies, notching up another victory with a 5-1 scoreline. Kicking off the match was a nine year old Judith Todd. The invitation to kick off the game originally went out to Judith's mother who was a prominent local figure in Liberal politics and war charities. She would have appeared to the organisers as a suitably distinguished female to officiate at the match. Perhaps Mrs Todd thought it highly undignified, as well as almost physically impossible, to stand in the middle of a football arena and kick a ball while wearing a long skirt, fur stole and large hat of the period. Consequently her daughter, Judith, was offered as a replacement. Judith remembered being very excited at the prospect and hoped to be allowed to wear a pair of blue shorts like the Dick, Kerr Ladies. But this was deemed out of the question and her final strip was a short navy skirt and white jersey. *"You're to come off directly you've kicked it"*, said her father. *"You're not to stay and play. Do you understand?"* She was rather disappointed at not being allowed to join in but was more enthusiastic after her father gave her a short lesson in the garden on the correct way to kick a football. "*All I remember of the actual event was hearing the referees whistle, successfully kicking the ball as instructed, and then obediently running back to the stands, weaving professionally as enormous figures rushed passed me in pursuit of the ball*". Children of that era were not encouraged to think too highly of themselves and it wasn't until some 30 years later that Judith's mother allowed her to see the letter received from Alfred Frankland, dated 3 April 1918. It reads: *Dear Miss Todd, I am instructed by the Ladies Football Committee at these works to thank you sincerely for so kindly taking the 'kick-off' on the occasion of the match played at Deepdale on Good Friday. You performed your duties in an excellent manner and in such a way that pleased the crowd. Faithfully yours, Alfred Frankland. Hon. Sec.*

The Dick, Kerr players were obviously very keen to keep up the momentum of their winning start and wanted to work harder to become fitter and faster than their opponents. The charitable nature of the games was very commendable and they wanted to do everything they could to help the needy, but make no mistake about it, these women wanted to play football, they wanted to win and their aim was to be the best. By the close of the 1917-18 season, the ladies had played four matches at Deepdale and although the records on gate receipts are a bit sketchy they were attracting significant numbers of spectators.

DATE	TEAMS	RESULT	CROWD	GATE
25 Dec 1917	DK v Coulthards	4-0	10,000	£600
26 Jan 1918	Lancaster v DK	1-2	?	?
9 Feb 1918	Barrow v DK	1-1	?	?
23 Feb 1918	DK v Lancaster	1-1	5,000	?
9 Mar 1918	DK v Barrow	2-0	2,000	?
29 Mar 1918	DK v Bolton	5-1	6,000	£200

Players grabbing the headlines during these games were: Florrie Redford, Alice Standing, Florrie Rance, and the press said of Alice Kell that she '*worked with a skill that no professional player could have excelled*'.

Florrie Rance was to find romance when she met an Australian soldier being cared for at the Moor Park Hospital. Hastings Booth had been wounded in France when his thumb was shot off by a German sniper. He was sent to Preston to recuperate and they met one day while she was out walking with her sister. He asked for directions to a local tea shop and invited them both to join him. Romance soon blossomed and after a whirlwind courtship, they were engaged and married. She continued playing for the team for the next few months as Mrs Booth.

In May of 1918, an application made from the Dick, Kerr Ladies to practice at Deepdale was granted by the Board and in August the ground was offered to them under the following terms:-

1. *£12.00 for a Saturday match.*

2. *£3.00 per week for training on Tuesday, Wednesday, and Thursday of each week during the daytime. Special arrangements to be made for holiday fixtures.*

By the start of the new season, Dick, Kerr's had once again approached the North End Board for use of the Deepdale ground. Extracts from the minutes are as follows:

27 August 1918 Resolved that Dick, Kerr Ladies Football Club could rent Deepdale for season 1918/19 on the following terms:-

1. *£12.00 for a Saturday match with Dick, Kerr's agreeing to take the ground for at least ten matches.*

2. *£20.00 for Christmas day.*

3. *£1.00 a week for training three days a week on Tuesday, Wednesday and Thursday during the daytime. The renting of the ground for training for the whole season or any part thereof is at Dick, Kerr's option. Payment to be made on the Monday following each match.*

In an article published in *the Lancashire Daily Post*, headed, **"LADIES FOOTBALL JUSTIFIED"**, it is interesting to note the sentiments of the reporters comments: *"When munition girls began to invade the football field, some of the old shell-backs scoffed at their usefulness both in a playing sense and as an attraction, and not even the fact that they were devoting their energies to the help of War charities seemed to abate the objections in some quarters. In Preston, the movement has been fostered instead of decried, and in the Dick, Kerr's eleven we have had perhaps the best ladies team in the country. The girls have had the benefit of enthusiastic sponsors and capable mentors in Jack Warner and now Bob Holmes, and the balance sheet of their last season's activities, furnished me by Mr A Frankland, to whom much of the success is due, is a convincing answer to those who derided or frowned upon their football existence. The statement shows that the fine sum of £804 10s 5d was raised, and that after amusement tax of £105 4s 7d, and rent of ground amounting to £61 4s 1d had been paid, together with general expenses that are eminently moderate, a net balance of £553 17s 1d remained. Of this £338 1s was given in July as a donation to the Moor Park*

Training at Deepdale

Left to right: Jessie Walmsley, Florrie Redford, Alice Kell, Molly Walker, Emily Jones, Nellie Mitchell, Jennie Harris

Hospital, and now £190 16s 1d of the residue has been divided amongst the War charities. The lump sum handed over to the Moor Park Hospital consisted of the proceeds of the match with Coulthards team at Christmas, in connection with which no expenses were paid, and it should be added that a further sum of £150.00 which does not appear in the accounts, was given to the hospital by the firm of Dick, Kerr & Co. This financial result can only be described as magnificent, and a tribute to those who have organised the team and have played in it. It is not necessary to consider here and now whether ladies football will survive the War. The point is that it is serving an altogether admirable purpose at the moment. I know that if one of the recognised League clubs had raised such a sum for charity it would have regarded it, and quite legitimately so, as a great achievement. How much more so, then, a body of girls who combine a means of exercise and relaxation from their arduous work, a means of helping a number of splendid charities? In the light of such a result, it is good to know that the club is going forward this season with greater zest and better prospects than before".

Questions arise from the figures quoted in this article which states that 'a fine sum of £804 10s 5d was raised'. Assuming the gate receipts for away games were kept by the home team, if £800 was raised from two games at Deepdale between Coulthards and Bolton, is it feasible that the remaining sum of only £4 10s 5d was raised from the other two games against Lancaster and Barrow with a combined gate of around 7000 people?

The Lancashire Daily Post, reported there was *'distinctly a public for ladies football',* and clearly the Dick, Kerr Ladies were building a good reputation and attracting big crowds at their matches. Alice Kell and Florrie Redford were emerging as two very skilful players and were frequently mentioned in match reports. However, the management at the club were keen to recruit talented lady footballers to help Dick, Kerr Ladies become the best and were always on the look out for new players to strengthen the team.

The new season began on 7 September 1918 and the ladies attracted a 'big crowd' at Deepdale for their match against Vickers of Barrow. They continued their unbeaten run recording a 1-0 victory over the Barrow side with a goal scored by Molly Walker, their new outside right from Lancaster Ladies. Molly must have impressed Alfred Frankland in their previous matches and for the purpose of our records Molly is likely to have been the first player transferred from another club to the Dick, Kerr Ladies.

7 September 1918   DK v Vickers   1-0
Team: E Clayton, Florrie Redford, Annie Crozier, E Birkins, Alice Kell, Miss Waring, Molly Walker, Miss Richards, Nellie Mitchell, Alice Standing, Lily Jones
21 September 1918 Whitehaven v DK 1-1 (Redford)
5 October   1918 DK v South Lancs Tramway (Atherton) 7-0 crowd 1500
Team: E Clayton, B Traynor, Annie Crozier, E Birkins, Alice Kell, Nellie Mitchell, Alice Standing, Molly Walker, Florrie Redford, Lily Jones, Miss Richards.

On 9 October 1918 the team suffered their first defeat at the hands of Whitehaven Ladies and it hurt them deeply. The match was played at Deepdale in front of a good 'gate' and they were beaten by 2-0. Team: E Clayton, B Traynor, Annie Crozier, E Birkins, Alice Kell, Miss McAvoy, Molly Walker, Alice Standing, Florrie Redford, Lily Jones, Miss Richards

2 November 1918   DK v Barrow   away win (3-0 @ half time) crowd 2000

The country was jubilant as it celebrated the end of the war and a welcome peace descended upon the nation. As the guns fell silent, the peace treaty was signed at 11 oclock on 11 November 1918. The cost of human sacrifice was unimaginable. A total of eight-and-a-half-million personnel had lost their lives. Never before in history had the world witnessed such a devastating conflict and life would never be quite the same again. As people tried to rebuild their shattered lives the demands placed on local charities was at saturation point and the need for charity football matches was just as great as ever it was before and the Dick, Kerr Ladies were more than willing to meet the challenge head on. They played their first peacetime match at Deepdale on 23 November 1918. Their opponents were from the British Westinghouse works, Manchester. The Manchester side were no match for the home team who had a comfortable 4-0 win. Once again, Kell and Redford stole the headlines and were the star players. Team: E Clayton, Florrie Redford, Annie Crozier, E Birkins, Alice Kell, Florrie Booth, Molly Walker, Alice Standing, Nellie Mitchell, Jessie Dickinson, Lily Jones.

Christmas was just around the corner and the need for charitable donations were hightend with the emotional demands placed on families over the festive season. The Dick, Kerr Ladies set about their task in earnest and a busy fundraising December lay ahead. A match was arranged at Deepdale on 8 December against L & Y Railway Co (Manchester). Team: Miss Walmsley, Florrie Redford, Annie Crozier, E Birkins, Alice Kell (capt) Florrie Booth, Molly Walker, Alice Standing, Nellie Mitchell, Elsie Arnold, Lily Jones. Result unknown.

They played Lancaster Ladies at Deepdale on 21 December and suffered only their second defeat going down 1-0. Lancaster had the two best players on the pitch in Jennie Harris and Jessie Walmsley. Annie Hastie in goal also gave a good account of herself. However, if Nellie Mitchell and Elsie

Lancaster Ladies

Arnold had taken the easiest of chances in the second half, Dick, Kerr's could have won the game. Team: Walmsley, Redford, Crozier, Birkins, Kell, Booth, Walker, Mclean, Mitchell, Arnold, Jones.

The skills of their opponents did not go unnoticed by Mr Frankland who wasted no time in strengthening the team for the Christmas day fixture with Bolton Ladies. His powers of persuasion had convinced more girls to play for the Dick, Kerr Ladies. The factory also seemed quite prepared to take on any of the girls wanted by Frankland to improve the squad. Four days after helping Lancaster to victory over Dick, Kerr Ladies, Annie Hastie and Jennie Harris, were in the line up with the Preston side. Jennie Harris had already carved out a well respected reputation for herself as a very skilful football player. She even had a song written about her during her playing days in Lancaster:

You've heard talk about professionals, that once got a rattling wage
But I will mention still another one, who is marked on history's page,
To play the game called football you would scarce believe your eyes
So just drop down to Lancaster, It will take you by surprise.
To see a bonnie lassie, friends by gum she's earning fame
She plays for the Projectiles and Jennie Harris is her name.
She really is a marvel and astonishes the crowd
For when she scores a brilliant goal, the spectators shout so loud.
You would think the heavens opened when Jennie does appear
For her dribbling down at Preston caused many a hearty cheer.
The toffs they do admire her, left their lady's in fine style
To fall in love with Jennie, the little wench from the Projectiles.

Eight thousand people went to Deepdale on Christmas Day 1918 and saw a thrilling game between Dick, Kerr Ladies and Bolton Ladies which resulted in a 2-2 draw. The score represented the merits of both sides and although the pitch was on the heavy side, the game was played at a remarkable pace. Bolton took the lead through Florrie Haslam who, after receiving the ball in her own half, outpaced all the opposition to score a very good goal. Molly Walker equalised for Dick, Kerr's just before half time. After the interval, M. Gibbons put Bolton in the lead, but Nellie Mitchell made it 2-2 after driving home a cross from Molly Walker. The receipts which totalled about £180 were divided amongst local charities. Team: Annie Hastie, Florrie Redford, Annie Crozier, E Birkins, Alice Kell, Florrie Booth, Molly Walker, Alice Standing, Jennie Harris, Nellie Mitchell, Lily Jones. This was the last match for Florrie Booth before she and her new husband left Preston to begin a new life in Australia. Hastings Booth was originally a dairy farmer from a small place called Temagog in New South Wales. At her farewell party she was presented with a silver purse engraved with the words: *Presented to Mrs F Booth by the players and committee of Dick, Kerr Ladies.* Her arrival in Australia actually caused something of a scandal as Hastings was already engaged to a girl in the village! Florrie soon settled into her new life and ran the post office from their home. She even rode around on horseback delivering the mail.

The first game of the new year was played against another Bolton team on 10 January 1919. Jessie Walmsley, playing at centre half, was yet another Lancaster player in their line up. They now had four players in their side who originally started with Lancaster Ladies. Team: Annie Hastie, Jessie Dickinson, Annie Crozier, E Birkins, Jessie Walmsley, Lily Jones, Molly Walker, Jennie Harris, Nellie Mitchell, Elsie Arnold, Florrie Redford (capt). Kell unfit. (No result given)

The Dick, Kerr Ladies 1919

Back row: Alice Norris, Alice Kell, Annie Hastie, Annie Crozier, Jessie Dickinson, Jessie Walmsley, Lily Jones, Lily Lee

Front row: Molly Walker, Emily Jones, Nellie Mitchell, Jennie Harris, Florrie Redford

One of seven children, Jessie Walmsley was born in Lancaster circa 1896. As a child she had a lucky escape after being struck by lightning and burnt down one side of her face, but the scars never detracted from her infectious smile that could light up a room. Jessie had also known the tragedy of war as her younger brother was killed in battle in 1914. The family were brokenhearted. He was just 16 years old. She was a nurse at the Lancaster Moor Hospital and this was her vocation. She risked her own life trying to save the lives of others during a major fire and massive explosion at the National Projectile Factory at White Lund, in October of 1917. Shrapnel travelled for several miles in all directions and local people had to be evacuated to the surrounding countryside. Ten bodies were recovered from the ruins. Jessie was involved in the rescue operation and later commended for bravery. To protect national security, the disaster was not reported in the press and the cause of the explosion was never discovered.

Jessie Walmsley

The 25th January 1919 saw the Dick, Kerr Ladies entertain Heywood Ladies at Deepdale. Heywood were asked to put together the strongest team from the area they could muster so that they would provide a good opposition to what was perhaps the strongest ladies side playing. The Heywood side were made up of some of the Bolton team and the Dick, Kerr Ladies were fielding their best team with Alice Kell now fit to play again. Team: Hastie, Kell (capt) Crozier, Birkins, Walmsley, Jones, Walker, Harris, Mitchell, Arnold, Redford. (Result not given)

Women's football was becoming increasingly more popular and teams were travelling further afield in order to meet fresh and stronger opposition. On 8 March 1919 Dick, Kerr Ladies played Newcastle United Ladies at Deepdale in their last home match of the season. The Newcastle team had built up a good reputation and they travelled overnight to play the fixture. Winnie McKenna was their leading goal scorer with 130 goals to her credit. The Preston team were taking no chances and strengthened their side with the inclusion of three members on loan from Bolton Ladies. They were Misses Rawsthorne, Hulme and Partington. Newcastle played in claret and white to avoid a colour clash. The game had been very well advertised but torrential rain had an adverse affect on the number of spectators at the match but there were still enough present to pay over £179 to support both teams. Nellie Mitchell scored the only goal in a 1-0 win for the home team. The Dick, Kerr eleven played strong and determined, and if Mitchell had been able to capitalize on other chances that came her way, they would have won by a bigger margin. This was the first time that the Newcastle side had been defeated. Walmsley, Jones, Kell and Harris were the pick of the home side but the whole eleven worked well and fully deserved their victory. Team: Hastie, Kell (capt) Hulme, Rawsthorne, Walmsley, Jones, Walker, Harris, Mitchell, Partington, Redford.

The return match at St James Park, Newcastle was played in front of 35,000 people. The Preston team included their new signing, Florrie Haslam from Bolton Ladies who came the closest to scoring in the 0-0 draw. In the first half, the home team had the advantage of both wind and sun, but the defence of Kell, Hulme and Hastie, especially the former, was splendid. The cleverness of Lyons in the Newcastle attack was always a source of danger. The second half however saw the Dick, Kerr team have all the play forcing five corners in quick succession, but they were still unable to find the net. The press reported that it was a memorable spectacle, reminiscent of the pre war League days due to the huge crowd and thousands of others being unable to get into the ground due to the inability of being able to cope with the crush.

The 29th March 1919 saw the Dick, Kerr team travel to Yarrow Bridge to play Bolton Ladies. The match was arranged by the local branch of the Chorley Discharged Sailors and Soldiers' Association and welcomed a good crowd who enjoyed a fine performance by the Preston team to secure a 2-0 victory with goals from Florrie Redford and Jennie Harris.

Plans were underway by the firm to organise a 'Peace Day' in memory of those employees of the Dick, Kerr works who fell during the Great War 1914-1919, and Ashton Park was dedicated to the fallen with a list of names of all the men who died. The 83 acre site was to be used as a sports and recreation ground for the company's employees. It had a cricket pitch, a nine hole golf course, tennis courts and a football pitch. There was a mansion house on the park where a memorial plaque with

Peace Day Programme

the names of the fallen were commemorated. The football pitch was situated at the corner of Blackpool Road and Pedders Lane and was surrounded by wooden hoardings to make it a private enclosure. It was known locally as 'Lively Polly Corner', due to posters advertising the washing powder of the day, 'Lively Polly', being pasted on the hoardings all around the exterior of the ground. The park was officially opened by Sir Charles Ellis GBE, KCB, at an opening ceremony on 2 August 1919. The event, which took months to arrange, was a large scale affair with large numbers of activities taking place all day.

Local girl Alice Norris began her working life at Dick, Kerr's in 1919 when she was 14 years old and was asked if she would like to play for the ladies team. She went with her father to meet with Mr Frankland and discuss the possibility. It was decided that she would be allowed to play on condition that it didn't interfere with the family. *"So I was put down as first reserve for when anybody finished",* she said. Born in Preston in 1905, she was employed by the company until her retirement in 1965. *"I worked at Dick, Kerr's until it was sold and became English Electric and then eventually it became BAC."*

Alice Norris

Alice remembered playing football with the apprentices at the back of the works. *"We used to play at shooting at the little square windows in the cloakroom. If the boys beat us at putting a window through we had to buy them a packet of Woodbines, but if we beat them they had to buy us a bar of 'five boys' chocolate. The senior foreman came down one day and said very firmly, 'If any more of those windows get broken, the next one responsible will be sacked!' Well, sure enough it was my turn to shoot and I was hoping and praying that the ball would miss, but knowing my luck, it didn't. The boss came down later and asked who had broken the window. I owned up to it but my chargehand (lady supervisor) didn't believe me, she thought I was shielding someone else. The boss decided to let it go but warned us we'd be sacked if it happened again."* Alice says of the team, *"There was a good friendly spirit at the club, you didn't hear anyone arguing with one another and it was a privilege to play for them. The older players took care of the younger ones and I remember Florrie Redford was very good to me. When we played on First Division grounds there would usually be a reception for us after* the game. On one occasion there was this lad who had taken quite a shine to me and he was making a bit of a nuisance of himself. I did my best to get away from him but he wouldn't take no for an answer. Florrie could see what was going on and came across to tell him to leave me alone. He told her, "Get lost, it's none of your bloody business", but she said, "I'm making it my business, she's my kid sister and if you bother her again, I'll have you outside!" That's the way they were all the time. Florrie Redford and Alice Kell would keep an eye on you to make sure you were alright. It was like being part of a big family. They were good days you know, we had some great times".

There was obviously a very good atmosphere at the club with a great camaraderie between the girls and success followed success. By the end of 1919 they were well and truly established as the team to beat and the next few years would see them achieve more than they could have ever dared to dream of.

At the beginning of the 'roaring 20s' the momentum for the team was beginning to build and more and more games were arranged for them. They were to lose their first match of the new decade to Liverpool Ladies by 2-0 on 7 February and they suffered a further defeat losing 1-0 at Wigan on 10th April. The goal scorer for Liverpool was a young lass named Alice Woods and she was to become the next major signing for the Dick, Kerr Ladies. Alice was already a top class sprinter, she could run a hundred yards in twelve seconds and became the first woman to win a race held under AAA laws (Amateur Athletics Association). This historic meet, the first in England to allow women runners, took place at Blackpool in 1918 when thirteen female athletes ran the race over 80 yards.

Alice began playing football while working at a munitions factory in Sutton, St Helens. She knew that her mother wouldn't approve of her playing and was worried what she would say if she found out. She confided in her older brother Jack about being asked to join the factory team because she was really keen to play for them. Jack played centre forward for Halifax Town and Alice always looked up to him. He said to her, "There's no need for Mum to know". He showed her on a blackboard what the positions were and taught her how to head, kick, trap and dribble with the ball. She learned quickly and her natural speed was always a great asset. Alice recalls, "We got this team up to play for charity, I captained the team and we won. We had heard about this Dick, Kerr's team who had been playing quite a while then and we played them a few times. They thrashed us 5-0 but we managed to beat them twice. We played them at Springfield Park, in Wigan (10 April) I scored a goal in the first half and we won 1-0. In the reception afterwards this Mr Frankland, who managed the

St Helens Ladies. Lily Parr back row 3rd player from right.

Dick, Kerrs, came to me and asked if I would like to play for them. At first I said I didn't think so but he contacted me during the week and after talking to my brothers, it was agreed that I could play for them". She was justifiably flattered with the attention from Mr Frankland and perhaps the imminent French visit made the decision more attractive. Alice became an immediate member of the team and decided to concentrate more on her football career rather than athletics. She scored her first goal for the Dick, Kerr Ladies against the French team on 1 May 1920.

Perhaps the most significant signing for the Dick, Kerr Ladies was that of 14 year old Lily Parr who arrived at the club only a short time after Alice Woods. Newsreel footage confirms that Lily was not part of the team for the first international match with the French Ladies at Deepdale. It is highly likely that she arrived soon after their match with St Helens on 8 May.

Lily was already playing football for St Helens and Alice Woods suggested to Alfred Frankland that she would be a good asset to the team. In her first season with the Preston side, she scored an incredible 43 goals.

Mr Frankland made all the arrangements for Lily to come to Preston and met her at the train station in St Helens. Alice Norris said, *"I can't just remember who we were playing but Lily was coming with us and we had to pick her up in St Helens. When the train pulled up at the platform she was sat on a skip reading a comic".* Alice goes on, *"My mother agreed to have Lily stay with us on*

Dick, Kerr Ladies 1920

Molly Walker, Daisy Clayton, Lily Lee, Alice Kell, Alice Woods, Lily Parr, Emily Jones, Jessie Walmsley, Jennie Harris, Florrie Redford, Annie Hastie

condition that she share my room. We lived in a three bedroomed house. I had my own room and my younger twin sisters shared the other but when Lily came to stay and we took her up to see the room she threw me out and my nightclothes came out after me! I didn't get back in my room much after that, not while Lily was staying with us. I think my mother must have felt sorry for her because when I tackled her about it she said, "Oh, she's alright, just leave her to it". She got another single bed for me and I slept in with the twins".

Alice and Lily were the same age, but from totally different backgrounds. Being thrown together as they were, an unlikely yet strong friendship grew between them. Lily was the young tear-away who was unaccustomed to rules or boundaries and Alice was bound by the rules and restrictions laid down by her father. There was perhaps a little envy between the two girls. Lily of Alice's family life and Alice of Lily's couldn't care less attitude wishing she could be more like her. Without doubt, there was a great deal of mutual respect between the two girls. Alice said, "*Oh, she did used to boss me about. Not in a nasty way of course, but let anybody else try it, and she were there like a shot!*"

Lily Parr was born on 26 April 1905. She was the fourth of seven children born to George and Sarah. The family lived in a rented property and life was pretty tough. Lily though was definitely a *'one off'* and the old saying of the mould being broken when someone was born was certainly true for this lady. A dominant football player, she would continue playing the game she loved until 1951 and was probably one of the greatest women players of all time. Standing almost six feet tall, with jet black hair, her power and natural talent were admired and feared, wherever she played. She was a totally unselfish player with amazing ball control and could pin-point a pass with amazing accuracy. Surprisingly though she was rather shy when meeting new people and found it extremely difficult to speak in public. When formalities were being exchanged at post-match receptions, she didn't have the confidence to speak to a room full of people, one sentence was about as much as she could manage. She would rather her feet did the talking on the pitch!

On one occasion the team were playing a match at Chorley, in Lancashire, and as they were warming up before the kick-off, Lily was challenged by a professional male goalkeeper. It was his opinion that a mere woman would never be a match for any man. He said, *"You might look good kicking in against other women, but you'd never score a goal against me".* Never one to shirk a challenge Lily suggested he stood in goal while she took a shot at him. She placed the ball on the penalty spot, ran up and kicked it towards him as hard as she could. As he put his hands up trying to save the shot, the sheer power behind her kick broke his arm. She had a satisfied grin on her face as she watched him being ushered away for treatment.

Lily Parr

Something of an enigmatic figure, Lily was the original 'rough diamond' with a heart of gold. Some described her as being a bit rough, and perhaps a little abrupt in her manner, but deep down she was a kind and decent human being. If you were her friend, you were a friend for life. She didn't worry about rules or regulations though and if she wanted to do something, she just did it. Coming from the poorer end of St Helens, she had to be strong to survive and she was used to looking after herself. There wasn't much work available in her home town so a move to Preston to work and to play football was a golden opportunity to improve her prospects. Alice Norris says of a teenage Lily Parr, *"She had an enormous appetite, she could eat for England. I'm sure my mother must have been out of pocket with her. What I found strange about her though, was during all the time she stayed with us, I never once heard her speak about her family. She seemed a bit of a loner and never mentioned anything about her home life. My Mum and Dad used to ask me if she ever talked about her parents, but she never spoke of anyone, she were a bit of a mystery really.*

When we played football with the apprentices, we used to club together to buy a sixpenny ball from Woolworths. One particular time, my twin sisters had been quite ill and were going to stay in a convalescent home near Blackpool. I thought it would be nice for them to have one of these balls to take with them. In those days we didn't have anything like as many toys as children have today and things were precious. So, as I was working overtime I asked Lily if she would take this ball and give it to father for the girls. When I got home and asked him about it I couldn't believe it when he said he'd bought it off her. "I paid her sixpence for it, just like she asked", he said. But that was Lily, you never knew what she was going to do next. You couldn't help but like her though".

But Lily really did care for Alice and was very protective of her. Alice goes on, *"One time we were playing up in Scotland and Lily was getting annoyed with this girl who kept running past her. It was a windy day and she had her hair in a plait. The next thing we knew, she ran past Lily again and Lily grabbed hold of her plait and pulled her back. The spectators thought it was really funny but when we were coming off the field after the match the girls mother got hold of me and she gave me a jolly good telling off. When Lily saw what was going on, she came to the rescue and sorted her out. She said, "You've got the wrong one mrs it was me, are you going to have a go at me?" But she wouldn't have a go at Lily".*

She had a deep voice, but was a quietly spoken lass with a droll sense of humour and she often had people in fits of laughter at her quick witted comments. This particular incident occurred around 1921 when it was fashionable to wear straw boater hats decorated with imitation fruit. The team were travelling home on the coach late one night and a couple of the girls needed a toilet stop. The driver pulled up by a wall but the girls were unaware that on the other side was a reservoir with a steep embankment. In the darkness Jennie Harris leapt over the wall and tumbled down the embankment, quickly followed by Lily Parr. Most of the others were still half asleep on the bus and were unaware of the commotion on the other side of the wall. After a few minutes, Lily strolled back on the bus and in her own inimitable way said, *"Oi, thy lot, wake up. Can any of you swim? There's a bloody hat floating about out there and I can't see Jennie Harris underneath it!"* They were all in fits of laughter at the sight of the hat and fake cherries bobbing about on the water, with poor Jennie coughing and spluttering as she was pulled to safety.

Joan Whalley, who signed for the team in 1937, recalled Lily's dressing room banter saying, *"You would have died laughing at her. She was the drollest person you ever met in your life. She was so funny, she really made me laugh. When the older players were getting ready for a match, there would be elastic stockings going on knee's and the strapping up of ankles, there were bandages here there and everywhere. Then Parr walked in,* (they would sometimes refer to one another by their surnames during this period) *and she stood looking at them all and said, 'Well, I don't know about Dick, Kerr Ladies football team, it looks like a bloody trip to Lourdes to me!'* She was a gem of a character was Lily Parr, a loveable rogue, who it seems, had a tendency to remove things from places.

Joan goes on, *"Parr was a rum devil. She was a devil for nicking things, she was for sure. We once went along to be photographed on Ashton Park and we all got changed in this big old fashioned house. There was nothing in the place, it was completely empty. After the photographs had been taken Parr said to me, 'Come here Whalley', she never called me Joan, all my life it was always Whalley. I knew she had something up her sleeve because she used to get me doing all her jobs for her, I was only young. 'Come here Whalley, come with me I've something to show you', and I went following along at her heels like a little puppy. She went into a room where there was an old sideboard, it was nearly falling to bits. She opened a drawer and there were all sorts of knives and forks in it. She had that look on her face, 'Do you think they're silver'? Of course they are, I said, they've got silver stamped on them. She asked me to help her get some but I didn't want to get involved. 'Come on Whalley, there's nobody wants them, they wouldn't be left lying around here if they did. I could make use of these, and with a bit of cleaning up they'd be lovely on the table'. But I told her I wasn't pinching for her and I left her to it.*

Wherever she went she used to try and take the football from the games. We always autographed the match ball and it would be raffled off to raise more money for charity. The game would be kicked off by some well known celebrity with the ball we all signed, then we would play the game with another new ball. After the

49

match someone would always come looking for the football, 'Where's the match ball, where's the ball'? But it was nearly always missing. I would say to Stella and Tich, it'll be that Parr again. She would be looking in all the corners, pretending to be searching for it and we would be daft enough to help look for it as well. How many balls she ever shoved in her grip I don't know but she would produce them on the bus when we were miles away from the venue. We never knew what she did with them".

After leaving the Dick, Kerr factory, like many of the other players, Lily began a career as a nurse at Whittingham Hospital, just outside Preston, where she stayed until her retirement in the 1960's. There too, she was not afraid of breaking the rules. In those days, the Matron was a fearsome woman who ran her hospital in a strict regimental order and had most lesser mortals shaking in their shoes. But not Lily Parr! For example, smoking on the wards was considered a serious offence and definitely forbidden. Lily however, enjoyed a cigarette and if she fancied a crafty smoke she wouldn't hesitate to 'light up' whenever the urge took her. There were occasions when she could be seen talking to the Matron with a lighted cigarette cupped in her hand behind her back! But she was a good nurse. She was kind and very caring and although they weren't supposed to have favourites, Lily often did. She had grown particularly fond of an old lady named Kitty. When Kitty passed away, Lily was quite upset and couldn't help shedding a few tears for the old girl. Of course she would never admit to anyone she had been crying and passed off her sniffles as *'having a bit of a cold'*. On another occasion, while out shopping, she came across an ex-patient and stopped to ask how she was coping at home. The lady confided to Lily that since leaving hospital she had been struggling to make ends meet and was about to have her electricity supply cut off. Lily asked how much she needed for the outstanding bill and immediately opened her purse and gave her the money. Squeezing the money into her hand she said, *"here you are lass, just get it sorted".*

A year or two in to her retirement she discoverd a lump in her breast and her worst fears were soon to be realised. The lump was malignant and she needed a mastectomy. Five or six weeks later, she discovered a lump in her other breast and had to undergo a second mastectomy. But her sense of humour shone through throughout her ordeal and she showed great courage. When speaking of her operations, Lily would joke, *"It's taken me 62 years to grow these, now they've taken the bloody things off me!"* A good friend who went to visit after the surgery wasn't quite sure what gift to take. Flowers or chocolates might have been an obvious choice but she decided to get what she knew Lily would appreciate most: A packet of Woodbines! True to form, her response was, *"Thank God for some bloody cigs, I can't get hold of any in here, they won't let me have them".* Lily lived for ten years after her second operation but was finally beaten by cancer and died at her home in Goosnargh, near Preston, on 24 May 1978, and this very special lady was laid to rest in her native St Helens. Without question, Lily Parr was one of the most influential and charismatic women ever to wear the famous colours of the Dick, Kerr Ladies. I feel sure that those whose lives she touched were perhaps a little richer for having known her.

CHAPTER THREE

GOING INTERNATIONAL!

By 1920, women's football had become accepted as a spectator sport. More and more charitable organisations were also recognising this fact and were placing considerable demands on the ladies to play more matches up and down the country. In France too women began playing football during the war and although not as experienced as their British counterparts, they were nonetheless very quick and skilful.

In 1917 discussions had already taken place in France and England exploring the possibility of female sporting events between factories. The committee of the Dick, Kerr Ladies club adopted this idea and hoped to invite a French ladies team over to England to play football. The defence of French soil by British troops during the 1914-1918 war had cemented strong ties between our two nations and what a wonderful gesture it would be for France to send a ladies team over to England to play football and raise funds for British charities.

The Dick, Kerr Ladies committee contacted the Federation des Societies Feminine Sportives de France to explore the possibility of staging a football tour between the two countries. The federation had been founded by Alice Milliat who was a staunch supporter of female sport in France and she agreed to arrange for a French representative team to play a series of matches in England in aid of the National Association of Discharged and Disabled Soldiers and Sailors. The committee were delighted that their invitation had been accepted and no doubt equally pleased that they would be the first club to announce such a notable coup. Meticulous planning went into arranging the whole tour and four matches were scheduled to take place in Preston, Stockport, Manchester and Chelsea. The Dick, Kerr girls were so excited at the prospect they could hardly contain themselves. They were counting down the days as they eagerly awaited their arrival. In an effort to ensure that nothing went wrong with the arrangements, Mr Frankland travelled to Dover to welcome the French team to England and he accompanied them to London. Having just experienced a very rough Channel crossing, the girls looked quite pale, cold and tired after their long journey as they descended from the continental train at Victoria Station. However, their spirits were soon lifted by the warm welcome given by a host of newspaper reporters and other officials. This was the first time any of the girls had been to England

and their manager Madame Alice Milliat said, *"We are very happy to be here and we are looking forward to a most pleasant visit. Of course, the girls are all very excited and full of it".* The party consisted of 17 players with ages ranging between 18 - 25 years. They were:

Mdlle Duray	*Shop assistant & interpreter*
Mdlles Lalas	*2 sisters - machine workers*
Mdlle Rigal	*Dressmaker*
Mdlle Pomies	*Dental student*
Mdlle Rinbaux	*Shorthand typist*
Mdlle Brule	*Shorthand typist*
Mdlle Bracquemonde	*Shorthand typist (captain)*
Mdlle Delpierre	*Student of Philosophy*
Mdlle Billac	*Bookkeeper*
Mdlle Patuneau	*Dressmaker*
Mdlles Trotmann	*2 sisters, English speaking, mother came from Leeds*
Mdlle Janiaud	
Mdlle Viani	
Mdlle Ourry	
Mdme Leveque	*the only married player in the team*

They arrived in Preston on 28 April 1920, and as the train pulled up at the platform, the Dick, Kerr Brass Band greeted the French football team with the 'Marseillaise'. The French girls gave a loud cheer as they stepped off the train and one of the players waved a toy rabbit which was their lucky mascot. A big crowd closed in around them and an hoard of press photographers jossled to get the best pictures of the girls before being introduced to the officials of the Dick, Kerr Ladies and greetings exchanged. A bouquet of flowers was presented to Madame Milliat. The French girls were mainly on the petite side but as most of them were all round athletes they were hoping their superior speed would give them an advantage in the coming matches with the Dick, Kerr Ladies. Madame Milliat already had considerable knowledge and experience of Association Football in France and she was probably unequalled by any other woman in her country. She said, *"In my opinion, football is not wrong for women. I do not think it is unwomanly to play football as they do not play like men, they play fast, but not vigorous football".*

A huge crowd had gathered at the station approach and thousands of people lined the streets to give an enthusiastic welcome to the French visitors. The Dick, Kerr band led the way up Fishergate, and they were followed by the French team who were driven up to their hotel in a wagonette drawn by four light bay horses (four in hand) which was draped with the French tricolour. At the rear of the procession, a motor charabanc had on board the Dick, Kerr Ladies and officials. The French ladies were visibly moved by the size and warmth of the welcome given them by the town and all agreed it was one of the most enjoyable and emotional experiences of their lives. The significance of the occasion could not have been lost on them. So soon after tens of thousands of British soldiers had lost their lives liberating France from German occupation in defence of their very freedom, the people of Preston had lined the streets in their thousands in appreciation of the French ladies making the long journey to their town.

French Team's arrival

They stayed at the Bull and Royal Hotel for the duration of their visit. This was the finest accommodation the town had to offer and it had been tastefully decorated with streamers of allied flags. On duty outside the hotel was local policeman PC Tomlinson who fortunately for all concerned, spoke fluent French. During the war he acted as an interpreter for British forces in France and he was delighted to help translate between the two teams. After dinner, the party were driven to the canteen at the Dick, Kerr works where a dance had been arranged for them. Madame Milliat thanked everyone for their wonderful hospitality and expressed her deep appreciation for the remarkable reception they had received on their arrival in the town. A full itinerary of events had been arranged for them during their ten day tour where they visited local beauty spots and other places of interest. They were also given a tour of the Dick, Kerr factory and saw the production line where tramcars were assembled. At the lamp works, a glass loving cup especially made to commemorate their visit, was presented to

The French team, 1920

Back row: Brule, Delpierre, Bracquemonde, A Trotmann, S Lalas

Middle row: Janiaud, J Trotmann, Viani

Front row: Rigal, G Lalas, Ourry, Pomies

the team. In the evening they left the hotel by charabanc, preceded by the Preston Military Band, en route to Deepdale for their first match against the host team. The Dick, Kerr band entertained the crowd before the start of the game and the teams were welcomed on to the pitch to the strains of Rule Britannia and the Marseillaise.

A crowd of 25,000, came to Deepdale to watch the opening match of the tour and Mr J Conner, MBE, General Manager at the factory, was delighted to perform the kick off to get the game underway. The match poster noted: **LEST WE FORGET** - *The French Ladies are playing the game here for the Lads who played the game over there!* The Dick, Kerr girls lined up in their now famous black and white stripes and the French team played in light blue jerseys with a red, white and blue cockade on the left breast, and navy blue shorts. Dick, Kerr's almost ran the French defence to a standstill with their superior play, but for all their possession they were still unable to score more than two goals. The highlight of the game was the excellent play from forwards Jennie Harris and Florrie Redford, and captain and right back Alice Kell. No player on either side could match the quality of performance set by these three girls but Jessie Walmsley played well in defence and easily broke up the French attacks. They were reduced to ten players just after half time when injury forced Molly Walker to leave the field. She had twisted her right knee earlier in the game and was unable to continue. Lily Lee, playing on the left wing, was carried off in the first half after a nasty kick on her foot. She came back on in the second half but struggled to keep up with play for the rest of the game. For the French team, Carmen Pomies and Mdlle Viani gave a good performance in defence, Mdlle Alice Trotmann and Mdlle Bracquemonde were the pick of the attack, and Mdlle Ourry, an alert and competent goalkeeper, frequently gained applause from the crowd. After the final whistle, Jennie Harris was carried shoulder high off the pitch by adoring fans who were impressed by her skilful play. The goals were scored by Florrie Redford and Jennie Harris and £1295.00 was raised for

Cartoon of game at Deepdale 1920

the ex servicemen's fund. Madame Milliat said afterwards that she had never seen such a big crowd at a match adding that they did not get crowds of that size at mens matches in Paris. Indeed it should be noted that never had a bigger crowd been seen at Deepdale's famous enclosure before this match.

Saturday saw both teams travel to Stockport for an early evening match. The 15,000 crowd saw an emphatic victory for the Dick, Kerr team with the French ladies going down 5-2. Goal scorers were: Redford 3, Walmsley and

Woods for Dick, Kerr's, Lalas and Bracquemonde for France. The total raised from the two games thus far was around £2000. Next day the visitors were welcomed at the home of Alfred Frankland. Mrs Frankland had been kept busy all morning making sandwiches and cakes for the occasion and endless cups of tea. The typically British hospitality was warmly appreciated by the French ladies. On Monday they were taken on a trip to Blackpool on what was an exceptionally windy day. The girls were having fun and enjoying themselves dodging the waves as they crashed against the sea wall on to the promenade. A sudden gust of wind took them by surprise when it blew off a hat from one of the French ladies. They all laughed as they watched it being swept away and swallowed up by the waves. The next day they enjoyed a welcome day of rest and took the opportunity to relax and prepare for the next match.

The game at Hyde Road, Manchester was played in front of 12,000 spectators who witnessed a well deserved 1-1 draw between the two teams. The French girls played very well, especially in attack and had it not been for the excellent work of the Dick, Kerr's goalkeeper, they could have scored at least two more goals. The French goalscorer had a novel way of celebrating her goal when she did a complete somersault and landed on her feet! The total raised from this game was £766 11s 5d and the Discharged Soldiers Association expressed their sincere thanks for the generous amounts raised at the matches and presented Madame Milliat with a manicure set as a small token of their appreciation.

The final match of the tour was played at Stamford Bridge, the home of Chelsea Football Club in front of 10,000 spectators. The French ladies recorded their first victory against the Dick, Kerr team by 2-1. Jennie Harris was knocked unconcious early in the game which reduced the Preston team to 10 players and gave the visitors an clear advantage. Mdlle Brule, the French full back was in very good form as was Alice Kell for Dick, Kerr's. It was a good game and the crowd were suitably impressed by the standard of play. *"I never thought girls could play till full time"*, was one spectators comment, *"Nor kick so hard"* said another. A quaint French touch was given to the victory when Mdlle Bracquemonde kissed Alice Kell, the Dick, Kerr captain, on the cheek and threw her arm around her opponents shoulder as they walked off the pitch together. Dick, Kerr team: Annie Hastie, Alice Kell, Sally Hulme, Annie Crozier, E Nixon, Lily Jones, Daisy Clayton, Emily Jones, Alice Woods, Jennie Harris, Florrie Redford. French team: Duray, Rinbaux, Pomies, Brule, Bracquemonde, Delpierre, Milliat, Patuneau, Lalas, Billac, Rigal.

The teams were honoured at a civic reception by the Lord Mayor of London at the Mansion House. Never in their wildest dreams could they

French and Dick, Kerr Ladies at the Mansion House

have imagined being welcomed in such esteemed company. Playing football had certainly changed their lives beyond all recognition and catapulted them into a whole new world. A day trip to Blackpool in those days was considered a great adventure, yet here we had these ordinary factory girls being welcomed by the country's 'top brass', politicians, sports stars, and entertainers alike. They were enjoying every single moment and their lives were never quite the same again. The Dick, Kerr Ladies were riding on the crest of a wave and would pinch themselves on a daily basis to make sure they weren't dreaming. They must have considered themselves to be the emancipated women of the 1920's.

As the tour came to a close both teams were very proud of a job well done. They had raised over £3000 for worthwhile charities and the French ladies had recorded a famous victory over a team who were recognised as being the best in the land. During the ten day visit, thousands of people had turned out to wish them well. Many friends were made both on and off the field and the whole tour was a resounding success. Addresses were exchanged between the teams and a promise to 'keep in touch' was warmly made and it was hoped that a return visit to France would be made by the Dick, Kerr team sometime in the autumn.

On their arrival home in Paris, the French team were given an incredibly warm welcome. Parents, friends and representatives of the girls athletic clubs were at the Gare du Nord to present the ladies with so many bouquets that there were several for each player. One railway porter was so moved by the reception given to them he was heard to shout *"Vive la France"*. Mdlle Bracquemonde, the team captain, was carried shoulder high by some of the wellwishers, and her mother was so proud she had tears in her eyes. The girls described their stay in England as, *"Enchanté"*, *"Magnifique"*, *"Epatant"*. Madame Milliat said the success of the tour had far exceeded their expectations. *"We were simply overpowered with kindness and we must give the English girls a welcome worthy of them when they come here in the Autumn. Our girls played well and everybody was very nice to them"*. A reporter asked if they had enjoyed their visit to England. The reply was an emphatic and unanimous Yes, *"but we found it very windy on Blackpool front!"* they said and giggled as they recalled the incident with the hat. Mdlle Ourry, the French goalkeeper returned to Preston not long after the tour. She played with the Dick, Kerr Ladies for a short time and received some valuable coaching from them.

Two days after the French team had returned to Paris, the Dick, Kerr Ladies were back on the victory trail. On Saturday, 8 May, a crowd of 15,000 came to Oldham to see them defeat St Helens by 2-0. A busy spring and summer lay ahead which saw them undefeated as they travelled throughout Lancashire, Cheshire and Yorkshire and with the exception of July, they played a match almost every Saturday. The final arrangements were underway for the return visit to France and the girls were undergoing intensive training as they prepared for the tour. They were grateful for some excellent coaching from the many footballers who were employed at the Strand road works. Bob Holmes, one of the original Preston North End 'Invincibles', Johnny Morley, ex Burnley and North End, Billy Grier, North End centre half and Jack Warner the North End and ex Portsmouth full back, were all willing exponents of their skill and experience.

George Birkenshaw had been appointed team coach. He was an enthusiastic man who always put the girls through their paces and training was as strict and thorough as with any First Division league club. The girls kept fit by sprinting, skipping and ball practice and they felt sure no other ladies' team in the country could be in better condition.

The girls were very excited and eagerly anticipating the trip to France. Team captain, Alice Kell said, *"We intend showing the people of France what fine sportswomen the English women are and we shall not allow sentiment to creep in quite as much as we did when the French team played over here earlier this year. Of course we didn't underestimate them, or allow them to win, but we didn't put in the 'last ounce' as you might say. And we were unlucky at having more than our fair share of injuries to our players in all the matches with the French ladies.*

Surely we will not have the same bad luck again. We have strengthened our team since last winter, and all our 'casualties' have fully recovered. If the matches with the French ladies serve no other purpose, I feel that they will have done more to cement the good feeling between the two nations than anything which has occurred during the last 50 years, except of course the Great War".

Alice's love of football began when she was a child. Her brothers were keen footballers and she had many a tough game with them on Preston marsh. Alice lived on Marsh Lane and went to the Hincksman Memorial School with her best friend Florrie Redford. The two girls were inseperable and later worked together at the Dick, Kerr factory where they both jumped at the chance of playing football in a ladies team.

The players who had lost brothers in the war were hoping they would have the opportunity to place wreaths in honour of their memory. Lily Lee had also lost a brother in the conflict. Gilbert Lee answered the call for recruits and enlisted with the Preston Pals. He was killed on the Somme in 1916 at just 19 years of age. There is no known grave for him and his name is listed among the fallen on the Thiepval Memorial. There were many memorials to British soldiers in the four towns where matches were scheduled and it must have been hard for them to see first hand the scale of the lives lost. It was also planned for the tour to take in visits of battlefields in the Ypres Salient where they hoped to pay a special tribute to Eddie Latheron, the former Blackburn Rovers star player. He was killed while serving with the Royal Field Artillery at Passchendaele. If at all possible they wanted to lay a wreath in his club colours on his grave at Vlamertinghe, a small town on the west side of Ypres.

The night before their departure to France they were invited to dinner dance in the works canteen with their family and friends. Guest's of honour were the Mayor and Mayoress, Alderman & Mrs T. Parkinson. Mr R. Livingstone, the new works manager, wished the team success on the trip and he paid tribute to their good work since its formation in 1917. In addition, chairman of the club Mr Adlington, spoke of the team's splendid work for charity and said that since its inception £8600 had been raised, mainly for local charities. The Mayor added his congratulations to the team and spoke of the towns efforts to help with the re-building of the war affected areas in France. In reply Mr Frankland paid tribute to the team's success and thanked the company for their kindness to them. He said that on the tour they hoped to uphold the traditions of the town and the firm, and win all four of their matches.

Letters had been regularly crossing the channel between the two teams since the French visit to England and the Preston girls were busy brushing up on their French in readiness for the tour. Florrie Redford and Jennie

Leaving for France, November 1920

Left to right: Jennie Harris, Alice Kell, Annie Hastie, Florrie Haslam, Flo Redford, Sally Hulme(?), Jessie Walmsley, Molly Walker, Alice Woods, Lily Parr, Lily Lee, Minnie Lyons(?) unknown, Emily Jones, Lily Jones, Daisy Clayton, unknown

Harris had been labelled in the press as Dick, Kerr's *'box o' tricks'* due to their impressive goal scoring record and recent signing 15-year-old Lily Parr, playing at full back, was said to kick like a first division male footballer. Lily Jones announced that she was to meet up with her fiance and finally tie the knot in London on their return journey.

On Thursday 28 October 1920, the Dick, Kerr Ladies left Preston en route for Paris. The streets were lined with cheering crowds as they were driven up to the railway station in a motor charabanc decorated with the Union Jack and the French tricolour. A large crowd had also gathered at the station approach to see them safely on their way and a loud cheer went up when the train pulled out of the station with Alice Kell waving the club's mascot, a teddy bear dressed in a union jack.

Those making the historic trip to France, to become the first British women's football club to embark on an overseas football tour were: Messrs Alfred Frankland, secretary, A.E. Howarth, treasurer, and George Birkenshaw, trainer. The 16 players were: Alice Kell, Annie Hastie, Lily Parr, Alice Woods, Jessie Walmsley, Sally Hulme, Florrie Haslam, Minnie Lyons, Daisy Clayton, Emily Jones, Lily Jones, Florrie Redford, Jennie Harris, Molly Walker, Lily Lee and Annie Crozier.

They arrived in London and made their way to the Bonnington Hotel for dinner and an overnight stay. They made the most of their whistle stop visit to the capital and were thrilled to have the opportunity to see a show at the world famous London Palladium. They didn't get to bed until after midnight but were so excited they hardly got a wink of sleep. Next morning they left Victoria station somewhat bleary eyed and arrived in Dover mid-afternoon. While going through customs Alice Kell and Florrie Redford bumped into an old school friend from Preston. Customs official Billy Maile had moved south several years earlier and was so pleased at meeting up with the girls he sailed

Alice Kell with her mascot

across to Calais with them to hear all about their success with the team. The Channel crossing was pretty rough and only five of the travellers avoided being sea sick, but their excitement helped them recover as soon as they landed on French soil.

The train journey from Calais to Paris was a much more pleasurable experience. It was a beautiful autumn day, the trees were just beginning to turn rich gold and deep red colours and the scenery was breathtaking. They had their noses pressed up against the carriage windows taking in every aspect of this foreign land. Unlike the more familiar Lancashire landscape with it's green hills and rolling fells, they could see for miles and miles as the train meandered through the picturesque countryside. They passed by Etaples Military Cemetery where row upon row of graves marked the final resting place for many British soldiers. Mr Frankland expressed his hope that it might be of some consolation to many British mothers to know that the cemetery was beautifully kept and full of flowers.

On their arrival in Paris they were greeted by Mrs Trotmann, an English lady originally from Leeds, whose daughters had been on the French team's tour during the spring. Mrs Trotmann was to travel with them acting as guide and interpreter. She said that of the 23 years she had lived in France, this was the happiest time she had ever had. As soon as the train arrived, the host players pushed past the police at the Gare du Nord station in their eagerness to welcome the Preston girls and they presented Alice Kell with a beautiful bouquet of flowers. Cheer after cheer rang out and they all began singing *'She's a lassie from Lancashire'.* The travellers were tired and hungry after their long journey and were relieved when they finally arrived at the Hotel Beau Sejour, where they quickly freshened up before coming down to dinner. This was their first encounter with French food and they were rather disappointed. Lily Parr would probably have been the most vocal saying something like, *"I don't know what the bloody hell this is but I'm starving, I could eat a scabby donkey!"* Although the majority would have quietly shared the same opinion they all manged to polish off their evening meal while hoping for something more familiar next day.

On Saturday they were taken on a sight-seeing trip around Paris. They saw the Chamber of Deputies, a fine building about 300 yards long. They drove along the Champs Elysees and climbed the 281 steps to the top of the Arc de Triumph. Next stop was the church of Notre Dame where they saw the actual spot where Napoleon was married to Josephine in 1804. Their attention was also drawn to the windows which contained around 300,000 pieces of glass which had to be taken out to protect them during 'Big Berthas' bombardment of Paris during the war. (Big Bertha was a huge German gun that was transported on railway lines. The gun shelled Paris from the Forest of Coucy, a distance of 76 miles away). There were still many British service personnel on active duty in the captial who were delighted to meet up with the girls and they gave them an incredibly warm welcome. Their presence in the city was causing quite a stir and they were regularly stopped by autograph hunters and people eager to have photographs taken with them. It seemed as though everyone in Paris wanted to be at the match in the Pershing Stadium the following day.

After their marathon tour of the city the weary travellers returned to the hotel very hungry and ready for their evening meal. There was a huge sigh of relief around the dining room as the waiter served up something much more suited to their palate. Steak and chips! *"That's more like it",* said Lily Parr, and the clatter of knives and forks soon took over from polite conversation. They met up later to discuss tactics for their first match and each was unanimous in wanting to field their strongest team. They voiced their determination not to lose any games during the tour and were ready for the challenges ahead.

Next day there was more sight-seeing on the agenda. They left the hotel after breakfast en route for the French Military Training School where they were welcomed by Colonel Seé and his Officers. After lunch they were shown a

WOMEN CEMENT ENTENTE.

Dick, Kerr's, Preston, women footballers, with some of their French friends, off for a tour of Paris. They met a representative French women's side, but after each had scored a goal the crowd stopped the game.—(*D.M.*)

Seeing the sights in Paris

demonstration in slow motion photography of famous French athletes in action. This was a new and special feature in the French Army as it showed men the correct way of perfecting the movements. Champion boxer Georges Carpentier was an instructor there during the war and Colonel Seé told them that Carpentier was one of his best pupils. (this would probably explain the reason for the slow motion newsreel footage from the 1920's, showing some of the Dick, Kerr Ladies boxing). Before leaving they were asked to sign the visitors book usually reserved for champion French athletes. The girls signed their names and Mr Frankland wrote, *'Dick, Kerr Ladies Football Club desires to place on record their grateful appreciation of the splendid manner in which they have been received by the Officers of our Brave French Allies. Long Live France'.* They walked the short distance to the Pershing Stadium to prepare for the opening match of the tour.

Twenty-two thousand people came to the stadium to watch the game. Lord Derby, the British Ambassador in Paris was invited to kick off the match, but his apologies were received by telegram and the French Air Minister stepped into the breach in his absence. Mr Frankland was asked to run the line and just after the kick-off he noticed his girls seemed rather nervous. They soon settled down though and kept the French team hemmed in their own half for the first 25 minutes but a breakaway goal was scored by Mdlle Laloz, whose superior speed saw her find the Dick, Kerr net. This spurred on the Preston side who put the French keeper, Mdlle Ourry, under tremendous pressure with shot after shot at her goal, only to find her playing as well as she had while with them in England. However, a brilliant 30 yard shot from Minnie Lyons gave Mdlle Ourry no chance. This was met by a huge cheer from the English supporters in the crowd who were heard to shout, *'Play up Dick, Kerr's', 'Play up Lancashire'*. The French team were lucky to be on level terms at half time.

The scores remained level throughout the second half and some good marking from the French defence kept out the industrious pairing of Redford and Harris. However, the game was to end in controversy when with only five minutes remaining, the French referee awarded a corner to Dick, Kerr's. A large section of French spectators disagreed with his decision and invaded the pitch in protest. Players from both teams were surrounded by the crowd and the referee was forced to abandon the game with four minutes still to play. Erring on the side of caution, he asked the police to clear the ground, but there was no malice intended and all the players were escorted away safely and the 1-1 scoreline seemed a fair result. Alice Kell said after the game that the French ladies were much better on their home ground and had improved since their visit to England. The Dick, Kerr team was: Annie Hastie, Alice Kell, Lily Parr, Alice Woods, Jessie Walmsley, Sally Hulme, Florrie Haslam, Minnie Lyons, Florrie Redford, Jennie Harris, Daisy Clayton

Playing football on a Sunday had seemed strange to the Preston team. Sunday in England was still regarded as the Sabbath Day. Mr Frankland had found it particularly odd given his Victorian up-bringing, and after the match he said, *"After our experience, we feel the English Sunday is something to be proud of. In Paris,*

Minnie Lyons in action in Paris

the market halls and theatres were open, something that is totally alien to us. Even the fairground was open, which was reminiscent of our Whitsuntide fairs. One wonders when the French get their rest".

They left Paris for Roubaix early next morning passing through some of the more devastated regions and saw for themselves first hand evidence of war torn France. Chappelle, Briebiers, Houplines, the Ancre District, Raimonte and Albert had all been reduced to ruins. They stared in disbelief at the desolation before them. They saw trenches still full of filthy water, exposing the dreadful conditions the soldiers had to endure for months on end. Discarded shell hobs and barbed wire entanglements still littered the area. They saw people living in makeshift huts made from oil drums picked up from the dumps, as they tried to rebuild homes destroyed by the bombs. Mr Frankland said that people who had not seen these parts could never conceive what Northern France must have suffered and endured, but rebuilding was going on at a fast pace.

The match in Roubaix was played at Parc Jean Dunbrulle in front of 16,000 spectators, a record for the ground doubling all previous attendances. The French team were given a tremendous ovation as they came out on to the pitch, but the reception given to the Dick, Kerr Ladies from the British spectators was reminiscent of a cup final. The French won the toss and played with the wind at their backs, but the Dick, Kerr girls probably played the best football of their lives and during the first half the French didn't get a look in. They could hear the crowd shouting *'Good old Dick, Kerr's', 'Play up Proud Preston'*. It was almost like playing a home fixture at Deepdale and it gave them a tremendous boost. The game throughout was played at a very fast pace and Dick, Kerr's were always on top. Alice Kell, Florrie Redford, Jennie Harris and Florrie Haslam all played some great football, but the first half remained goalless. After the interval the Dick, Kerr girls carried on from where they left off with the forwards outwitting the French on all sides. Florrie Redford opened the scoring with a well taken goal and the crowd went wild. Union Jacks and black and white colours were being waved all over the ground. Then, with ten minutes to go, Dick, Kerr's were awarded a penalty. Florrie Redford took the kick and scored with a great shot just wide of the left hand of the goalkeeper. The 2-0 scoreline didn't reflect the quality of their play and at the end of the match the whole team were carried shoulder high off the field by the British spectators who were so delighted with the English victory.

They returned to the hotel later that evening to discover a large crowd of British soldiers and Lancashire workmen, the latter there to help with the rebuilding programme, waiting to meet and greet the victorious team. The crowd gave the girls the most wonderful reception and they were rather taken aback with the warmth of the good wishes they received. There was also quite a number of Englishmen staying at the hotel who had travelled from all parts of Northern France to get a glimpse of the players. Mr Frankland said, *"Words fail to describe how glad they all were to see our team, I cannot describe their hearty greetings, I have never seen a team get a better reception than ours did"*.

On Tuesday, the team went to pay their respects and lay a wreath at the Cenotaph in Roubaix for the many soldiers who had lost their lives during the War. The wreath measured an incredible twelve feet in diameter and was placed at the foot of the memorial by Alice Kell, Jessie Walmsley and Lily Lee. It was a difficult and emotional moment for the girls as each was reminded of their own personal loss.

The rest of the week had a busy sight-seeing itinerary. Wednesday saw them reach the top of the Eifel Tower. Thursday was a trip to Versailles with a guided tour of the Royal Palace and saw the historic table on which the peace treaty was signed on Armistice Day. They also went through the famous Hall of Mirrors before having lunch at the Villa d'Array. Later they visited the State China and Porcelain factory, where the celebrated Serres pottery was made. In the evening they went to a show at the Alhambra Variety Theatre in Paris, made all the more enjoyable as the performers were English and they could understand what was going on! Friday morning they had some free time to hit the shops to buy souvenirs for family and friends at home. After lunch they placed a beautiful wreath in the cemetery Pere Lachaise in Paris, before leaving the French capital for Le Havre.

After breakfast in Le Havre the next morning they began preparations for the afternoon match with the French ladies. A crowd of 10,000, the smallest of the tour, saw the Dick, Kerr team record a very convincing 6-0 victory. In Rouen the next day they were taken on a visit to the tower where Joan of Arc was imprisoned and later made their way to the Lilas Stadium for the final match of the tour. The game was watched by a crowd of 14,000 who enjoyed a good performance by The Dick, Kerr girls who defeated the French ladies by 2-0.

A farewell party was held before their departure and promises to keep in touch were warmly made. The girls could reflect on the resounding success of the tour and be especially proud of achieving their goal of going home undefeated. Their only criticism was that they hadn't had enough time to see as much of the country as they would have wished as most of their free time was taken up on organised tours in the city. They were also bitterly disappointed at being unable to lay flowers on the grave of Eddie Latheron of Blackburn Rovers, but they did discover the grave of one young Preston soldier and most were reduced to tears. It was a touching scene as the girls paid tribute to this brave young man and they covered his final resting place with a beautiful blanket of colourful flowers.

They left Rouen for Dieppe and much to everyone's relief, the return Channel crossing to Newhaven was much smoother than the outward journey. They arrived back at the Bonnington for another overnight stay. The next morning they were at the register office to witness their team mate Lily Jones tie the knot with her childhood sweetheart before leaving Euston station on the last leg of their marathon trip in which they had covered over 2,000 miles. They arrived in Preston early evening and as they stepped off the train they were greeted by a large crowd of supporters, family and friends. They made their way to the station entrance and the Dick, Kerr Band played 'See the Conquering Hero Comes'. Outside a charabanc was waiting to take them to the Dick, Kerr factory and as they drove away they received a rousing cheer from the crowd. The band marched in front of the charabanc, which made a tour through the streets before arriving at the factory. The team was enthusiastically cheered and welcomed by crowds all along the route and the players waved Union Jacks and Tricolours in acknowledgement.

Arriving at the canteen, players and friends were guests of the firm to a dinner hosted by Mr Livingstone, the works manager. He welcomed them home and spoke of the pleasure it had given everyone concerned to know that not only had they maintained the traditions of the team, but they had all played the game splendidly. Mr Frankland said that it was his personal opinion that the tour had done something towards cementing *Entente Cordiale*. Afterwards, in an interview with a newspaper reporter, Mr Frankland said that, "*With the exception of slight colds, the girls returned with a clean bill of health and we were able to field the same team in every match. The French Ladies had improved a great deal in their playing ability compared with their performances when they visited England, but they were somewhat inferior to the Preston players*".

The tour had reached its conclusion and the bond of friendship made between the two teams would see them through a second World War and continue well into the 1950's when many more visits would be made between the two countries and lots more money would be raised for the many worthwhile charities they supported.

CHAPTER FOUR

THE RECORD MAKERS

By 20 November 1920 the team was back on the road travelling to Leicester for a fund raising fixture against St Helens. Twenty-two thousand spectators came along to see another 4-0 victory recorded by the Dick, Kerr Ladies with a hat trick being scored by Florrie Redford and Jennie Harris netting the other.

Team picture 1920

Back row: unknown, Lily Lee, Alice Woods, Emily Grice?, Jessie Walmsley, Daisy Clayton

Front row players: Florrie Haslam, Alice Norris, Florrie Redford, unknown, Lily Parr

Matches played at night were pretty much unheard of in those days. The technology of floodlighting an arena simply wasn't available and the ability to play football by night was considered a novelty idea. The Dick, Kerr Ladies however, were once again to be the first when it came to breaking new ground. The local charity for unemployed ex-servicemen were appealing for donations to provide food hampers for Christmas. Mr Livingstone, the Dick, Kerr work's manager, came up with the unusual idea for the ladies to play a match by searchlight to help raise funds for this worthy cause. Local MP, Colonel Stanley, and Councillor Tom Shaw, were keen to support the idea and made the approach to the War Office for the loan of two anti aircraft searchlights and generating sets, along with forty carbide flares, to be used for the occasion. Permission was granted for their use by the Secretary of State for War, Mr Winston Churchill. They had only ten days to prepare for the game and arrangements were made for it to be played at Deepdale against a team made up of the best players from the rest of England.

It turned out to be a great success. On 17 December 1920, 10,000 spectators came along to witness this unique match. Pathe News cameramen and a barrage of press photographers in true papparazi style, were also there to record this most unusual spectacle. Matches by artificial light had reputedly been played by professional mens teams in the past but according to those present in the crowd who had seen those games, none had been as successful as this one turned out to be. The two military searchlights were placed at either end of the ground and they threw powerful beams of light above the playing area and close to the touchline the carbide flares were placed all around the pitch. Owing to an air-lock and a petrol shortage, the searchlights temporarily went out of action just before the start of the match and once during the first half, but there was still sufficient illumination for the game to be followed by both players and spectators. The match finally kicked off at 7.15 p.m. Much to the amusement of both teams and the crowd, it was so dark that no one could find Jennie Harris, the smallest player on either side. One of the photographers obligingly set off one of his flash lights and the missing player was found! Bob Crompton of Blackburn Rovers kicked off the match, which was refereed by Mr W Taylor of Longridge. In order to help the crowd see the brown leather ball from every corner of the arena, former PNE 'Old Invincibles' star Bob Holmes, suggested whitewashing the ball so that it could be seen from all parts of the ground and he kept himself busy throwing a newly painted white ball on to the pitch at regular intervals.

Bob Holmes was born in Preston in 1867. He became captain of Preston North End and the Football League XI, and also won seven caps for England. He made his debut for the club in their first ever league game against Burnley in September 1888 and he also played in the FA Cup Final of the same year. An ever present member of the team, he eventually retired from professional football at the end of the 1899/1900 season, but continued to play as an amateur. He was president of the Football Players' Union and later took up refereeing and coaching. Without doubt, Bob Holmes is one of the most celebrated players in the history of Preston North End. In his later years he could still been seen around Deepdale working as an assistant groundsman. He died in 1955. He was 88 years old.

The game could hardly have taken place under better conditions. The night was windless and clear, and not too cold to cause discomfort. A touch of white frost remained on the surface and the pitch was hard, but the game was played at a good pace by both teams and few passes went astray. The Preston side showed an all round improvement in their performance since they had last played a match in their home town and the players most prominent once again were the famous trio of Harris, Redford and Kell. The Dick, Kerr eleven were the same side which played in all four games in France and they lined up as follows: Annie Hastie, Alice Kell, Lily Parr, Alice Woods, Jessie Walmsley, Sally Hulme, Florrie Haslam, Minnie Lyons, Florrie Redford, Jennie Harris and Daisy Clayton. The Rest of England team were : Waine (St Helens), Hickson (Horrockses), C Wagstaffe (Barrow YWCA), Willis (Newcastle), Rance (St Helens), P Scott (Chorley), D Bates (Stoke), Yates (Horrockses), Benyon (Verdin & Cooks, Middlewich), M Seed (Blyth Spartans), Dickinson (Vickers, Barrow)

There were several amusing incidents during the game. On one occasion, the operator of the searchlight at the Spion Kop end of the ground turned his searchlight on an exciting duel between the Preston forwards and the opposing defence. As a result, the players were so blinded by the brightness they temporarily lost all sence of direction. The players were sometimes distracted in front of goal by the over zealous enthusiasm of press photographers and newsreel cameramen. In an effort to faithfully record every aspect of the game they set off a number of flashlights when an attacking player had a goalscoring opportunity. This led to some bad finishing when they were startled by the camera's flash bulbs. One such victim was Jennie Harris for Dick, Kerr's. Her first attempt to find the net was from close range, but much to the amusement of the crowd and players alike, her shot travelled so high over the goal that the ball struck the top of the south stand and fell behind it. She soon made up for her misfortune and scored two goals later in the first half. In the second half, Florrie Redford and Minnie Lyons added goals in the last few minutes of the game. The Dick, Kerr goalkeeper Annie Hastie, didn't have one shot to save all evening.

The crowd showed they were well into the spirit of the game when a free kick was given against a 'Rest' player and a female spectator jokingly shouted, *send her off ref*'! The Rest of England played well together on the whole, but they couldn't stop the might of Dick, Kerr's as they recorded yet another 4-0 victory. Their best player on the night was Miss Waine, the goalkeeper from St Helens. She made several excellent saves and even injured herself saving one attempt on goal and needed treatment before the game could continue. Miss Dickinson and M Seed were the pick of the attack, but they were outclassed by a vastly more experienced team with Florrie Haslam and Daisy Clayton also playing exceptionally well. Before and after the game both sets of players happily posed for the cameras and kicking about near one of the goals for the Pathe News reporters. A crowd of young lads gathered round them and managed to get the match ball and raced to the other end of the pitch, quickly pursued by the searchlight and a posse of policemen! The whole event was an enormous success which amply repaid all those who had a share in organising this unique method of raising funds. Financially, the proceedings far exceeded the expectations of the organisers and there was an added collection of £14, 5 shillings made at half time by ladies at the ground. After the match, both teams and officials were special guests at a supper in the canteen at the Dick, Kerr works. A vote of thanks was made by representatives from the Unemployed Ex Servicemens Fund. They were to receive in excess of £600 as a result of the game. In response, Mr Frankland said that future activities of the team would be devoted to helping unemployed ex-Servicemen in various parts of the country.

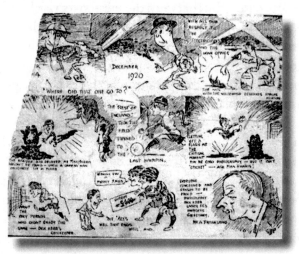

Cartoon of Night Match 1920

A chance meeting in 1993 with ninety year old Charles Newton who was a spectator at the match told me, "*I had never seen lassies play football before and they were quite adept. They had some very good players and I remember they overplayed the opposition. I thought that Alice Kell was the player most outstanding*".

Undoubtedly the biggest crowd ever to attend a ladies football club match was the one played at Goodison Park, Everton on Boxing Day 1920. Mr Frankland was advised by a reporter from the 'Topical Times', that they would raise over £1000 for charity if they played a game on Merseyside. His advice was taken and what occurred that day far exceeded anyone's expectations and will probably stay in the record books forever.

This was probably one of those stand alone moments in history, especially when you consider that since the inception of women's football there had been a misconceived belief that it was nothing more than a novelty for ladies to play the game, and an even bigger novelty for the public to actually dare to choose to come and support them. Surely the Goodison match in particular surpasses any suggestion of mere novelty. Without the benefit of mobile phones, twitter, facebook, television and any media hype, it was without any gimmicks that an astonishing number of spectators turned up that day to watch women play football.

The clever choice of opponent for this match on Merseyside was St Helens Ladies. Quoting from an extract in Mr Franklands scrapbook describing a previous match with the St Helens side when a crowd of 22,000 came to watch them it highlights the growing popularity of the women's game, it reads: *"It's co-incidental to think that in leading the way among ladies teams of the land, Dick, Kerr's are but emulating what "Proud Preston" did in mens football way back in the 1880's. Preston North End were then known as 'The Invincibles': Dick, Kerr Ladies are the Invincibles of today. Monday's experiences constitutes a distinct call. It is perfectly clear that something will have to be done, both at Goodison and Anfield to increase the public accommodation".*

Perhaps they heeded the warning, or maybe not enough as 53,000 spectators were packed inside Goodison Park, with between 10,000-14,000 unable to gain admission. There were so many people about the players had to have a police escort to get them safely to the changing rooms. But notably, if the ground *had* been able to accommodate everyone who wanted to get in to watch the match, there was a potential audience of approximately 67,000 people willing to pay to watch women's football. Not an Olympic event with a National team, but an ordinary bunch of factory girls from Lancashire. Phew! Quite phenomenal.

They had all come to see Dick, Kerr Ladies play their closest rivals, St Helens. Both teams had already met seven times in this year, with the Preston side being the victors on each occasion. But with St Helens at home on Merseyside, could they dent the armour of the invincible Dick, Kerr Ladies in front of their own crowd? Team captain Alice Kell, did her best to keep them calm but hearing the sound of that huge crowd from the dressing room could never have prepared them for the stomach churning experience they encountered when they ran out on to the pitch. They couldn't quite believe what they saw as they entered the arena that day. It was an unbelievable atmosphere playing in front of such an enormous crowd, an experience they would no doubt remember for the rest of their lives.

Florrie Redford had been in Paris and narrowly missed the train to Liverpool and was therefore unavailable for selection. It was a bitter blow for the team and St Helens were hoping they could capitalize on Dick, Kerr's being without one of their most prolific goalscorers. The game was kicked off by music hall star Ella Retford. Ella was a top comedienne and pantomime principal boy. She had also written a number of wartime songs but her most famous one was *'She's a Lassie from Lancashire'*. To compensate for the missing fire power of Redford, the diminutive Jennie Harris was moved to centre forward, and at the interval, Dick, Kerr's were leading by 1-0 thanks to a goal scored by her. A second half reshuffle saw right back Alice Kell, switched to the centre forward position. It was a superb tactical decision as Alice played a blinder and scored a remarkable hat-trick to help her side achieve a memorable 4-0 victory. Afterwards, the Lord Mayor of Liverpool presented the team with a silver cup, while each member of the team received a medal as a gift of thanks from the ex servicemens organisations. An amazing total of £3115 was raised for charity that day, which far exceeded the expectations of anyone involved and was an achievement unlikely to be equalled. (www.thisismoney.co.uk calculates a comparison value today to be worth £118,151)

Given the benefit of hindsight, this is probably **the** match that sealed the fate of the ladies game. Not only was it the biggest crowd ever to attend a women's match, it was in fact the largest crowd recorded at **any** game in the football league since records began in 1888. If we look at the figures, the picture becomes clear. Newcastle United came a distant second in the 1920/21 season when they had the biggest crowd in men's football with a gate of 41,265. Next came Chelsea with 38,520, and in third place was Everton with 37,215. In the newly formed Division Three, Millwall had the biggest crowd with 18,160. (Through the Turnstiles by Brian Tabner) The Goodison game was unprecedented and must have sent huge shock waves resounding throughout the whole of football. All this attention for a bunch of factory girls? It couldn't last, could it?

74

PLAYED 30	WON 25	DRAWN 2	LOST 3	GOALS FOR 133	AGAINST 15

DATE	VENUE	RESULT	CROWD
7 Feb	Euxton	DK 0 Liverpool 2	?
13 Mar	Leyland	DK 4 Aintree 2	?
23 Mar	Burnley	DK 5 Liverpool 0	?
10 Apr	Wigan	DK 0 Liverpool 1	?
24 Apr	Wigan	DK 4 Aintree 0	?
30 Apr	Preston	DK 2 French 0	25,000
1 May	Stockport	DK 5 French 2	?
5 May	Manchester	DK 1 French 1	12,000
6 May	London	DK 1 French 2	10,000
8 May	Oldham	DK 2 St Helens 0	15,000
15 May	Blackpool	DK 6 Bolton 2	14,000
22 May	Blackburn	DK 6 St Helens 0	13,000
12 June	Winsford	DK 5 Cheshire 0	3,000
26 June	Crewe	DK 3 Verdin & Cooks 0	10,000
21 Aug	Bostock	DK 3 Verdin & Cooks 0	3,000
28 Aug	Chorley	DK 6 Verdin & Cooks 1	5,000
4 Sept	Morecambe	DK 6 St Helens 0	6,000
11 Sept	Harrogate	DK 7 St Helens 0	10,000
18 Sept	St Helens	DK 9 St Helens 1	5,000
29 Sept	Blackpool	DK 7 Irish 0	15,000
9 Oct	Accrington	DK 9 St Helens 0	14,000
31 Oct	Paris	DK 1 French 1	22,000
1 Nov	Roubaix	DK 2 French 0	16,000
6 Nov	Rouen	DK 6 French 0	10,000
7 Nov	Le Havre	DK 2 French 0	14,000

20 Nov	Leicester	DK 4 St Helens 0	22,000
11 Dec	Nelson	DK 12 Verdin & Cooks 0	8,000
16 Dec	Preston	DK 4 Res 0	10,000
18 Dec	Accrington	DK 7 Chorley 0	10,000
26 Dec	Liverpool	DK 4 St Helens 0	53,000

Goal scorers to date:

Florrie Redford	56	*Alice Mills*	5
Lily Parr	43	*Florrie Haslam*	4
Jennie Harris	24	*Alice Kell*	4
Alice Woods	14	*Jessie Walmsley*	1
Lily Lee	11		

Above details from the 1920 diary of Alice Stanley, nee Woods. The goals scored could have been listed since her arrival at the club. Not mentioned are the goals already documented in earlier matches before she joined the team: Nellie Mitchell (3), Florrie Rance (3), Lily Jones (2), Molly Walker (2), Miss Whittle (1), E Birkins (1), Alice Standing (1), Minnie Lyons (1) With a tally of 56 goals scored by centre forward Florrie Redford it is easy to see why Mr Frankland regarded her as the best goal scorer in the women's game.

N.B. In an effort to give some scale of the monies raised at these matches if a rough estimate of around £1000 is taken as an average per game, there could be a potential not far short of £30,000 for this one season alone.

CHAPTER FIVE

KICKED INTO TOUCH

Arrangements were finalised for a match to be played at Old Trafford, the home of Manchester United, on 8 January 1921 against Bath Ladies in aid of Manchester Unemployed Ex-Servicemen. This was to be the first meeting between the two clubs and Bath were a team the Dick, Kerr girls were keen to play against. Another game against a southern team had been arranged to be played in Leicester towards the end of 1920 but they withdrew from the game because Dick, Kerr's had refused to weaken their side. Luckily their local sparring partners St Helens, sportingly stepped into the breach so as not to disappoint the charities or the public. Bath Ladies though were anxious to meet the Preston team at full strength in order to compare their own level of skill against them. They were recognised as one of the best teams in the south and had earned the reputation of being among the best sides in the country. They were coached by Charlie Slade who played half back (midfield) for Huddersfield Town.

Following the success of the Goodison match, this game was causing a great deal of interest and extra trains, trams and buses were laid on. The pre match press publicity stated that Florrie Redford and Jennie Harris, the Dick, Kerr's 'box o tricks', had scored 260 goals between them. A crowd of 35,000 came along to see yet another victory for the Dick, Kerr Ladies in which 15 year old Lily Parr scored four of her teams goals in a convincing 12-0 scoreline. Lily had been moved from full back to left wing and this was probably the most inspired tactical decision in the club's history. Other goals came from Florrie Redford 3, Jessie Walmsley 2, Jennie Harris 1 and local girl, 17 year old Alice Mills, scoring 2 goals.

Alice Mills was born in Preston at 149 Marsh Lane on 15 June 1904. She was the eldest of five children born to William Mills and Mary Ann Martin. William was a master shoemaker and was very good at his craft and they were soon able to open their own shop on North Road in Preston. The family lived above the premises and Alice's sister Winnie was born there in 1907. The business was thriving when an opportunity arose for William to open another shop in Hyde near Manchester. The family moved again and it was there where brother Joe and sister Elizabeth Ann were born in 1908 and 1910 respectively. Things were going pretty well for the Mills family and they had a good standing within the community. They were a church-going family with Alice's mother being of a strong Catholic bias. (Mary Ann Mills was a prejudiced woman but Alice was just the opposite and grew up to be very tolerant). However, tragedy was to befall the family when William became seriously ill with a degenerative lung disease. Mary Ann did her best to care for him but having recently fallen pregnant with their fifth child she was finding it increasingly difficult to cope. They had no option but to return to Preston to be closer to family during his final months. William died on 14 August 1913, he was just 34 years old. Three months later, still devasted from the loss of her husband, Mary Ann gave birth to their daughter, Mary. At only nine years of age, Alice Mills often found herself in charge of her siblings. Mary Ann didn't know which way to turn and was finding it hard to make ends meet but with five hungry mouths to feed she knew she had to carry on. She was determined to keep the family together and take care of her children. Pride went out the window as she took in laundry and cleaned at the local bakery and although they were extremely tough times, she made sure that the family unit stuck together and survived. Alice went to work as a weaver in the cotton mills when she was just 12 years old. She later worked at the Dick, Kerr factory where the opportunity arose for her to join the ladies football team and she became a regular player during what would probably be its most successful era. Her uncle, Jack Martin, spent a lot of time with Alice and he was something of a father figure to her. He shared her love of football and taught her how to play the game. He had played centre half for Preston North End in 1903-04 and also captained St Helens for several years. Alice played for the Dick, Kerr Ladies against her mother's wishes but with the support of uncle Jack, he persuaded Mary Ann that she would be alright. He said ,*"Go on sis, let her play".* Mary Ann eventually relented and no-one could have realised at the time just what a life-changing event her joining the team would turn out to be for all the family.

Many years later Alice recalled her life in Preston during the First World War. She often talked of her visits to the Protestant Orphanage after her fathers death. She felt the family would not have survived had it not been for the good Protestants. It had a big impact on her life and taught her discipline and tolerance.

"The years 1914-1918 were war years. Times were hard and anything that was free, I was there to grab! A free meal, Canadian flour or a hunk of cheese which I had half eaten before I got it home. If memory serves me correctly, every two weeks or so we got a large bag of flour and being as we were one of the poorest families in the Sacred Heart Parish, we were assured of fresh bread and cheese. Nothing in this world has ever tasted quite as good as those free meals whether

they came from the Canadian government or the Weslyan Church soup kitchen. That was the closest I ever came to the Protestants. Poor as we were mother would not let us mingle with who she considered to be, the dirty Protestants. Nothing or nobody was quite as good as a crummy Catholic. Being ten years old and the eldest in a family of five children, the youngest born only three months after my father died, I was always the one who did the flour carrying, or the one that took the other kids for free meals. Thank God for those free meals. They sure filled a corner of stomachs that could stand anything that went into them!

The Clay family who lived across the street had poor appetites. Mrs Clay was a good cook and she always gave us the leftovers and unlike Julia Child who always said Bon appetit, I used to pray that they would come home with bad ones! The Lord must have heard my prayers because we ended up more often than not with ample food for all. One meal I will remember all my life is Shepherds Pie. I have tried many times to recapture that delicious flavour, but never quite made it. However I am glad to have had such an outstanding meal. Many thanks to the Wesleyans! My mother took in washing for one rich family in our parish and looking back over the years, I realise how lucky we were to have had such a good friend in Mrs Brown. She used to save me drippings from the roast beef and the best creamery butter on earth does not compare with a slice of bread fried in beef dripping! Luck must have been our constant companion. My mother

Alice Mills in action at Leeds 1921

also got help from the St Vincent Society. Sacred Heart was a rich parish and we were the poorest family in it, so we got a ticket for food every two weeks or so. The shopkeeper, Mrs Fuller, always saved us the bacon ends, or bits of ham and cold cuts. Many a silent prayer I said for that good old soul! Another thing that helped out was the biscuit factory. For a few pennies you could take a pillow slip and get it filled with broken biscuits. That was another way of eating good. Saturday nights, mother cleaned the local bakery and always came home with the leftovers. Every little bit helps and sometimes she brought home rice pudding made with real cream. A gift from the Gods".

In the early 1920's the national enthusiasm for the Dick, Kerr Ladies had in some ways paralleled that seen by the rapid expansion of the professional male game during the same period. In 1920 Divisions one and two of the men's football league were each expanded from 20 to 22 clubs and in the 1920/21 season a new Division Three was formed from southern clubs soon followed by a Division Three North in 1921/22.

Despite the growth of the men's game after the war the national interest in

Team picture 1921

Back row: men unknown, Molly Walker, Lily Parr, Alice Kell, Annie Hastie, Daisy Clayton, Alice Woods, Annie Crozier

Front row: Alfred Frankland, Lily Lee, Alice Mills, Florrie Haslam, Jessie Walmsley, Jennie Harris, Florrie Redford

women's football was still quite substantial. It was however, a state of affairs that wouldn't be allowed to last. Women's Football offended the middle class propriety of the FA's ruling Council, but perhaps more importantly it was taking away too much of the spotlight from the male game. The conspiracy instigated by those within the football establishment had begun in earnest with an unstoppable momentum. The women were naively oblivious and time was quickly running out for ladies football. But by 1921 the popularity of the Dick, Kerr Ladies was at its height and they were the team that everyone wanted to see. They had been booked to play an average of two games a week all over the British Isles until the middle of August and there was even talk of a tour to Canada. Many charities had realised what a *little gold mine* these girls represented and they were inundated with requests to play more matches. In fact they received so many requests that they regretably had to refuse at least 120 invitations from Lord Mayors and MP's from all parts of the land.

The dedication and love these girls had for their sport was remarkable. They were working full time at the factory *and* playing football almost every Saturday. For a midweek match they were still expected to work before travelling to the venue to play the game. Compare that with the professional male footballer today who gets tired if he has to play a couple of games a week. Alice Norris recalled, "*It was sometimes hard work when we played a match during the week because we would have to work in the morning, travel to play the match, then travel home again and be up early for work the next day. But I was proud to be a Dick, Kerr's girl, it was worth all the effort we put in*". And let's also remember that travel was much more time consuming in those days. These girls weren't able to whizz up and down a motorway in an executive coach or charter a private aircraft, they often had a rickety old bone shaker to contend with. But they still enjoyed their journey, each one being a new adventure, and they would sing songs together to while away the time. They even had a song of their own:

When upon the field of play we go, thousands come to cheer us on our way
And you will often hear them say: Who can beat Dick, Kerr's today?
When the ball is swinging merrily, faces are all beaming happily
So play up girls and do your best, for victory is our cry.

Pre match publicity in the Stalybridge Reporter on 5 February 1921 for a match between the Dick, Kerr Ladies and St Helens, once again highlighted the goal scoring prowess of Florrie Redford and Jennie Harris, but 'the new kid on the block', Lily Parr, was taking her first steps towards carving her own unique place in history. Of the 15 year old starlet they said, *'Taking age and sex into consideration, there is probably no greater football prodigy in the whole*

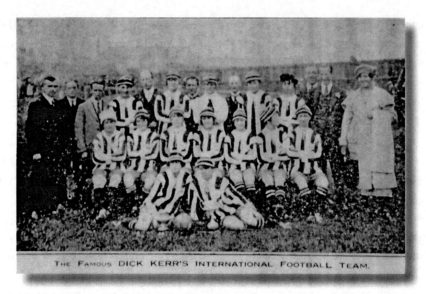

Stalybridge 1921

Back row players: Alice Woods, Jessie Walmsley, Annie Hastie, Lily Parr, Molly Walker, Annie Crozier (trainer)

Middle: Lily Lee, S Hulme, Florrie Haslam, Alice Kell, Alice Mills, Lily Jones, Daisy Clayton

Front: Florrie Redford, Jennie Harris

country than Miss Parr. Not only has she speed and excellent ball control, but her admirable physique enables her to brush off opposing defenders. She amazes the crowd where ever she goes by the way she crosses the ball clean across the goalmouth to the waiting forwards'. The game was another resouding success and a crowd of 12,000 saw a comfortable 9-0 victory for the Preston side with goals from: Lily Parr 3, Jennie Harris 3, Florrie Redford 2, Alice Mills 1

During the same period, music hall comedian Harry Weldon was in Liverpool appearing in pantomime. He came up with an idea of organising a Charity Fancy Dress Carnival and a ladies football match, with all proceeds going to Unemployed ex Servicemen, Liverpool Hospitals and the Variety Club Benevolent Fund. Time was short and they appealed for volunteers to accompany the procession and sell programmes en-route and for car owners to join the parade with suitably decorated vehicles. The Dick, Kerr Ladies were invited to play against a team made up of the best players from the rest of the UK. Harry thought of getting the opposition together in a good humoured attempt to 'put one over' on the invincible Dick, Kerr's. The Rest of Britain team (or Team GB) was made up of the best individual players in ladies teams throughout the country and distance was no object. One player even came from the Island of Unst in the Shetland Isles! Both teams were invited to take part in the carnival procession through the streets of Liverpool. He donated a trophy, aptly named The Harry Weldon Cup, to be presented to the winners. The date was set for 14 February 1921 and the directors of Liverpool Football Club agreed for the match to be played at Anfield in the afternoon.

The Dick, Kerr team was: Annie Hastie, Alice Kell, Daisy Clayton, Alice Woods, Jessie Walmsley, Lily Lee, Florrie Haslam, Jennie Harris, Florrie Redford, Alice Mills, Lily Parr.

Rest of Britain, chosen from: Waine, capt (St Helens), Macpherson (Scotland), Gee (St Helens), Jones (Horrockses Crewdson), Ransome (St Helens), Dickinson (Barrow in Furness), Swift (Sutton Oak), Bartholomew (Southampton), Bennion (Cheshire County) Leviconte (Lyons, London) Walker (Scotland), Riddell (Scotland)

Twenty-five thousand people came to see if the invincible Dick, Kerr Ladies could be beaten by the Rest of Britain team. When Ella Retford kicked off the match there seemed to be more photographers than players on the pitch with newspaper reporters and newsreel cameramen (Pathe News) all fighting for the best view. The Preston team soon took control of the game and quickly went into a three goal lead thanks to a hat-trick from Lily Parr but Miss Riddell, the Scottish centre forward replied with a goal for the Rest of Britain. Just before half time Daisy Clayton, the Dick, Kerr left back went down injured. The crowd cheered as Annie Crozier ran on to the pitch to treat her with the customary bucket of water and magic sponge. Goals came quickly in the second half, two more from Lily Parr, taking her total to five, two from Florrie Redford and another two from Jennie Harris. The final score was an emphatic 9-1 victory for the Dick, Kerr Ladies and they were delighted with their perfomance against a team representing the best of the rest. A grand total of £1500 was raised in gate receipts alone. After the match both teams and officials were invited to a gala performance of the pantomime Dick Whittington at the Olympia Theatre. At the end of the show the Dick, Kerr team were invited on stage to receive the 'Harry Weldon Cup' from the man himself. Alice Kell accepted the trophy on behalf of the club and they received a standing ovation from the audience.

The team were invited to play a couple of matches north of the border to raise funds for ex servicemen in Scotland. They played at Celtic Park in Glasgow on 1 March against a Scottish side who were really no match for them. The scoreline was a very comfortable 9-0 victory. It was a similar

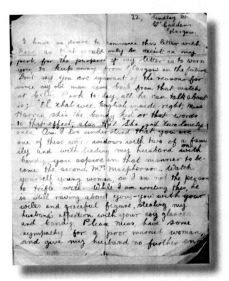
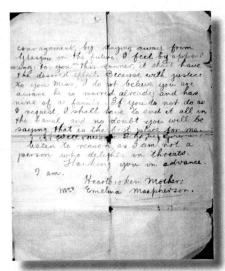

Letter from Mrs Macpherson

story in Edinburgh too when in front of 23,000 spectators, the Dick, Kerr girls ran the opposition ragged with a 13-0 scoreline. Not long after they returned home from Scotland, Jennie Harris received a letter from an extremely distraught wife of a very enthusiastic supporter who perhaps had an over zealous appreciation of her exceptional skills on the football field. (see below)

The letter reads: *I have no desire to commence this letter with Dear, as that would only be deceit on my part, for the purpose of my letter is to warn you to keep away from Glasgow in the future. Don't say you are ignorant of the reasons, for since my old man came back from that match at Celtic Park today, all he can talk about is:- "Oh that wee English outside right, Miss Harris, she's the Candy Kid" or words to that effect, also that, "She got two lovely ones". Am I to understand that you are one of these war widows with two of a family and with feeding my husband on Candy, you aspire in that manner to become the second Mrs Macpherson. Watch yourself young woman, as I am not the person to trifle with. While I am writing this, he is still raving about you, - you with your wiles and graceful figure, stealing my husband's affection with your coy glances and Candy. Please Miss, have some sympathy for a poor married woman, and give my husband no further encouragement, by staying away from Glasgow in the future. I feel by appealing to you in this manner, it shall have the desired effect. Because with justice to you Miss, I do not believe you are aware he is married already and has nine of a family. If you do not do as I request, I shall have to end*

Jennie Harris

it all in the Canal, and no doubt you will be saying, that is the best place for me. Well Miss, I hope you will listen to reason, as I am not a person who delights in threats. Thanking you in advance. I am, Heartbroken Mother, Mrs Emelina Macpherson.

Amusing as this incident may seem and all joking aside, it does confirm that there was a genuine appreciation from the public for the athleticism of these girls. Let us hope though that Mrs Macpherson decided against 'ending it all in the canal' and that she and Mr Macpherson were reconciled and they all lived happily ever after!

The French team made a welcome return to England later in the year but during this visit they mainly played against other teams in the south. They did travel up to Staffordshire on 17 May when they played Dick, Kerr's in front of 15,000 spectators. Lily Parr scored all five goals in a 5-1 victory and the Dick, Kerr bandwagon continued to roll. Later that year, Carmen Pomies was another of the French players to return to Preston and play football with the Dick, Kerr team. She lived and worked in the town for several years and for some time stayed at the home of Florrie Redford. Carmen was a champion javelin thrower in France and also a versatile footballer, playing either in goal or out field. She was to enjoy a long affinity with the Preston team.

Dick, Kerr Ladies v Yorkshire Ladies 1921

Centre second row: Georges Carpentier

The Dick, Kerr Ladies were going from strength to strength and other prominent sporting personalities were more than happy to show their support for ladies football. The photograph above shows Georges Carpentier posing with them before kicking off the match. Carpentier was considered the greatest European boxer of all time. On 5 June 1921 he fought Jack Dempsey for the championship of the world. Dempsey won the fight after a knockout in the fourth round, but Carpentier was not disgraced and went on to be the light heavyweight champion until 1925.

The fixture list was growing and in August they went on a three day tour to the Isle of Man with St Helens Ladies. They played in Ramsay, Port Erin and Douglas and they were the victors on each occasion. On 9 August they played a match in Derby at the Baseball Ground, defeating Coventry Ladies by 3-0 in front of 20,000 spectators with goals from Florrie Redford 2, Alice Mills 1. The match report reads: *'When the teams had been photographed and the Mayor had started the game, there was a disposition on the part of the crowd to treat the struggle in a holiday spirit and extract fun from every move. But they began to look at things from a different viewpoint when Lily Parr tricked her way, by deft footwork, past a couple of defenders and shot the ball goalwards with surprising force. Excellent passing between Jennie Harris, Florrie Redford and Alice Mills, coupled with the capital centres of Florrie Haslam, completed* the disillusionment and the spectators settled down to a serious exposition of the game. Dick, Kerrs showed themselves to be a team carefully coached in the best points of the game, with a penchant for hard shooting, and exceptionally evenly balanced, it being impossible to point to any department where weakness was shown. The halves (midfield) were excellent, and the full backs, particularly the captain, Alice Kell, so near impregnable that the goalkeeper was unbeaten without saving a shot. Coventry lacked the training and skill of the champions. The heroine of the evening was S Sidwell in the Coventry goal. She played with the coolness of a veteran and saved shots that would have added to the reputation of a mere male professional. Rounds of applause greeted her display and there was delerious enthusiasm when, in the closing stages, she kept out the redoutable Lily Parr.' At the end of the game, the players autographed the match ball which was offered up for auction and the Mayor's Hospital Fund were expected to reach a total in excess of £600.

They were soon back on the road again travelling north of the border for another visit to Scotland. The 10th September saw them play in Aberdeen and the next day they had a match in Dundee. Other fixtures followed in the North West, and later that month they played Wales at Blackpool, beating the representative side by 4-0, with goals from the 'box o' tricks', Redford (3) Harris (1). They were later entertained at a Banquet and the menu card below illustrates how these women were held in very high esteem and once again mixing with top stars of the era.

Dinner Menu Card 1921

(Autographed by Jennie Harris and 'Wee' Georgie Woods. Standing only 4 foot 9 inches tall, Georgie Woods was one of the most famous stars of music hall. He also starred in the film, 'Two Little Drummer boys' in 1928)

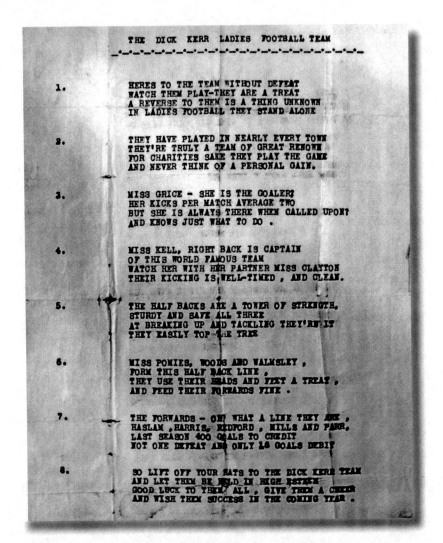

THE DICK KERR LADIES FOOTBALL TEAM

1.
HERES TO THE TEAM WITHOUT DEFEAT
WATCH THEM PLAY-THEY ARE A TREAT
A REVERSE TO THEM IS A THING UNKNOWN
IN LADIES FOOTBALL THEY STAND ALONE

2.
THEY HAVE PLAYED IN NEARLY EVERY TOWN
THEY'RE TRULY A TEAM OF GREAT RENOWN
FOR CHARITIES SAKE THEY PLAY THE GAME
AND NEVER THINK OF A PERSONAL GAIN.

3.
MISS GRICE - SHE IS THE GOALER,
HER KICKS PER MATCH AVERAGE TWO
BUT SHE IS ALWAYS THERE WHEN CALLED UPON,
AND KNOWS JUST WHAT TO DO .

4.
MISS KELL, RIGHT BACK IS CAPTAIN
OF THIS WORLD FAMOUS TEAM
WATCH HER WITH HER PARTNER MISS CLAYTON
THEIR KICKING IS WELL-TIMED , AND CLEAN.

5.
THE HALF BACKS ARE A TOWER OF STRENGTH,
STURDY AND SAFE ALL THREE
AT BREAKING UP AND TACKLING THEY'RE IT
THEY EASILY TOP THE TREE

6.
MISS PONIES, WOODS AND WALMSLEY ,
FORM THIS HALF BACK LINE ,
THEY USE THEIR HEADS AND FEET A TREAT ,
AND FEED THEIR FORWARDS FINE .

7.
THE FORWARDS - OH! WHAT A LINE THEY ARE ,
HASLAM ,HARRIS, REDFORD , MILLS AND PARR,
LAST SEASON 400 GOALS TO CREDIT
NOT ONE DEFEAT AND ONLY 18 GOALS DEBIT

8.
SO LIFT OFF YOUR HATS TO THE DICK KERR TEAM
AND LET THEM BE HELD IN HIGH ESTEEM
GOOD LUCK TO THEM ALL , GIVE THEM A CHEER
AND WISH THEM SUCCESS IN THE COMING YEAR .

Poem for The Dick, Kerr Ladies FC

Nineteen twenty-one must surely have been their halcyon year and everything they touched turned out to be a great success. One of the club members wrote a poem about the team which further illustrates their achievements. The author of the verse is not clear.

However everything wasn't all sweetness and light. Storm clouds were gathering and in spite of all the success there were still many critics of women's football. Indeed, throughout the life of the sport the negative opinions from those within the male game were never very far from the surface. It seemed that women's football *had* to be stopped at all costs and by the end of the year it would be seen in a very different light.

Dick, Kerr Ladies 1921

Emma Grice, Alice Mills, Jennie Harris, Daisy Clayton, Alice Kell, Florrie Redford, Florrie Haslam, Alice Woods, Carmen Pomies, Jessie Walmsley, Lily Parr

A resentment was growing within the male soccer establishment due to the size of crowds women's football, and in particular the Dick, Kerr Ladies, were attracting. Despite the fact that worthy charities were benefiting from the ladies matches, the uncomfortable truth was that they were drawing bigger crowds than men. The Football League had only just been expanded and there was a new Division Three to populate, so perhaps they thought there wasn't enough spectators to go round. There was too much support for women's football, the boys didn't like it and the two were on a collision course that would dramatically change the course of history.

Suggestions were also being made regarding the misappropriation of monies raised at ladies matches and this was causing considerable concern. No-one really knows where the rumours began or who indeed was responsible for any alleged misappropriation, but something needed to be done in order to try to quell the speculation. Consequently, the FA took steps to gain some kind of control regarding the finances at specific matches. Permission for a game with Dick, Kerr Ladies v South of England, at Bristol City FC on 16 September, was only granted on condition that the Club be responsible for the receipts and payments and a Statement of Account be sent to the FA showing how the whole of the receipts were apportioned. These conditions were strictly adhered to but the rumours did not go away and the FA took further action. On 10 October they stated that rather than just for specific games, Clubs must not permit matches between **any** ladies teams to be played on their grounds, unless sanction for such matches had first been obtained from the FA. It was also to be a condition of any application granted that Clubs abide by the same requirements as stated above. It seems that the FA wanted to make it increasingly more difficult for women to continue playing the game.

But continue they did and in November the Dick, Kerr Ladies played Lyons (London) Ladies at Hyde Road, Manchester in aid of the Lord Mayor's Charity Fund. The match raised in excess of £500 for the French town of Charleville-Mézières and the proceeds went towards the rebuilding of the hospital which had been totally destroyed during the war. With the help of the people of Manchester, the hospital was eventually rebuilt and it is still called the Manchester Hospital today. Also this month they played in Skipton to raise funds for the town's hospital. The game raised £145 for the hospital fund and the press said, *'Just to put that into context, the Skipton Gala is the biggest source of fund raising for the hospital which would normally only raise that amount in a year'.*

Despite the good will of the ladies, the plot to bring down women's football had begun and in real terms the writing was already on the wall, but they protested their innocence vehemently. Yes, they received expenses for loss of time at work and travel costs: who wouldn't expect some recompense for that? But they never received a penny piece more than what they had spent and they were deeply hurt by the allegations. As far as the ladies were concerned what happened to the money after the match was nothing to do with them. Their interest went no further than the good causes they were helping and their performance on the pitch. But the finger of suspicion had been pointed at women's football and it was only a matter of time before the bubble was to burst. The FA met again in November and one of the items on the agenda was a match that had taken place between Plymouth and Seaton Ladies, played at Winchester City FC. The club were reprimanded for having allowed the match to be played on their ground without first obtaining permission from the FA. The club were ordered to donate their share of the gate receipts to a local charity.

Opinions regarding the playing of football by women were also obtained from the medical profession and it was just what the FA wanted to hear. Some doctors were of the opinion that football *was* a dangerous pursuit for ladies and it could cause them serious physical harm. It seems rather contradictory that they thought it safe enough to run around a hockey pitch yielding a big stick to be acceptable but football on the other had was dangerous. However, the campaign was gathering momentum and the FA finally dealt the fatal blow to the ladies game and effectively changed the course of women's football forever.

The FA Council consisted of around 60 members. President of the Association was Lord Arthur Kinnaird and there were six vice presidents. They also had ten divisional representatives, forty county association reps and seven other affiliated association reps. It was this band of merry gentlemen who were responsible for what can only be described as the biggest miscarriage of justice ever meted out by a sporting body. On 5 December 1921, they unanimously passed the following resolution:

"Complaints having been made as to football being played by women, the Council feel impelled to express their strong opinion that the game of football is quite unsuitable for females and ought not to be encouraged.

Complaints have also been made as to the conditions under which some of these matches have been arranged and played, and the appropriation of receipts to other than charitable objects.

The Council are further of the opinion that an excessive proportion of the receipts are absorbed in expenses and an inadequate percentage devoted to charitable objects.

For these reasons the council request clubs belonging to the association to refuse the use of their grounds for such matches".

It was as easy as that. The axe had fallen and despite the ladies denials and assurances regarding finances and their willingness to play under any conditions laid down by the FA, their decision was irreversible. The chauvenists, the so called medical 'experts' and the anti-women's football lobby had won. Their threatened male bastion was now safe and the opportunity for equal growth and prosperity from the game of football was gone forever.

The *Lancashire Daily Post* quoted Alfred Frankland, as expressing his disgust at the FA's decision, he said, *"The women's game would continue if organisers of charity matches would provide them with grounds to play on."* When questioned about payments to players he said, *"Dick, Kerr's were only paid expenses for travelling, accommodation and for loss of time at work. The girls were in no way paid for playing football."* Commenting on the FA's opinion that the game was not suitable for women, he said, *"Dick, Kerr Ladies Football Club do not think the FA are capable of judging whether the game is harmful or not. Most of the girls have been playing for four years, and a recent mishap to Miss Kell's wrist was the first real accident, and this was due to a fall while running".* He went on to say that the club had raised something like £50,000 for charity which was mainly for ex servicemen and hospitals.

Alice Kell said, *"Girls have a right to play football if they desire. We play for the love of the game and are determined to go on. It is absolutely impossible for working girls to afford to leave work to play matches in Scotland, Ireland and up and down the country and be the losers. I can see not the slightest reason why they should not be recompensed for loss of time."*

Shock waves resounded throughout the land. Arguments for and arguments against, but nothing would reverse the decison of the Football Association now that they had succeeded in bringing down the ladies game. But such serious action does seem to be based on some pretty flimsy opinions. The truth is that up to the ban being enforced, the Dick, Kerr Ladies had played 65 games of football that year and almost 900,000 people had come to watch them. Isn't that the real reason for the ban? Clearly they were victims of their own success

Doctor Elizabeth Sloan Chesser said, *"I do not believe in placing a ban on any pleasures. If women want to play football let them. On the other hand, there are physical reasons why the game is harmful to women. It is a rough game at any time, but it is much more harmful to women than to men. They may receive injuries from which they may never recover."* But this was contradicted in the *Lancashire Daily Post,* when it reported, *'One of Dick, Kerr's best players is a nurse at Whittingham Hospital. Recently she was on duty all night in charge of a ward. When she came off duty she cycled the seven miles to Preston in the rain, travelled by train to the Midlands, played a fine game of football in the afternoon in front of a record crowd, and was back on duty at the hospital the same evening.'* However they couldn't prevent the medical profession voicing even more absurd opinions. Again it was the *Lancashire Daily Post* who printed this article from an undisclosed source: *"A Doctor who has been associated with football, both professionally and as a keen follower of the game for some years told a 'Post' reporter that from every point of view it was undesirable that girls should play such a strenuous game as football. He had himself had to attend to three girl footballers who had been affected internally by playing, and he is convinced that physicologically it was most harmful, whilst the risks were very much greater than in the case of men players. He does not believe that women are fitted for violent leg strain, and even professional dancing on the stage, which of course, is not associated with the same dangers from external causes as football, is objectionable on this account. The periodicity of a woman's life and their delicate* organism emphasises the danger of accident strain, and the ordinary risks of violent exertion. As a spectacle too, he does not think it is at all satisfactory, but only attractive as a novelty, so that when this phase has passed, he thinks people will realize that it was not nice to see girls taking part in the strenuous practices of the football field."

And Dr Mary Scharlieb, a Harley Street Physician said, "I consider it a most unsuitable game, too much for a womans physical frame." Mr Eustace Miles also said, "I consider football quite an inappropriate game for most women, especially if they have not been medically tested first. The kicking is too jerky a movement for women and the strain is likely to be rather severe."

Looking at things objectively, no one can deny that these very same women had played their part in keeping the country going during those terrible years of 1914-18. They were considered 'suitable' enough then to undertake any challenge required of them and do all manner of dangerous and heavy work necessary in helping the nation win the war. Our country would indeed have been defeated without their contribution. Where were these doctors when the women were lugging hundredweight sacks of coal from the mines or being slowly poisoned by toxic fumes from TNT? It does rather strengthen the argument that the football establishment simply did not want women playing football at any price.

The ladies were convinced the FA had taken this action because they were drawing bigger crowds than men and there can be no doubt that this was one of the reasons. Alice Woods said, "We were all disgusted with the FA after we had played all those games for charity. They said it wasn't a game for ladies, but we all thought it was because we were getting the spectators that the men didn't get, especially in the outlying districts on the small grounds. We always had terrific crowds." And she was right. The figures speak for themselves. In the 1921/22 season, the largest crowd in the First Division was at Chelsea with 37,545. Second Division West Ham 20,100, Division 3 South, Millwall 16,650 and Division Three North, Stockport 11,050. The remainder of the new division north and south, could only attract crowds of between 2500-9500. (Through the Turnstiles, Brian Tabner) Alice Norris added, "It was a terrible shock when the FA stopped us playing on League grounds. Everybody was upset because we were drawing the crowds. We just ignored them when they said it wasn't a suitable game for ladies to play. It was petty. I think it was jealousy."

The case for the women was put very fairly in a letter to the secretary of the FA from Major Cecil Kent, former honorary secretary of the Old Westminsters FC. In his letter, Major Kent said: "I may mention that in present and past seasons I have watched about 30 ladies football matches between *various teams and I have met the players. I have travelled with them frequently by road and rail and I have attended the various functions to which they have been invited and I have met the Lord Mayor's and also the officials of the local charities and football clubs concerned. On all sides I have heard nothing but praise for the good work the girls are doing and the high standard of their play. The only thing I now hear from the man in the street is, "Why have the FA got their knife into girls football? What have the girls done except to raise large sums for charity and to play the game? Are their feet heavier on the turf than the men's feet?" (Lancashire Daily Post)*

Support also came from other quarters within the game itself. Harry Hampton, ex Aston Villa and Birmingham forward told of his support for the women's game in an article in the *Sunday Mercury and News*, when he said: *"It is not often I find myself in disagreement with members of the Football Association but, candidly, I do not see eye to eye with them in their attempt to suppress ladies football. They have not attempted to stop it - they have not the power to do it - but they have put obstacles in the way of its growth. We English people are steeped in conventions; We refuse to change. We have been so long without ladies football that we object to it and say we will not have it. To bolster up our objections we say that it is unbecoming to a lady; it is much too rough for them. That is because we, unfairly I maintain, judge it from the men's point of view. If we are beaten in our contention we attempt to defend our conservatism by saying that the women players look ugly or that they are watched by men out of curiosity. That, in my opinion, is an ungallant 'get out'. By all means let the girls play but they must play against each other and not men and women being pitted against one another."*

How were the FA able to justify their actions with that kind of support? But of course this wasn't what they wanted to hear and they chose to ignore all the positive comments. The success of women's football was sentenced to be buried in history. But what about the financial side of things? Was there really some unscrupulous person, or persons, taking advantage of ladies football for their own gain? Apparently, this is what usually happened. The secretary/ manager of a team would estimate their costs for travel, accommodation and loss of time at work and then claim this amount from the gate receipts from the charity for which they were playing. The secretary/manager would then reimburse the girls their expenses.

Let's be honest, there's no smoke without fire and there probably was some element of truth in the allegations regarding the finances, so why wasn't an enquiry set up to get to the bottom of all the speculation and punish those who truly were responsible? With the huge amounts of money being generated, temptation may have been far too great for some and there is no doubt at all that the women *were* exploited.

Lydia Ackers, a St Helens player who later played for, and worked at the Dick, Kerr factory, remembered vividly some very interesting facts. Lydia said, *"Well, there won't be many people remember this, but I witnessed it and this is the truth. We were playing a match near Manchester against the West Cheshire's. As we were getting dressed, the man who had brought the West Cheshire team came in and asked how much we got when we played. We told him ten shillings each match. But he was asking for much more. The team he brought to play against us were supposed to be the West Cheshire's but we didn't recognise them. He must have thought that because there had been a big crowd at the game, he would put in for a big lump sum and get more than he was entitled to, but he didn't get it. It wasn't long after this that the FA stopped us from using league grounds."*

Let's try to figure it out. At the time of the FA ban the Dick, Kerr Ladies had been playing for four years and Mr Frankland was quoted as saying they had raised £50,000 for charity since their inception. But only £50,000? In 1920 they played 30 games of football and roughly could have averaged around £1000 per match, give or take. In 1921 another 67 games of football were contested which again, give or take, could roughly have averaged close on £1000 per match. Thats 97 games of football in just two years, with a potential maximum figure of £97,000. Take off a few grand for over-estimating, but if this is anywhere near correct, what could have happened to the remainder of the money?

The ladies game wasted no time in fighting back against the FA ban. A report in the *Lancashire Daily Post* stated that a Ladies Football Association had been formally inaugurated at a meeting in Liverpool on 10 December. The meeting resolved to form a Ladies FA and its main priorities were to promote the game among young girls, give aid to charities and deal with the gate receipts so that there would be no possible grounds for complaint. It went on to say: *"A league of ladies clubs is being formed in the Doncaster district and another in the Coventry area. An East Riding and North Lincolnshire league is also in contemplation. Representatives of some 60 clubs will meet this weekend to draft rules and decide upon modifications of the game which are considered desirable".* The Dick, Kerr Ladies had heard nothing of the Liverpool meeting, although Alfred Frankland did travel over in an effort to gleen some information. It seems there were over twenty clubs present at the inaugural meeting (had the Dick, Kerr Ladies been deliberately excluded from taking part?). They quickly set out their stall with new rules and regulations and put out a statement saying, *"The Ladies Football Association is most concerned with the management of the game and intend to insist that all clubs in the Association are run on a perfectly straightforward manner so that there will be no exploiting of the teams in the interest of the man or firm who manages them"* (one wonders if they had anyone in mind with that statement)

The next meeting of the LFA was held at Blackburn on 17 December and the number of teams represented had increased to almost sixty. The newly elected President was Leonard Bridgett, the manager of Stoke Ladies. There were five other Vice Presidents on the management committee with Mrs Barraclough of Huddersfield Atalanta being the only female member. New rules were agreed and perhaps the main stumbling block for the Dick, Kerr Ladies was regarding players not being allowed to play for a team if they lived a distance of more than 20 miles from the club's headquarters without obtaining permission from the Association. Now this really did put a spoke in the wheel for Frankland. He had been used to calling the shots as he had already brought in players from further afield, so it might be possible that they did decided to 'go it alone'. Fortunately for the players the Dick, Kerr factory had provided them with their own pitch to play on and they were keen to get on with playing football.

On 26 December 1921, only three weeks after the FA's momentous act, they welcomed Fleetwood Ladies to their first home game at 'Lively Polly' corner on Ashton Park in Preston. The match was played on behalf of the Clog Fund for Poor Children in the town and all the arrangements had been made without any expense whatsoever falling on the gate receipts. Every penny raised would go to the Poor Children's Fund. The match was supported by the Guild Mayor and Mayoress, Mr & Mrs Astley-Bell. Due to the controversy caused by the statement from the FA as to football being unsuitable for females, team captain, Alice Kell, invited local members of the medical profession to come along and witness the game for themselves to see what their verdict would be. About twenty of them accepted the invitation and Dr Mary Lowry kicked off the match. Fleetwood Ladies were considered to be among the best in women's football and a crowd of 3,000 came along to witness yet another victory for the home team by 3-1. Although Dick, Kerr's were the superior side, the play ran fairly evenly and it was only due to an own goal by Jessie Walmsley in the closing stages that Fleetwood got some consolation. Mistakes in front of goal cost the Dick, Kerr team a hatful of chances but they always had the game well in hand. Their goals were scored by Lily Parr (2) Florrie Redford 1. The referee was J W Ashworth from Preston. The Dick, Kerr team was : Emma Grice, Jessie Walmsley, Daisy Clayton, Carmen Pomies, Alice Woods, Lily Lee, Florrie Haslam, Jennie Harris, Florrie Redford, Alice Mills and Lily Parr.

Interviewed after the match, Dr Mary Lowry said, *"From what I saw I do not think the playing of the game by women would be any more injurious to a woman than a heavy days washing, or, for instance the working of a wringing machine. Those girls come on the field perfectly trained, and in the game they get no more wrenches than they would in tennis. They are so trained as to be able to stand any slight strains, and, indeed, we should be poorly made individuals if we could not bear a few wrenches. An open air life is better for girls than a heavy life indoors. I can't see any harm in the game if it is played under any decent sort of supervision."* The *Lancashire Daily Post* reporter covering the match asked the Doctor's for their opinions of football as played by women. None of them had any adverse criticism and the general opinion was unanimous that football was physically no more harmful for women than either tennis or hockey. A Nonconformist minister also present added that he didn't think there was anything to be depreciated in women's football.

In spite of the FA ban the public still turned up in their thousands to watch women's football and at New Brighton on 27 December, 7000 people went along to watch St Helens v the Dick, Kerr Ladies. The game was in aid of the British Legion and was kicked off by the Mayor of Wallacy. The Preston team recorded another 2-0 victory with goals being scored by Alice Woods and Jennie Harris. Alice Kell had sent out invitations to members of the FA Council to attend the match but not surprisingly, there is no mention of their attendance. As the new year approached there was much work to be done if women's football were to continue on its own. No one knew what lay ahead and the future was uncertain. But the Dick, Kerr Ladies were determined to push forward as they always had in the past, and new challenges for them were just around the corner.

MATCH FACTS 1921

PLAYED:	WON:	DRAWN:	LOST:	GOALS FOR:	AGAINST:
67	67	0	0	448	22

Goalscorers:

Florrie Redford	*170*	*Alice Woods*	*17*
Lily Parr	*108*	*Lily Lee*	*11*
Jennie Harris	*89*	*Jessie Walmsley*	*6*
Alice Mills	*27*	*Molly Walker*	*2*
Florrie Haslam	*17*	*M Dickinson*	*1*

Florrie Redford is way ahead as leading goalscorer during this period. 170 goals in one year, while still working full time at the factory, is no mean feat and worth a mention by anyone standards. Her achievement should be acknowledged and documented in world statistics. Perhaps the longevity of the career of Lily Parr may overshadow her contribution but she was the original archetypal centre forward with a touch of glamour, exceptional football skill and could kick the ball with either foot. What value would be put on that kind of talent today? In more recent times, Sylvia Gore, MBE, scorer of England's first goal in the first recognised international match against Scotland, in 1972 actually scored 134 goals in one season when playing for Fodens during the 1970's. These stats are part of women's football history and the players deserve due recognition in the record books.

Florrie Redford

DATE	VENUE	RESULT	CROWD	RECEIPTS
1 Jan	Clitheroe	DK 17 Rest of Lancs 0	5,000	?

Scorers: Florrie Redford 6, Jennie Harris 4, Florrie Haslam 4, Lily Parr 3

8 Jan	Manchester	DK 12 Bath 0	35,000	£1962

Scorers: Lily Parr 4, Alice Mills 2, Jessie Walmsley 2 , Florrie Redford 3, Jennie Harris 1

22 Jan	Gt Harwood	DK 10 Horrockses 0	5,000	£140

Scorers: L Parr 3, A Mills 2, Flo Redford 2, Jennie Harris 2, Jessie Walmsley 1

29 Jan	Macclesfield	DK 9 St Helens 1	7,000	£385

Scorers: Jennie Harris 5, Lily Parr 2, Alice Mills 1, Florrie Redford 1

5 Feb	Nelson	DK 10 St Helens 0	6,000	£325

Scorers: Florrie Redford 4, Jennie Harris 2, Lily Parr 3, Alice Mills 1

8 Feb	Stalybridge	DK 9 St Helens 0	12,000	£763

Scorers: Lily Parr 3, Jennie Harris 3, Florrie Redford 2, Alice Mills 1

9 Feb	Chester	DK 4 St Helens 0	11,000	£700

Scorers: Jennie Harris 2, Florrie Redford 2

12 Feb	Rossendale	DK 13 Horrockses 0	8,000	£500

Scorers: Florrie Redford 7, Alice Mills 2, Lily Parr 2, Jennie Harris 1, Florrie Haslam 1

14 Feb	Liverpool	DK 9 Rest of Britain 1	25,000	£1500

Scorers: Lily Parr 5, Florrie Redford 2, Jennie Harris 2

19 Feb	Wrexham	DK 2 St Helens 1	10,000	?

Scorers: Florrie Redford 1, Lily Parr 1

26 Feb	Coventry	DK 8 St Helens 1	27,000	£2000

Scorers: Lily Parr 3, Florrie Redford 3, Jennie Harris 1

1 Mar	Glasgow	DK 9 Scotland 0	6,000	?

Scorers: Lily Parr 4, Florrie Redford 3, Jennie Harris 1, Alice Mills 1

2 Mar	Edinburgh	DK 13 Scotland 0	23,000	£700

Scorers: Lily Parr 5, Florrie Redford 3, Jennie Harris 2, Molly Walker 2, Florrie Haslam 1

5 Mar	Burslem	DK 12 Cheshire/Staffs 0	10,000	?

Scorers: F Redford 4, J Harris 3, Lily Parr 2, Alice Woods 1, Florrie Haslam 1,
Jessie Walmsley 1

12 Mar	Lancaster	DK 4 Lancaster 0	8,000	?

Scorers; Jennie Harris 2, Florrie Redford 2

19 Mar	Hull	DK 4 Hull 1	20,000	?

Scorers: Florrie Redford 2, Jennie Harris 1, Alice Woods 1

25 Mar	Dudley	DK 2 St Helens 0	18,000	£700

Scorers: Florrie Redford 1, Jennie Harris 1

28 Mar	Coventry	DK 3 Stoke 0	12,000	?

Scorers: Florrie Redford 2, Jennie Harris 1

Date	Team		Score		Attendance	Amount
29 Mar	Cardiff	DK 4	Cardiff 0		18,000	?
Scorers: Florrie Redford 3, Alice Mills 1						
31 Mar	Swansea	DK 6	Swansea 1		25,000	?
Scorers: Jennie Harris 3, Lily Parr 3						
6 Apr	Leeds	DK 7	Yorks&Lancs 0		27,000	£1700
Scorers: Jennie Harris 3, Alice Mills 3, Florrie Redford 1						
7 Apr	Stoke	DK 2	Stoke 0		20,000	?
Scorers: Florrie Redford, Jennie Harris						
9 Apr	Standish	DK 5	Lancaster 0		2,000	?
Scorers: Florrie Haslam, Jennie Harris, Florrie Redford, Alice Mills, Lily Parr						
13 Apr	Bradford	DK 6	Lister Ladies 0		20,000	£1150
Scorers: Florrie Redford 3, Jennie Harris 2, Florrie Haslam 1						
14 Apr	Rotherham	DK 7	Bradford 0		20,000	£1000
Scorers: Lily Parr 2, Jennie Harris 2, Florrie Redford 2, Alice Mills 1						
16 Apr	Kilmarnock	DK 7	Scotland 1		15,000	£700
Scorers: Florrie Redford 4, Alice Mills 2, Lily Parr 1						
19 Apr	Bury	DK 8	Ellesmere Port 0		27,000	£1000
Scorers: Florrie Redford 5, Jennie Harris 3						
20 Apr	Bolton	DK 8	Bolton 0		33,000	£1500
Scorers: Florrie Redford 5, Lily Parr 2, Alice Mills 1						
23 Apr	New Brighton	DK 3	Ellesmere Port 0		15,000	£600
Scorers: Florrie Redford 3						
26 Apr	Rochdale	DK 4	Fleetwood 0		18,000	£800
Scorers: Florrie Redford, Jennie Harris, Florrie Haslam, Lily Parr						
28 Apr	Barrow	DK 14	Barrow 2		12,000	£600
Scorers: Florrie Redford 7, Jennie Harris 4, Lily Parr 3						
4 May	Sheffield	DK 4	Atalanta 0		20,000	?
Scorers: Florrie Redford 3, Lily Parr 1						
5 May	Hull	DK 2	Hull 0		19,000	£900
Scorers: Florrie Redford, M Dickinson						
11 May	Middlesboro	DK 3	NE Coast 1		25,000	£1200
Scorers: Florrie Redford 2, Florrie Haslam 1						
14 May	Preston	DK 3	Yorkshire 0		12,000	£600
Scorers: Jennie Harris 2, Florrie Haslam 1						
17 May	Longton Staffs	DK 5	French 1		15,000	?
Scorers: Lily Parr 5						
21 May	Nottingham	DK 11	Wales 0		20,000	£800
Scorers: Florrie Redford 7, Jennie Harris 2, Alice Mills 2						

Date	Venue	Result	Attendance	
4 June	Crewe	DK 8 Wales 0	10,000	?
Scorers: Jennie Harris 2, Lily Parr 2, Florrie Redford 2, Alice Mills 1, Florrie Haslam 1				
1 Aug	Ramsay IOM	DK 5 St Helens 3	5,000	?
Scorers: Florrie Redford 3, Lily Parr 1, Alice Mills 1				
2 Aug	Port Erin IOM	DK 3 St Helens 0	6,000	?
Scorers: Florrie Redford 2, Lily Parr 1				
3 Aug	Douglas IOM	DK 4 St Helens 0	2,000	?
Scorers: Lily Parr 2, Jennie Harris 1, Florrie Redford 1				
4 Aug	Leeds	DK 9 Heys Brewery 0	20,000	?
Scorers: Florrie Redford 5, Lily Parr 2, Jennie Harris 2				
5 Aug	Southport	DK 4 Fleetwood 0	16,000	?
Scorers: Florrie Redford 2, Lily Parr 1, Jennie Harris 1				
6 Aug	Birmingham	DK 4 Coventry 0	15,000	?
Scorers: Florrie Redford 2, Lily Parr 1 Jennie Harris 1				
7 Aug	Batley	DK 11 Listers 0	10,000	?
Scorers: Florrie Redford 5, Lily Parr 2, Alice Mills 2, Jennie Harris 1, Florrie Haslam 1				
8 Aug	Halifax	DK 6 St Helens 1	15,000	?
Scorers: Lily Parr 3, Florrie Redford 2, Alice Mills 1				
9 Aug	Derby	DK 3 Coventry 0	20,000	?
Scorers: Florrie Redford 2, Alice Mills 1				
10 Sept	Aberdeen	DK 6 Aberdeen 0	18,000	?
Scorers: Jennie Harris 2 Lily Parr 1, Florrie Redford 1, Alice Woods 1, Florrie Haslam 1				
11 Sept	Dundee	DK 6 Dundee 1	8,000	£300
Scorers: Jennie Harris 2, Lily Parr 2, Florrie Redford 1, Alice Woods 1				
12 Sept	Bury	DK 3 Bolton 2	3,000	?
Scorers: Florrie Redford, Jennie Harris, Lily Parr				
13 Sept	Birkenhead	DK 4 St Helens 0	6,000	?
Scorers: Lily Parr 2, Florrie Redford 1, Lily Lee 1				
14 Sept	Rochdale	DK 2 Mrs Vizards 1	?	?
Scorers: Lily Lee, Lily Parr				
16 Sept	Bristol	DK 5 Sth of England 0	8,000	?
Scorers: Florrie Redford 2, Jennie Harris 1, Lily Parr 1, Lily Lee 1				
21 Sept	Blackpool	DK 4 Wales 0	12,000	?
Scorers: Florrie Redford 3, Jennie Harris 1				
17 Oct	Huddersfield	DK 10 Atalanta 0	8,000	?
Scorers: Florrie Redford 5, Lily Lee 3, Lily Parr 2				
18 Oct	Scarborough	DK 12 Scarborough 0	5,000	?
Scorers: Florrie Redford 6, Lily Parr 4, Jennie Harris 2				

19 Oct	Ormskirk	DK 18 Horrockses 0	9,000	?
Scorers: Lily Parr 5, Florrie Redford 5, Jennie Harris 3, Lily Lee 3, Florrie Haslam 2				
20 Oct	Warrington	DK 11 Farnworth 0	8,000	?
Scorers: Alice Woods 6, Jennie Harris 2, Lily Parr 2, Lily Lee 1				
21 Oct	Southport	DK 10 Farnworth 0	5,000	?
Scorers: Alice Woods 4, Jennie Harris 3, Lily Parr 2, Jessie Walmsley 1				
22 Oct	Bradford	DK 4 Heys Brewery 1	10,000	?
Scorers: Lily Parr 2, Jennie Harris 1, Florrie Redford 1				
23 Oct	Dumfries	DK 8 Dumfries 0	6,000	?
Scorers: Florrie Redford 4, Lily Parr 2, Lily Lee 1, Alice Woods 1				
24 Oct	Belfast	DK 6 Belfast 1	12,000	?
Scorers: Lily Parr 3, Florrie Redford 2, Alice Woods 1				
25 Oct	Wigan	DK 4 Heys 0	6,000	?
Scorers: Florrie Redford 3, Jessie Walmsley 1				
Nov	Manchester	DK 13 Lyons 0	?	£550
Scorers: Florrie Redford 9, Jennie Harris 3, Lily Parr 1				
26 Nov	Skipton	DK 1 Heys 0	3,000	?
Scorer: Jennie Harris				
28 Dec	Ashton Park	DK 3 Fleetwood 1	3,000	?
Scorers: Lily Parr, Florrie Redford, Jennie Harris				
29 Dec	New Brighton	DK 2 St Helens 0	7,000	?
Scorers: Alice Woods, Jennie Harris				

All match facts from the diary of Alice Stanley, nee Woods, (except undated November match with Lyons). The gate receipts for the 25 matches that are listed totals £22,525. Information documented by Herbert Stanley, who acted in an official capacity for the club during that time.

CHAPTER SIX
ACROSS THE ATLANTIC

Dick, Kerr Ladies started the new year with the same enthusiasm they had always displayed as the new era of ladies football got underway. They may no longer have been allowed the use of association football pitches, but as one door closes another one opens and they were welcomed to play their matches on rugby grounds. They met Heys Brewery from Bradford on 7 January 1922 at Wakefield Trinity Rugby Ground in aid of the Wakefield Workpeoples' Hospital. Heys Ladies were the champions of Yorkshire and had earned themselves a good reputation. Eight thousand people came to watch the match and £250 was raised for the hospital. The game ended in a 1-1 draw with Florrie Redford scoring the Dick, Kerr goal. The result brought to an end a remarkable run of 75 straight victories. Their last draw being against the French Ladies in Paris in October 1920. Their unbeaten run had continued since then and this was their 89th unbeaten contest since the defeat at Stamford Bridge in May 1920.

If women's football was to succeed without the support of the FA they needed to get their own house in order. The new English Ladies Football Association met in Manchester on 7 January 1922, the same day the above match was taking place. It is not known whether the Dick, Kerr Ladies were deliberately excluded from taking any part in the new association but it seems incredulous that they wouldn't have wanted to be involved in some way. The meeting discussed the size and weight of the standard ball and agreed that it should be a size 5 and weigh 12 ounces, which is not unlike that used today. They also discussed the size of the pitch, drew up cup competition rules and selected their first representative team which was to play against Grimsby and District Ladies. Notably none of the players selected were members of the Dick, Kerr or Heys team. President of the association, Len Bridgett, presented a cup for which all affiliated clubs would be invited to compete. The teams in the hat for the first round of the English Ladies FA Cup were: Stoke, Newcastle, Smallthorne, Chell, Birmingham, Dunlop, Coventry, Aston, Fleetwood, Manchester United, Mersey Amazons, Rochdale, Plymouth, Marazion, Ediswan, Osram, Grimsby, Doncaster Bentley, Huddersfield, Huddersfield Atalanta, Boston, Lincoln, and Stoke United. (Research by Patrick Brennan)

The final of the competition was played between Stoke and Doncaster on 24 June 1922 in front of only 2000 spectators. Stoke won the game by 3-1.

This transitional period within the sport was not as easy as they had initially anticipated and the English Ladies FA turned out to be a short lived affair. It became much more difficult than first thought to recruit new teams and the weekly struggle to find a pitch to play on did take its toll on even the most dedicated organiser. Without all the glitz and glamour that went hand in hand with playing at all the top stadiums, many of the girls did turn their back on the game and even before it had really taken off, the Ladies FA went into decline. The women were still very angry at the treatment meted out to them by the FA and without the resources and readily available football pitches and officials, it would have been virtually impossible to sustain a national league. What is clear is that for the next 50 years it remained extremely difficult for women to play football because of the FA ban. It was easier for teams like Dick, Kerr's who had the support and backing of a big company and did not have to struggle to find a pitch to play on every week but other teams like their old sparring partners St Helens were less fortunate and eventually fell by the wayside. There were though, many charitable organisations still in need of help and the Dick, Kerr Ladies were more than happy to give of their services.

In the meantime the Dick, Kerr Ladies welcomed the French team on yet another of their visits to England. The first match of the tour was played in Cardiff on 22 March in front of 15,000 spectators who saw the Preston team record another 3-0 victory. Jennie Harris (2) and Florrie Redford getting the goals. The return match at Lively Polly Corner on Ashton Park saw new goalkeeper May Graham keep a clean sheet in a 4-0 victory. A hat trick was scored by Lily Parr and Jennie Harris added the other. At the Stanley Athletic Ground on 27 March, another 4-0 scoreline was recorded with goals from Florrie Redford (3) and Alice Mills. The penultimate match of the tour was played at Burnley and despite the enforced ban by the FA there was still a lot of support and admiration for women's football. An extract from a letter (in Franklands scrapbook) from the Mayor of Burnley to Mr Livingstone, the Dick, Kerr work's manager, emphasises his support for the team when he says: *"I was very grateful at having the opportunity of meeting the French Ladies and when I saw that the Dick, Kerr Ladies were also present I was more pleased. I love your team of Preston lasses, and whenever I find them within a measurable distance of Burnley you may rest assured I shall be at the match if at all possible. They are so cheerful that it does one good to be about them."* The final match of the tour was played at Planters Recreation Ground in Hyde and achieved another victory by 5-1. Afterwards they were guests of the Mayor at a reception in the town hall and proceeds from the day were in aid of the Hyde YMCA.

The seeds planted early in 1921 for a proposed trip to Canada were to come to fruition in 1922. Prior to the trip taking place, Mr Frankland had been doing his homework and contacted the Dominion Football Association (Canadian Soccer Assoc). A newspaper article in the original scrapbook, tells of the Dick, Kerr Ladies wish to visit Canada.

TEAM OF LADY FOOTBALLERS HAVE THEIR EYES ON CANADA – **Dick, Kerr Girls Ask Dominion Body If Soccer Tour Could Be Arranged – Would Bring Two Teams** It says: *"The Dick, Kerr lady footballers who attracted some big crowds in England, desire to visit Canada. The DFA, through Tom Guthrie, has been asked by Alfred Frankland to furnish advice regarding the possiblities of a tour throughout the Dominion this summer. Mr Guthrie has submitted the matter to the President of the Association Dan MacNeil and secretary, Davie Roy at Winnipeg. A visit from a team of players selected from the Scottish League and another from the Dick, Kerr Ladies in one season would arouse a new and deep enthusiasm in the game throughout Canada. Such a departure from the beaten track would boost the sport and widen its circle of friends. The question of securing suitable grounds to stage such games would be more difficult a solution than any financial problem. A good team from the Scottish league would more than pay its way, and the novelty attached to the ladies would help swell the 'gates'. The difficulty is, that in Canada we have **not one** team of ladies to oppose the Dick, Kerr girls; but this difficulty has apparently been forseen by Mr Frankland, who offers to bring out a second team if necessary, which of course would add to the expense. The Dick, Kerr Ladies are not novices at the game. Last season they played 20 games, won 19 and drew 1, scoring 118 goals, and only 5 against. If it can be arranged, the Ladies will play matches in the principle cities throughout the Dominion."* (For the purpose of trying to compile as accurate a playing record of the team as possible we will assume that these statistics represent the 1922 season. This would bring their unbeaten run to an incredible 109 games!)

Another clipping from The *Toronto Evening Telegraph* published a photograph of the Dick, Kerr Ladies stating that they wished to tour Canada and could bring with them the champion ladies of France or Ireland to provide the opposition. It is obvious that Mr Frankland *was* aware before they had even set sail that there were infact no ladies teams for them to play against but plans went ahead regardless and the girls were given the impression that there were lots of them. For some unknown reason the Dick, Kerr team were initially referred to as Newcastle United Ladies. A possible explanation could be due to their black and white stripped shirts, and Newcastle might have been a more familiar name than theirs. The report below from the *Toronto*

Evening Telegram on 2 September 1922 suggests that games had already been arranged which must have been against men's teams given that it has already been identified that there were no women's teams.

LADY FOOTBALLERS ON TOUR WANT A GAME IN TORONTO

The Newcastle lady footballers who are touring the United States are anxious to play in Toronto before their return to England in November. In the Old Country they did very well as far as women's football goes, and have met with good receptions across the border, and will tackle the famous Bethlehem team on September 13. The only game arranged for Canada so far is their meeting with Grand Trunk at Montreal on October 28 and if at all possible they would like to link up with some Toronto team soon after the latter date. They ask for a guarantee of $1000.

The same newspaper reported on 6 September 1922:

OPPOSE LADY SOCCER TEAMS – DFA ANNUAL SESSION OPENS

The Dominion Football Association went on record as opposed to lady soccer teams and will not permit any clubs to play against the ladies team which propose to tour Canada.

Extracts from the minutes of the AGM of the DFA, held in Winnipeg on 5 September 1922 read as follows:

Arising out of a letter from the United States regarding the proposed tour of footballers into this country President MacNeil wanted to know whether Ladies Football was to be approved of or not.

Mr Steven did not approve of Ladies Football.

Mr Lyne was also against Ladies Football.

Mr Swain desired to know the reason of disapproval.

In reply, Mr Lyne said that a woman was not built to stand the bruises gotten in playing football.

Mr Dean quoted an instance of ladies football having been played in Hamilton. He said that the first two games played were alright but after that the people became against it entirely. He regarded it as a shame to be allowed. He thought such games should not be permitted.

Moved by Mr Lyne, seconded by Mr Dean, that we do not approve of the proposal of Ladies Football. Carried.

Mr Steven, seconded by Mr Russell, wished to go on record as not approving of Ladies Football.

This was consented to. Moved by Mr Mitchell, seconded by Mr Lyne, that we join with the Football Association and pay fee for same.

It isn't clear what that last statement refers to but the mention of the Football Association could imply 'The' FA in England.

Meanwhile, back in Preston, plans were going ahead in earnest and the girls were full of anticipation for their transatlantic adventure. They were on the verge of embarking on an amazing journey to the other side of the world to play football and they could hardly believe how incredibly fortunate they were. However, one young lass was about to have her heart broken. Lydia Ackers, a former St Helens player, had been invited to travel with them and was all set to make the trip, eagerly looking forward to all the new experiences that lay ahead. Coming from a small rural village in the Lancashire countryside, things like this didn't happen to ordinary folk like them, this was the stuff of fairytales. She had her passport at the ready and couldn't wait to wear all the new clothes her mother had bought for the trip. She was so happy. But then came the news that would shatter her dreams. Mr Frankland told her that they couldn't take everyone with them, someone had to be left behind and it was to be her. There were some issues with those promoting the tour and problems with the finances. Either way it was poor Lydia who had to pay the price. Words could never express her disappointment.

Leaving Liverpool

On 15 September 1922, the Dick, Kerr Ladies sailed from Liverpool aboard the SS Montclare, across the Atlantic to the shores of Canada and the United States of America. Pathe Gazette were there to film the occasion and the joyous band of travellers happily performed for the cameras on the deck of the ship. Two of the girls were turning a skipping rope for Alice Mills and Alice Woods and they were soon joined by Carmen Pomies, Alice Kell, Jessie Walmsley and Florrie Redford. The next sequence was of Carmen Pomies holding one of the ships lifebelts while Jennie Harris and Florrie Redford kicked a ball toward her trying to aim for the centre of the lifebelt. Painted on the ball in white letters was, 'Dick, Kerr's off to Canada'. The final sequence shows all the party waving excitedly from the upper deck before setting sail.

Another article in Franklands scrap book, written by Major Cecil Kent just as the party had left England, reads as follows:

"CHARITY BEGINS" - In America for Girl Footballers

Dick, Kerr's famous football girls have started their greatest adventure, leaving Liverpool by the C.P.S. Liner Montclare, for Montreal. They will be away for four months, in which they will play 24 matches at the following places:

New York	Richmond	Philadelphia
Brooklyn	Harrison	Norfolk
S Louis	Detroit	Cleveland
Milwaukee	Chicago	N Bedford
Fall River	Boston	Baltimore
Bethlehem	Bridport	Washington
Rochester	Toronto	Ottawa
Montreal	Hamilton	Winnfer

The full strength of the club has been mobilised with the exception of Peggy Mason, the goalkeeper, who has experienced the hardest luck possible in not being in the party. Miss Mason has lost her mother and although not yet twenty one, besides being all day in the works, she runs the house for her father and small brothers and sisters. Everybody on route yesterday had a kindly and cheery word for the lady footballers.

Interviewed just before departure, Alice Kell said: *"In the last five football seasons our team has raised £50,000 for English charities, chiefly ex servicemen and hospitals, but the English FA, by forbidding their clubs to allow us the use of their grounds have prevented us from raising more. The American and Canadian FA's hearing of this, invited us to visit them, so now we are going to play for American charities instead of English ones. The harsh treatment we have received from the English body, has been a means of giving us the tour of our lives. We do not expect to return to Preston until 1923. We shall have plenty of opponents in America because girls football has caught on over there, and in one state alone, Massachusetts, there are already eleven girls football teams. The English FA got nothing out of our 'gates' because the proceeds were entirely for charity, so they don't mind losing us, but at the same time they don't think we ought to go, and they have even tried to stop us, but failed. They certainly rule English football but not the world, thank goodness. We are all wondering what sort of gates we shall get on the other side, and whether we shall beat our record of the Boxing Day match at Goodison."* The lucky girls chosen to make this momentous journey were:-Florrie Haslam, Molly Walker, Alice Woods, Jennie Harris, Alice Kell, Lily Lee, Florrie Redford, Jessie Walmsley, Lily Parr, Carmen Pomies, Daisy Clayton, Alice Mills, Annie Crozier, May Graham.

The newspaper articles are necessary to document as many facts as possible in order to paint an accurate picture and uncover the truth surrounding their transatlantic adventure. With 24 matches arranged and the promoters asking for a guarantee of $1000 per match, it would appear that someone was intent on making a considerable amount of money. But just who were the opposition supposed to be? Looking at all the evidence, it does point towards the fact that they had deliberately gone ahead and arranged all those games knowing full well the ladies would be playing against men, yet Alice Kell was quite specific in her statement regarding the growth in women's teams in

Pictured aboard the SS Montclare

(left) Florrie Redford, Carmen Pomies, (right) Jennie Harris, Alice Kell, May Graham?, Lily Lee

America. Exactly who gave her that information and why, is open to speculation, but it is clear that *someone* had deliberately lied.

Alice Woods also recalled the journey, *"We had a really nice time in America but we didn't know until we got there that we had to play against men. It was a terribly rough crossing and all the girls were seasick. We saw the beautiful icebergs and they reminded us of the Titanic."*

As history has frequently documented, Titanic was launched on its maiden voyage from Southampton on 10 April 1912, heading for New York and everyone said it was unsinkable. Four days after its launch the ship hit an iceberg 400 miles off the coast of Newfoundland and 1503 people perished. Despite any fear of a similar fate, nothing could dampen the ladies spirits as they embarked on the biggest adventure of their lives.

Among the party on this historic trip was 21-year-old Harold Stanley who was an active committee member at the club. He later made a tape recording of a very interesting story which occurred on board the SS Montclare. It sheds more light on the shady dealings that were at the heart of this trip. This is a transcript of Harolds recording. The man he refers to as David, is in fact David Brooks, the joint promoter of the tour.

"All the arrangements for the tour had been in the hands of an American Jew and an Irish International football player who happened to be captain of a famous north of England club. He will be nameless. He was a very fit, fine, upstanding figure of a man; good looking with curly hair and I was eventually apportioned the same cabin as him when we got on board ship. There were only two classes, cabin and what was known as 2nd class. We travelled cabin. David, I'll refer to him as David, was I afterwards learned, a man who had left his wife and family and cleared the country without saying a word. He had been doing all the negotiating for the tour in secret and this was his getaway. I first met him when we were on board the ship. He was a likeable fellow. I didn't know his history or his background except through the press and his football career. His one ambition in life I soon learned, was to make love to women, any woman provided he could gain his own ends. And there was I thrown with him for a period of ten days on this ship! Two days out we hit a heavy storm and most of the passengers were seasick but on the third day all began to recover and the life of the ship went on.

David, I learned, was broke. Now in those days, before you could land in Canada you had to have in your possession at least £25 in English money. I knew David had nothing but he told me not to worry. He was happy and carefree, he wasn't concerned and knew he would make out. He asked me how much money I had and I told him that I didn't have £25 either. I personally didn't know how

I was going to get through the immigration authorities when we got to the other side. He asked again, "Well, how much have you got?" I told him how much I had and by his charming manner, he borrowed £2 from me. I didn't see much of him for the next two or three days except at meal times, but I knew he was making love to a very rich elderly woman and the way he was carrying on, anyone would have thought they were teenagers!

Dick, Kerr Ladies were well known and their autographs were sought. It was one of my duties to see that autographed photographs of the team were sold for charity or given to important people whenever possible. One day, soon after breakfast, David came to me and said, "When I beckon you on deck, come to me and stand between the cabin behind, and where I am stood. I'll tell you my reasons for it afterwards." Sure enough, he had his lady love engaged in the usual loveable dialogue leaning over the ship's rail. Presently, he pulled out his wallet, extracted one of the photographs of the team and said he would get all the players to autograph the picture for her and would start off with his name. He called me over and I stood where he had told me to stand and he said, "Will you get this photograph signed by the rest of the party," I said I would. He half turned, and with a deft flick of his right wrist he flicked his wallet into the sea and cried, "My wallet!" I was the only one who had seen this action. He had attracted the attention of some of the crew and a number of the passengers and we all watched the wallet as it was swallowed up in the waves. Then came the most pathetic story you have ever heard about him being destitute, his world of wealth was in that wallet, how would he pass the authorities at the other side? The Purser organised a collection amongst the first class passengers and when David was asked how much he had in the wallet he said it was just over £50. The collection raised about £45 and during the dance on deck that night the money was presented to David. With grateful thanks and with something of an apologetic manner, he said the remainder of the money did not matter. In the cabin later that night he returned me my £2. The whole of his scheme had been really well organised and looking back I feel that for a most plausible rogue, David took the cake."

They arrived in Quebec on Friday 22 September 1922. Local newspaper, the *Daily Star*, covered their arrival:

LADY SOCCERITES TO PLAY MANY MATCHES – WILL ALL BE ACROSS THE BORDER – DFA WILL NOT ALLOW CANADIAN TEAMS TO PLAY.

Mr A Zelickman of New York, representing the USFA was at the landing to welcome the ladies team and conduct them to New York city where they will play their first match. Dick, Kerr Ladies Football Club are not in America to *play matches with the object of making money. They have come as champions to meet all-comers and will play matches with the gate money to go to charity. They expect to play 24 matches in the US, several of which will be played in the Fall River district where so many people from Preston and other Lancashire cotton towns are now residing. Matches will also be played at New York, Philadelphia, Boston, St Louis, Baltimore, Washington, Detroit, Chicago and Winnipeg, and probably Ottawa, Montreal and Hamilton.* Mr Zelickman was joint promotor of the tour along with David Brooks. It is a safe assumption that these two men are the American Jew and Irish International football player mentioned at the beginning of Harold Stanley's story.

They had no sooner set foot on dry land when they were met with some devastating news. Mr Zelickman informed them he had been given the cold shoulder by the Dominion FA and they had refused permission for them to play football in Canada. He said although not having received official notification from them, he had been told by the affiliated clubs in the Association that they had been forbidden to play against the visiting English lady players. (Surely the affiliated clubs in the association would have been men's teams?) It was at this point that he finally came clean and told them there were in fact no ladies teams for them to play against and they would have to play against men's clubs in exhibition matches in the United States.

We can only begin to imagine what must have been going through their minds. Before they left England, they were given the impression that ladies football had really caught on in America and there were plenty of ladies teams for them to play against. They must have been utterly devastated to discover the truth but left with little alternative but to agree. They had to play to pay their way or they would have been stranded. They decided the best way forward would be to regard the tour as an experiment and try to enjoy their once in a lifetime trip. They travelled the 442 miles to New York by train with Mr Zelickman where they were to begin the tour and he accompanied them during their early travels in America.

It was hardly an ideal situation. Their first game in the United States took place on 24 Sept 1922 only five hours after they arrived in the city. The girls where exhausted after the long journey but still turned out against Paterson FC, at the Olympic Park in New Jersey, in front of 5000 spectators.

The *New York Times* reported: *The crowd gave a tremendous welcome to the ladies from Preston as they entered the arena to the sound of loud cheering and the tooting of horns. Dick, Kerr's won the toss and they impressed the onlookers with their skill and open style of play. The Jerseymen contented themselves by copying the methods of their gentler opponents and there was no rough play and few falls. McGuire, the noted one armed forward from Brooklyn, was the first to be brought down when Alice Woods, the sturdy centre back, was responsible for the tackle, and she seemed just a little proud of it. Mlle Carmen Pomies was the first to earn a round of applause as she saved an onslaught from Patersons left wing. Jennie Harris at inside right, and the smallest of all the players, soon showed herself to be the speediest. Her passing was splendid and the way she followed up would put many a veteran male to shame. The other outstanding figure among the English girls was Lily Parr at outside left. Her driving from the wing and the accuracy of her shots left little to be desired. Alice Kell was a steady full back and coached her team well. Florrie Redford was the pivotal point in the forward line. A tall stately young woman filling the important position of centre forward.* The girls put up a gallant fight, but lost the game 6-3. The Dick, Kerr goals were scored by Florrie Redford, Jessie Walmsley and Lily Parr. Goals for Paterson were scored by: McKenna (3) Fryer, McGuire, and Heminsley. Dick, Kerr's: Carmen Pomies, Alice Kell, Lily Lee, Molly Walker, Alice Woods, Jessie Walmsley, Florrie Haslam, Jennie Harris, Florrie Redford, May Graham, Lily Parr. Paterson FC: Renzulli, Reynolds, Whitehead, Scott, Fryer, Irvine, Duggan, McGuire, Heminsley, McKenna and Sweeney.

Next they travelled 186 miles north from New York to Pawtucket, Rhode Island,for their match against J & P Coats for which 5000 tickets had been sold in advance. They were met by John Walmsley, President of Coats A A, who escorted them to their accommodation and officials of the YWCA arranged for the full use of all their leisure and fitness facilities during their stay. The second match of the tour was played on 30 September at Lonsdale Avenue, Pawtucket, in front of at least 9000 spectators. They marched on to the field to the strains of 'Annie Laurie', played by the Sayles band who had entertained the spectators before the game. The crowd gave a rousing cheer as the Dick, Kerr team, led by capt Alice Kell, ran out from the clubhouse. A battery of cameras were focused on the players but the girls were extremely business like and kept their concentration only posing for team photographs when required by the persistent photographers. Alice Kell shook hands with Ferguson, the Coats captain, and won the toss. It was a warm day and the heat affected the girls performance but they still managed a 4-4 draw. Press reports documented: *Everything pointed to J&P Coats winning the match 4-3, but with about five minutes remaining, Lily Parr lifted the ball and shot goalwards. It travelled so fast to the back of the net that Joe Knowles in goal didn't see it coming. The vast crowd seemed perfectly satisfied at the end of the game and gave the girls a great ovation. Judging from the excellence of their team work and the stellar offensive play of the forwards, it is easy to believe that this line up is the fastest women's team in England. Few outside lefts are capable of playing better than Lily Parr. Carmen Pomies in goal, was another shining light as she made several really brilliant saves during the game.* The goals were scored by: Florrie Redford (2) Jennie Harris and Lily Parr. Goals for Coats came from: Fleming (2) Reid and Gallagher. The Dick, Kerr team was: Carmen Pomies, Alice Kell, Lily Lee, Daisy Clayton, Alice Woods, Jessie Walmsley, Florrie Haslam, Jennie Harris, May Graham, Lily Parr. J & P Coats: Knowles, Stevenson, Ferguson, Lappin, Neilson, Brookes, Gallagher, Morley, McAvoy, Reid, Fleming.

Pawtucket USA 1922

Florrie Haslam, Molly Walker, Alice Woods, Jennie Harris, Alice Kell, Lily Lee, Florrie Redford, Jessie Walmsley, Lily Parr, Carmen Pomies, Daisy Clayton

Making the return trip of 186 miles back to New York and only twenty four hours after their last match, the girls were once again taking to the field, at the New York Oval in New York city. They took on Centro-Hispano FC, a team made up of Spanish Americans in front of a crowd of 7000 spectators. The Dick, Kerr team walked on to the field wearing their now familiar black and white shirts and blue shorts and were immediately surrounded by a host of photographers. They ran for cover until the pitch was cleared and they were able to limber up. At the start of the game a large bouquet of flowers from the State League was presented to Florrie Redford who was acting captain in place of Alice Kell. A brass band played the American and British national anthems.

114

J&P Coates FC

After going down 2-0 early in the game, at the half time whistle the Dick, Kerr team were leading by 3-2. Clever passing regularly brought them salvo's of applause from the crowd. During the match Lily Lee, playing at left back, was injured in a collision with one of the Hispano players and was out for the count. When they realised she was unable to get up, her team mates rushed to help her and she was soon back on her feet again thanks to the help of Annie Crozier with her magic sponge! A generous round of applause was given as she resumed play. The Centro-Hispano's lost no time in equalising and soon made it 4-3. The final score being 7-5 to the Hispano's. Defeated they may have been, but by no means humiliated for with only 24 hours since their game in Pawtucket, they showed remarkable speed and staying power against the Centro-Hispano eleven who were runners up in the Metropolitan Football League. Carmen Pomies again received praise in the press for her goalkeeping skills: *"She was equal to every emergency when it was not downright impossible".* The scorers for the ladies were, Florrie Redford (2) May Graham, Jennie Harris and Lily Parr. The Hispano goals came from: Urizar (4), Rosabal (2) and Plaja. The teams were: Carmen Pomies, Daisy Clayton, Lily Lee, Molly Walker, Alice Woods, Jessie Walmsley, Florrie Haslam, Jennie Harris, Florrie

Redford, May Graham, Lily Parr. Centro Hispano: Caravaglio, Nelson, Mozetes, Gonzales, Plaja, Blanco, Solano, Petrillo, Urizar, Rosabal, Ororez.

They now had several days without a game and took the chance to relax and check out the local area. One of the male members of the party was hoping there might be somewhere close by where they could get a beer. It could be that he wasn't aware that prohibition was in force at that time and alcohol was definitely off legal limits. Perhaps it was someone's idea of a joke as they were directed to a bar a few blocks away. Lily Lee later told of it being raided by the police and she ending up hiding under a table! However they all appear to have escaped unscathed and the tour went ahead without further incident. She also said they were given an allowance of a few dollars per day and the chaperones accompanying them were rather strict.

During their games in New England, some of the girls were guests of local families. There were a number of cotton mills in the area and some of the girls had relatives already living there. The salaries paid to workers in the US cotton industry were significantly higher than in English mill towns and this would probably have accounted for the large number of ex-pats out there. The standard of living in America was a great talking point among them as most agreed it was much better than in Preston. Alice Mills was particularly taken with life in the new world and Lancashire life for her had little to offer by comparison. The whole experience left a lasting impression on the young teenager.

Enjoying free time in USA

Lily Parr, May Graham, Alice Kell, Carmen Pomies, Florrie Redford, Jessie Walmsley, Alice Mills, Jennie Harris

They travelled to Washington DC on 8 October where they took on Washington Stars FC. The result was a 4-4 draw. Some years later it was reported in the *Lancashire Daily Post* that the President of the United States, Warren G Harding, kicked off the match and autographed the match ball before presenting it to team capt, Alice Kell.

Next stop on their travels they arrived at New Bedford on 10 October for a game against the New Bedford All Stars. It was a welcome change to have a couple of days to rest and prepare for the match and they hoped this would put them in good shape for their big contest with the New Bedford team.. The *Fall River Evening Herald* reported their arrival and said: *Negotiations are now underway to bring the team to Fall River next Sunday if it is possible to arrange an agreement with the management. The girls*

USA 1922

Jessie Walmsley, Carmen Pomies

Alice Kell, Lily Lee, Florrie Redford

Football autographed by President Harding

Lucy Hoyle, Edith Hutton, Margaret Thornborough, May Helme, Lily Parr, Alice Cook (Kell) Joan Whalley

expressed their surprise at meeting so many men's teams in this country. They expected that they would at least meet one or two women's clubs on tour, but to date they have been matched only with men's clubs, and in nearly every instance it has been teams of the highest reputation. The team is being coached by David Brooks. Thomas Bagnall, a member of the National Challenge Cup Committee is acting as the delegate of the USFA on the trip. In the evening they were dined at a banquet tendered by the officials of the Soccer leagues in the city.

The match between Dick, Kerr Ladies and the New Bedford All Stars took place at Sargents Field in New Bedford, Massachusetts, on 12 October. The New Bedford team had a collection of star players picked from some of the best in the city. A crowd estimated at over 6000 packed the sidelines and climbed on everything possible to give them a better view. Not only was New Bedfords English colony represented, but a large number who had never seen a soccer match before, turned out to see the girls in action. It was the biggest crowd ever seen at Sargents field.

The *Evening Herald* covered the match. *A storm of applause greeted the girls as they were led on to the field by Alice Kell. The All Stars won the toss and elected to play with the wind at their backs and Jennie Harris kicked off. The All Stars entered the game not giving enough respect to the skill of the Preston team, and were not taking the game too seriously. The girls showed that they had a perfect knowledge of the game, and their passing the ball to one another was a lesson to some of the local league players. Every one of the forwards knew how to shoot and Misses Walker, Harris and Redford, sent in shots that did them credit. When it came time to go out and get the goals, the New Bedford team found that the ladies could defend as well as go forward, and try as they would they could not break down the solid Dick, Kerr defence. The Lady soccer team showed the way to the pick of New Bedfords finest when they beat William Beardsworth's eleven by 5-4. Miss Kell gave the New Bedford boys a goal to help them out, and the referee played an extra 4 minutes and 44 seconds at the end of the second half.* The Dick, Kerr goals came from: Florrie Redford (2) Jennie Harris (2) Molly Walker. New Bedford: Beardsworth (2) Howarth and Alice Kell o.g. The teams were: Carmen Pomies, Alice Kell, Daisy Clayton, Lily Lee, Alice Woods, Jessie Walmsley, Florrie Haslam, Molly Walker, May Graham, Florrie Redford. New Bedford: Wilkinson, Whalley, Cross, C Green, Stewart, G Green, Woolley, Wilson, Howarth, Beardsworth, Salt.

Negotations to have the Dick, Kerr Ladies play in Fall River were successful and the *Evening Herald* reported that they were expecting a crowd of about 8000 to come and see them. *'The Dick, Kerr team is one of the biggest things in soccer that has visited the United States. Fall River has witnessed many championship games yet there has never been a ladies club play in this city. Sam Mark has decided that the public of Fall River should be given this attraction and accordingly the Dick, Kerr team was booked to play here on Sunday at an enormous expense. The team has had many other offers and were asked to come to this city before fulfilling their other engagements. Advice from other cities where the team have played warrant that the fans will be given a wonderful show for their money. This team is as near to perfection in every aspect of the kicking game. Carmen Pomies was compared with one of the best goalkeepers in the area, Jennie Harris won praise in every game she played, and Lily Parr was said to be capable of showing any of the big leaguers a thing or two! Fall River were taking no chances with this combination and the team's best players were to take the field against the ladies. Special courtesy is to be shown the ladies of this city who are interested in seeing the game. A half section of the grandstand will be reserved for ladies and those accompanied by gentlemen only. This will accommodate 2000 people. A special price of 25 cents will be placed on ladies tickets. The men folks will pay the regular charge.*

A journey of 212 miles back to New York came next as they took on New York FC on 14 October, and they achieved a remarkable victory against the New Yorkers as they recorded a scoreline of 8-4. Next there was another long journey of 196 miles back to Fall River, Massachusetts for a game the next day.

The venue was at St Marks Stadium in Fall River, where Dick, Kerr Ladies earned a 2-2 draw with Fall River FC in front of more that 4000 spectators. Due to the length of the journey they were late arriving at the ground and the kick off had to be delayed for almost an hour. The match report in the local paper said that the men were willing to let the girls win the game, *'The bobbed headed and pretty Miss Redford scored the first goal early in the game. Duncan, the Fall River goalie, deliberately let it go by him. When Miss Redford turned for the kick-off, she showed that she was aware of Duncan's kindness. During the second half, Jock Lindsey twice gave her a chance to score. She passed it up indicating that any goal she scored had to be earned and not gifted. Of course the girls were no match for the men, for girls they are very good and each one clearly proved that she had considerable experience. However, their visit had helped to promote soccer immensely but the fans would have liked to have seen them play against a women's team. Had that been the case, their skill would have been more evident.'* Dick, Kerr team: Lily Parr, Daisy Clayton, Jessie Walmsley, Carmen Pomies, Alice Woods, Alice Mills, May Graham, Jennie Harris, Flo Redford, Florrie Haslam, Molly Walker. Fall River: Duncan, Lindsey, Collier, Lyon, Clarke, Houlker, Cairney, Pepper, Brittan, Lorimer, Miller. Dick, Kerr goals scored by Flo Redford (2) Fall River goals: Brittan, Pepper.

It comes as no surprise that the team's bookings had not been handled properly. The scheduling of matches, finances and other details of the tour organised by Zelickman and David Brooks were ridiculous. The girls were rather unhappy at being expected to play a game immediately after a long journey, and some of the hotels they stayed in were shabby and infested with cockroaches. Of course, the accommodation costs would probably have been deducted from the appearance fee, so from the promoters point of view, the cheaper the better. The tour wasn't working out as planned and in order to protect them from being stranded in the country, Thomas Bagnall from the USFA was asked to take control. Things were re-organised and plans for games in Chicago, Detroit, Cleveland and other mid western states were dropped and the others were reduced and confined to the Atlantic coast. This was possibly the time when David Brooks did a runner, as according to verbal evidence from the family of Alice Mills, she said, *"he just disappeared into thin air"*. And as Harold Stanley previously mentioned in his tape recording, *"David was a man who had left his wife and family and cleared the country without saying a word. He had been doing all the negotiating for the tour in secret and this was his getaway."* Added to that is the evidence from the newspaper articles documenting that Alfred Frankland was fully aware there were no ladies teams for them to play against, it becomes clear that this tour was based on lies and deceit. With David Brooks and Zelickman out of the picture, they can justifiably cop the lot with no case to answer. Interestingly though, the passenger list for the Montclare on the outward journey states the occupation for David Brooks and Alfred Frankland as both being Farmers, and Harold Stanley is listed as Trainer. Even more interesting are the listings of address for David Brooks and Harold Stanley. They are both the same. One wonders which of all of these gentlemen had the most to hide.

With the new arrangements in place, the next stop on the tour was in Maryland and the team were taken on a visit to a college in Baltimore. While being shown around the grounds, they stopped to watch the college football team in training for their next game. The team coach was explaining the rules of American football to the Dick, Kerr party when one of the players inadvertently kicked the ball towards them. Lily Parr instinctively kicked the oval shaped ball back towards them and although she had seldom kicked a ball of that shape, it flew right over the posts. The coach thought this was the biggest fluke of all time and thought she would be unable to repeat the feat. Confident that she could, Mr Frankland asked, *"How many dollars will you bet?"* The two men had a wager and the coach shouted to one of his players to kick the ball back towards them. It came over at quite a pace and once again Lily kicked the ball but this time kicked it even further, leaving the unsuspecting coach open mouthed in amazement. On Sunday 22 October, they took on Baltimore SC and recorded another victory winning the game by 4-3.

There were reports they had departed New York aboard the SS Scythia on 26 October but there must have been a change of plan, as Mr Frankland took time out to visit his sister in Ontario. He was interviewed in *The Standard* newspaper and said, "The *Dominion Football Association had given permission for the team to tour Canada, but for some reason best known to themselves, they withdrew their permission.*" He went on to say that he felt, "*some explanation was due them from the DFA*", and it was "*distinctly understood that they would play ladies teams but so far they had to play against men.*" He also found time to write to the *Lancashire Daily Post*, who published his letter in November. Once again he claimed to have no knowledge of the fact that there were no women's teams and said, "*We have drawn record crowds for the soccer game in America. We were informed by the promoters of the tour when it was arranged that we were to play ladies teams, but on our arrival at Quebec it was suggested that we should play men's teams in exhibition games as there were not enough ladies teams. Under great pressure we gave way on that point, and regarded the tour as an experiment. Not a single girl has received any injury and we have done really well against the men's teams. In New England our girls were greeted by the Lancashire people in great style, and I certainly have never seen so many automobiles at a match before. Nearly all the workers seem to have their own cars and telephones. We play our last match at Philadelphia on Saturday, 4 November on the Baseball Ground. There is seating capacity for 45,000 people and the ground is the best in America. We have got accustomed to playing on no more than dust heaps! There is a big demand here for English and Scottish footballers and plenty of opportunities for good men to earn big money*".

His penultimate sentence speaks volumes for the standard of organisation on this tour, and perhaps another insight into what were the underlying motives. Of course it must have been a great thrill for them to play at such a wonderful stadium again. But the last match of the tour ended in a 5-4 defeat. However, they had a marvellous opportunity before the game when they finally had some female opposition. Alice Kell spoke of their pre-match contest: "*Before the game at the Baseball Ground, four members of the team raced the American Women's Olympic team in a relay race. The Preston team comprised of Florrie Haslam, Jennie Harris, Molly Walker and Lily Parr. The Preston girls led all the way. Molly Walker established a lead of about three yards which was slightly reduced against Lily Parr. Jennie Harris increased it again to three yards, but the last American runner made a great effort a few yards from the tape which Florrie Haslam breasted just before her."* The lassies from Lancashire jumped for joy and were delighted with their victory over the Olympic team. They were finally able to prove to the Americans that when on a level playing field, there were few other sportswomen who were their equals. Not even Olympic Athletes! (The inaugural Women's Olympic Games took place in Paris, in April of 1922, when eighteen athletes broke world records in front of 20,000 spectators. The games were the brainchild of Alice Milliat, founder of La Fédération Sportive Féminine Internationale (FSFI) who first brought the French Ladies team to England in 1920).

The trip lasted for nine weeks and during that time they played 9 matches, won 3, drew 3, and lost 3. The newspapers reported that: *"The Dick, Kerr Ladies showed remarkable spirit in their games even though they were pitted against some of the strongest men's clubs in the country. They displayed great stamina, clever combination play and considerable speed. The individual performances of several players, compared favourably with the skills of the men. Lily Parr displayed great speed and a terrific kicking power."* One paper even quoted her as being the most brilliant female player in the world. Interestingly though, none of the newspaper reports included any reference to charitable donations being made during the tour.

As for the teams the ladies played against, they were some of the best in the United States with many of the players having had experience in the Football League. On the Fall River team, Harold Brittan, the centre forward, played for Chelsea and Alec Lorimer, the inside left, played for Kilmarnock. The J&P Coats team of Pawtucket, Rhode Island, won the championship of the Professional American Soccer League in the 1922-23 season. The inside right, Fred Morley, played for Blackpool and Brentford, while outside left, Tommy Fleming played for Morton. The outside right for J&P Coats, James Gallagher, later played for the U.S. in the World Cup of 1930 in Montevideo, Uruguay. Pete Renzulli who played in goal for the Coats team, a member of the National Hall of Fame, and US International and American Pro League player during the 1920s, said of the skill of the Dick, Kerr Ladies: *"Here is something. I played against them in 1922 in goal for the Coats team. We were national champions and we had a hell of a job beating them 6-3."*

Their transatlantic adventure came to an end and they departed New York aboard the SS Adriatic on 9 November 1922 and arrived back in England at Liverpool on Friday 17 November.

Homeward bound

Back row, ladies: Alice Woods, Carmen Pomies, Daisy Clayton, Jennie Harris, May Graham

Front: Florrie Haslam, Molly Walker, Jessie Walmsley, Lily Lee, Alice Kell, Lily Parr, Alice Mills

Pictured on the right holding the Stars and Stripes, is an unhappy looking 18 year old Alice Mills. She was so taken with life in the USA she fell completely in love with it. As she set foot on American soil she was heard to say, "*This is my country!*" When the time came to return to England, Alice couldn't be found on board the ship. Some representatives from Travellers Aid were asked to search for her. She reluctantly made it back on board but vowed to return to make a new life and her homecoming to Preston would be relatively short lived. Upon her arrival she threw her bags on living room floor and said, "*I'm out of here!*" She would soon make plans to change her life and realise her dream.

Interviewed in the press on their return, Alice Kell gave a more informed view than her comments before their departure and said, "*The tour has been a fine experience and holiday. We went out to meet ladies teams, but on arrival found there were none, so all our games were against men. But we have had a splendid time. Soccer is only a new game out there and the average attendance at men's matches is about 4000. We played before 8000 and 10,000. In America, football is not the same as ours. It is all individual play, they don't pass the ball* as we do and players all try to go through on their own. *We played our usual game and Lily Parr was always an outstanding player and our leading goalscorer was Florrie Redford. Girls are learning football at the colleges in America and possibly teams will be formed. We visited two colleges in Baltimore and found girls learning football. The tour has been well worth while.*" Everyone agreed the tour had been a great success and were pleased to report that there were no injuries to any of the players.

On Friday 1st December they were officially welcomed home by the management of Dick, Kerr & Co Ltd but due to recent changes, the company was now known as English Electric Ltd. The team were guests at a social evening and dance held in the works canteen, which was appropriately decorated for the occasion and the guest list read like a who's who in local dignitaries. Quoted in the press, works manager Mr Livingstone said: "*On behalf of the whole management team we are glad to see our players again and notice that all the girls look so well after their strenuous American tour. The team has brought back a most interesting trophy, a football signed by President Harding, and they captured an American flag by conquering the hearts of the Americans. The Company is very proud of the charitable services of the club and we hope in the future the team would again give their services generously in aid of deserving causes*". Maybe the Canadian Football Association had a change of heart after their refusal to let the girls play in Canada as Mr Livingstone also announced they had received an offer from Edmonton, Canada, requesting that the part of the tour which had to be curtailed should be continued in Canada and the States next fall.

Councillor Ellison added, "*I am delighted to be able to welcome the players home. I had half expected to find them all having picked up American expressions such as, 'I guess' and 'I reckon', but such a habit it seems must have been left behind. Some people do not like ladies playing football, but a subject on which the medical profession disagreed must be judged by laymen. I feel it is right and proper for ladies to play football, especially in support of charitable institutions.*"

Alderman Whitehead, ex Mayor of Burnley, also added a welcome and said, "*I am sorry that the FA have placed a ban on women's football and I hope they will soon see the error of their ways.* This was met with cries of '*Hear, hear*' from all present. *I have been connected with football for many years and always believed that the presence of lady spectators had a good influence on the game. I am delighted with the Dick, Kerr Ladies play. Ladies play football without a loss of temper and furthermore, I feel that they have as much right to play as men, and hope that they will soon be on grounds where they ought to play.*"

In reply, Mr Frankland gave an amusing and interesting account of the tour, in which he described the pains and the joys of the sea voyage. He said that it had been a great shock when they arrived in Quebec, to learn that they had to play against mens teams. The players made the decision on their own to play the men and they gave a magnificent account of themselves. The tour though, he said, was badly managed by those on the other side, with the players having to make long journeys immediately prior to a game. They were however, greeted with remarkable enthusiasm everywhere and their proudest achievement was the victory in a relay race over the American Ladies Olympic team.

There is no doubt the tour was a resounding success and history makes it a remarkable achievement but it does become apparent that the girls were exploited. Whether they realised it or not, they still had the most fantastic experience of their young lives. The past year had seen them survive everything that had been thrown at them and their dignity remained intact. But could they face up to standing alone as the women's game became almost extinct with no official body to support them? The Dick, Kerr Ladies had already shown their resilience and the FA must have been aware that they were still fighting back. One thing was for sure, these girls weren't going away quietly, but what did the future hold for this trailblazing team? Would their tenacious spirit see them through the tough times ahead, being constantly up against the establishment, and if so, how much longer could they survive?

CHAPTER SEVEN
A NEW ERA

The French ladies made a return visit early in 1923 for what had evolved into an annual event and during this tour they played against the Dick, Kerr Ladies at Cardiff Arms Park. The proceeds of match went to the Rheims Cathedral Fund and the Railwaymen's Benevolent Association.

Cardiff Arms Park 1923

Back row: Daisy Clayton, Carmen Pomies?, Alice Woods, Annie Marsland,
Alice Kell, Jessie Walmsley

Front row: Florrie Haslam, Jennie Harris, Florrie Redford, Alice Mills, Lily Parr

Following the tour of America, some of the girls were soon to end their playing days with the team and there began a time of rebuilding at the club, but there was no shortage of girls queuing up to join them, all hoping for the same opportunities. New players joining the team in 1923 included Hilda Parkinson and Lily Buxton. Both girls came from Blackpool and they could often be seen playing football together on the beach and during the winter months were even seen swimming in the sea! Lily Buxton was so dedicated to the Dick, Kerr Ladies that she actually gave up a dancing career to enable her to play for the team. She had previously been a dancer with the John Tiller Troupe and performed as one of the Tiller Girls at the Winter Gardens in Blackpool.

More girls from St Helens had also joined the team including Lizzy Ashcroft, Sue Chorley and Lydia Ackers. The ladies team had disbanded soon after the FA ban and this could explain the high number of St Helens players moving over to Preston and Lydia had obviously put the disappointment of the USA trip behind her. There was little work available in their home town and in Preston they not only had a job at the Dick, Kerr factory, but they could also continue playing football. Lydia recalled that her mother felt she was too young to leave home and didn't really want her to go away. Mr Frankland assured Mrs Ackers that her daughter would be well taken care of because they wanted them all together at the factory in Preston. Lydia said, *"They eventually got us all together and they found us 'digs'. I had a very good place in Avenham. The first thing I can remember was the 'knocker up' knocking at the window. I came from the countryside and it was something I had never heard of before."* The 'knocker up' was the chap who's job it was to extinguish the gas lamps in the streets at first light. With the long pole needed to 'snuff out' the lamps, he could also knock on the upstairs bedroom windows to waken people who worked on early shifts, and he would do this to earn an extra few shillings every week.

Lizzy Ashcroft played full back for the team. She was rated as the best defender at the club since Alice Kell and was nicknamed 'Tommy' by her team mates. Some years later, her son Alec Bolton recalled: *"My mother was a very good player and she used to embarrass me with her skills. I would be playing football in the street with a bunch of kids and many a time she would come home laden down with shopping bags in each hand, but she could easily take the ball off us, dribble round the kids and score a goal."*

In June of 1923 the team took part in the Blackpool Carnival and played a match for fun at Squires Gate against a representative side made up of the rest of the United Kingdom. Prior to the game they took part in the carnival procession on a wagon that displayed their remarkable playing record, where they claimed to be *The World's Champions*. The wagon was decorated with goal posts and a large globe of the world. During the parade the team were completely overwhelmed by a gesture made by the ex servicemen who were on another wagon representing their Association. Alice Norris explains: *"Our*

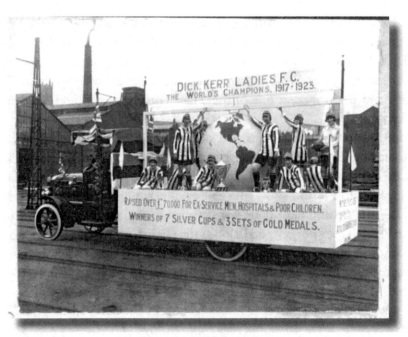

Blackpool Carnival Float

Annie Crozier standing right of globe: Alice Norris seated

Alice Kell far right holding ball

Souvenir Programme

wagon was going down the road one way and the ex servicemen were coming up the other way. For some reason both wagons stopped opposite each other and the ex servicemen stood up and saluted us, they actually saluted us! I can't tell you how much it meant to us all. We were as proud as punch". The Dick, Kerr Ladies had raised an enormous amount of money for the Ex Servicemen's Association and it was a lovely gesture by them paying their own tribute in return. Alice treasured that moment for the rest of her life.

In some ways it could be said that the FA ban in trying to stop women from playing football had been a failure. Although they had succeeded in preventing them from playing on League grounds, the never say die attitude of these girls was quite remarkable and their spirit could not be broken. They would play anywhere they could and the crowds still turned up in their thousands to watch them. By 1923 it was claimed they had raised £70,000 for charitable causes.

This year was also a momentous year in the life of 19 year old Alice Mills as she made the brave decision to travel alone and begin a new life in the United States. Unable to settle back into Lancashire life after returning from America with the team, she left her home town of Preston forever. Just short of twelve months after the US tour, she sailed from Liverpool aboard the Cunard ship Samaria and landed in Boston, Massachusetts on 1 September 1923. She went to live in Pawtucket staying with a lady named Mrs Fleming who sponsored her emigration to the USA. Alice got a job in a textile mill and it wasn't long before she met her future husband, J Aime Lambert. He was born in Rhode Island and they were married on 11 November 1925. Alice and Aime worked extremely hard until they had saved enough money to bring out the rest of her family. Her mother, Mary Ann, sisters Winnie, Elizabeth, Mary and brother Joe, all arrived in America before the birth of their first daughter Irene, who made her entrance into the world on 3 October 1926. Five more daughters were to follow: Louise, Winnie, Terry, Frankie and Rose.

Aime became a barber, but with Alice's encouragement they opened a hardware

Mr & Mrs Lambert, 11 November 1925

store in Pawtucket. They later moved to Seekonk, Massachusetts where he and Alice built and ran another successful hardware store. *Lambert Hardware* had a large clientele. The building was later expanded to include a gift shop and a drug store and it became one of the first strip malls on Central Avenue, Seekonk - a far cry from the days of being the poorest family in Sacred Heart Parish!

Meanwhile, back home in Preston, the football continued and other new arrivals at the club included local girl 15 year old Lily Martin and Elsie Yates from Fleetwood. The team may not have played as many games as in the early days, but their dogged determination to continue to play football was a credit to them. In a match programme from a game at Colne on 22 September 1923 against Stoke Ladies, there are interesting cameo sketches of some of the players.

Alice Kell, captain and goalkeeper:- *Modest and unassuming off the field, cool and capable on it. Kicks with beautiful accuracy and judgement. Strangers who meet her in private life express surprise that she is a footballer. They little know that the quiet, charming girl to whom they are speaking is captain of the most famous girls' team in the world, and that she only occupies that position by virtue of her consistent and excellent play.*

Florrie Redford, centre forward:- *Can shoot with tremendous power and accuracy, and has scored more goals than any other girl playing football. Has returned specially from Paris to play in this match.*

Lily Parr, outside left:- *A phenomenal player, and quite young. Big, fast and powerful, is tricky and can take corner kicks better than most men, and scores many goals from extra-ordinary angles with a left foot cross drive, which nearly breaks the net. Is the tom-boy of the team, who always says exactly what she thinks about everybody and everything - often to the amusement of the other members of the side.*

Teams for the game were: Stoke: J Longshaw, T Cooper, Lizzie Carroll, Lily Bridgett, Dolly Cooper, Ida Bridgett, Ada Derricott, Elsie Stavier, Tilly Wagg, Daisy Bates, E Bridgett. Dick, Kerr's: Alice Kell, Lily Lee, Lily Buxton, Lily Martin, Lizzy Ashcroft, Hilda Parkinson, Sue Chorley, M Moran, Lily Parr, Florrie Redford, Lydia Ackers. Reserves: J Lancaster, E Frankland, Elsie Yates, Alice Norris, Miss Riding.

The team continued to play throughout the 1920s and although not as frequently as before, their games were now played mainly during the summer months. It was recorded at the Annual General Meeting of Dick, Kerr factory in 1924 that the football team was undoubtedly more well known than the company!

After the First World War many of the women who had been employed at Dick, Kerr's on war placings, were released from the factory. The need for munitions had ceased and they were also expected to make way for the men who were returning home from the conflict and resuming their place in the workforce. Details surrounding the employment of the girls in the football team at that time are rather vague but a safe assumption might be that they would have left the factory after the armistice and perhaps with some gentle persuasion from Mr Frankland, they may have been brought back into the works to continue with the football team. Lydia Ackers spoke of working at the factory, but exactly how long they were all there together after the war isn't clear. Mr Frankland did his best to find work there for all team members and we do know that Carmen Pomies, from France, worked in the offices.

It was probably during these years that a long association began between many of the Dick, Kerr Ladies and Whittingham Hospital. Whittingham was the largest psychiatric hospital in Lancashire. The work was long and hard, and the nurses employed there needed to be fit and healthy, and the girls from the football team certainly fitted that criteria. The nurses were also expected to 'live in', and this may well have made the idea of working there a more attractive proposition for members of the team who had come to Preston from other towns. On numerous occasions over the years Alfred Frankland was responsible for getting jobs at the hospital for many of the girls. Whether it was his direct influence or that of his sister who was already a ward sister there is uncertain, but many of them were able to have permanent full time employment because of their association with the football team. Alec Bolton, who's mother Lizzy Ashcroft, worked there said, *"It was easy to get jobs at Whittingham because they needed muscle. I can remember watching the patients during the war years (WW2). I remember one patient called Edith. She used to wear about ten cardigans, she would wear everything she had. But if she threw a fit or was having a bad turn, they could have her stripped off and in a padded cell within seconds. They needed people like my mother and Lily Parr. It's all sedation nowadays, but they didn't have the drugs back then."*

Dorothy Nightingale relates some experiences of her sister Joan Whalley, and the possible dangers they encountered there during the second world war. *"On her first day on duty she went off looking so prim and proper wearing her lovely new uniform. She was walking down the middle of the ward, when all of a sudden she felt something hit her with a splat! One of the patients had thrown faeces at her. It was all over her, she was covered in it. She could see the funny side though, well you had to hadn't you! She worked night shifts more often than not and during the black outs, the lights had to be kept very dim. She was on a* ward with over forty patients, all with suicidal or murderous tendencies. You can imagine what it was like sat there with all the lights dimmed, you could hardly see a thing it was so dark. The girls would have done anything rather than be in that place. Joan said that one night she turned round and there was a face staring at her from behind and the patient was just about to grab her. It scared the living daylights out of her, but she was tough and always tried to laugh things off. But she wasn't so lucky while once escorting a patient to the toilet. When the patient came out of the cubicle, she grabbed Joan by the throat and tried to strangle her. She was black and blue with bruises and had to wear a silk scarf around her neck to hide the marks until they faded."

The committee at Whittingham were very sports minded and encouraged the girls to be involved in playing all manner of sporting activities. Quite a number of those who were members of the football team also represented the hospital cricket and hockey teams. Some of the players known to have worked at the hospital in the early days of the football team were, Florrie Redford, Lily Lee, Jessie Walmsley, Lily Parr, Lizzy Ashcroft, Lydia Ackers, Eva Gardner and Lily Martin. Jessie Walmsley was already nursing before she came to Preston.

Matron Jessie Walmsley

Lydia Ackers said of Alfred Frankland, "He got me my job at Whittingham. He was in with everybody. After the war there was no work at Dick, Kerr's and

132

when the team were finishing at the factory, they all went to work at the hospital. I worked there for 32 years." Lily Parr worked there too until her retirement. It does seem that playing football changed the lives of these girls for the better and brought opportunities they would perhaps have been unlikely to experience had they remained in their home town of St Helens.

In the summer of 1925, the French Ladies made yet another of their regular trips to England when they played a series of nine matches with Dick, Kerr Ladies. Incredibly and without the benefit of television, news of the trip had travelled as far afield as Australia. The *Brisbane Courier* published a photograph of the two teams lining up before the kick off.

FAMOUS FRENCH GIRLS' TEAM PLAYS BRITISH GIRLS.

The famous team of girl football players, from the Femina Sports Club of Paris, recently played nine match In England with the Dick Kerr's women team of Preston, Lancashire. The photograph shows the French ar English captains kissing before the toss-up.
Central News phot

Cutting from Brisbane Courier 19/6/25.

Brisbane Courier 1925

The tour also took in some matches in Scotland and interestingly the game in Kilmarnock was played on Kilmarnock FC's ground despite the ban being in force, so it appears that north of the border they were, to some extent, ignoring the wishes of the English FA. The Dick, Kerr Ladies won the game by 2-1 and Polly Scott was dubbed as *'the girl McCracken'* due to her knowledge and use of the off-side rule. Another paper said, *"Lily Parr is a really amazing player and would undoubtedly be playing 1ˢᵗ League if the English FA would permit it".*

They travelled to Ireland to play an International match in Belfast. Feted as 'England', they played an Irish representative team made up of players from leading Belfast clubs. The game was kicked off by the Rt Hon, Sir Dawson Bates MP and was refereed by Alf H Shepherd. The linesmen were Fred Mckee and Mickey Hamill a legendary centre half at Belfast Celtic. (result not available). Preston team: Maggie Shaw, C Howarth, Lizzy Ashcroft, Lily Buxton, Edith Hutton, A Marsh, Lydia Ackers, Jennie Harris, Sue Chorley, Hilda Parkinson, Lily Parr. Ireland: Sleator, Donaldson, Cree, McKelvey, Molly Seaton, Herbert, Gibson, Smyth, Hinds, Kearney, Morris.

Alice Norris recalls: *"We had a really good time when we played in Ireland. Mr Frankland told us we were to be shown round a works and we had to go through this place where they were making boats. Lily Parr, Tommy (Lizzy) Ashcroft, and Lily Martin were all friends and went around together and they wouldn't come with us. They were smokers you see and they liked their cigarettes. So we go through this here yard where the boats were being made, but we finished up at a tobacco factory (Gallaghers?). We were given a guided tour and when we came out they gave each of us a souvenir parcel of cigarettes. Well, when Lily found out she was fuming and she wouldn't let me keep my parcel. She were bigger than me and she took them off me. No, you didn't argue with Lily! Mr Frankland said to her, 'That serves you right, you should have come with us,' but she just said to him, 'She doesn't smoke, so she's not having them and that's that.'*

In 1926 they were forced to change their name and became Preston Ladies. This enforced change is likely due to an incident that had occurred some time earlier at the Dick, Kerr works.

Alice Norris explains, *"There was some trouble because Dick, Kerr's stopped us from playing on Ashton Park. One day while we were working, someone said that we all (the team) had to meet in the watch house. Something must have gone wrong because it was all so sudden that afternoon at the works. There was a strange atmosphere and there must have been some rumours going round. The men were saying, "What have you lot been up to?" It was our training night and Mr Frankland told us not to go anywhere near Ashton Park any more. Something must have gone wrong between him and the firm. I don't know what it was, but the girls didn't come in to work the morning after, they all went with Mr Frankland. He knew he had a place where the girls could go to keep them all together. When I went home, Lily had gone. She didn't say anything. She didn't* come home, I've no idea where she went. *When they all left, Mr Frankland was still calling the team Dick, Kerr Ladies for a while, but one of the workmen said he heard that he hadn't to use the name Dick, Kerr's anymore, so they changed the name to Preston Ladies, but Mr Frankland was always with them. He wanted me to go and take over as trainer. Annie Crozier was the trainer and I used to help her with first aid and massaging. She was leaving and Mr Frankland asked me if I would take over and he offered to pay for me to learn the job properly, but I wasn't prepared to give up my job. My father always said, it doesn't interfere with the family and when I went home and told him, he said I'd done the right thing.*" Alice went on, "*There was one time when we were playing up in Scotland and two players from the other team told us that we wouldn't be asked back again as we were too expensive. We didn't really understand what they meant because we were only given what it had cost us to get there. I think that's when all the trouble must have started down at the works.*"

Lydia Ackers recalled: "*We trained on Ashton Park. We bought it in the first place but the men kind of took it over. They shoved us off our training ground and we went on a little place down by the river.*"

We will never know exactly what happened at the factory that day. We can only speculate what the 'trouble' was all about. The truth has gone to the grave with those who could shed any light on the mystery. But the actions of everyone not going back in to work afterwards would suggest it must have been pretty serious. Could there be any substance to Lydia's claim that *they* had bought Ashton Park? Where could she have got such an idea from?

Lydia remembers: "*He had a greengrocer's shop on Sharoe Green Lane and his wife used to run it. He was a good manager but we had a bit of difficulty getting our expenses from him. He would try to get away with it if he could, but I wouldn't let him. I used to say, we want paying or we won't play. Well that did it, when we said we wouldn't play he gave us our expenses. He came to see my parents when they wanted me to play for them. He was always well dressed. Of course he was looking after himself wasn't he. I think that's how he bought his fruit shop.*"

Alice Norris said, "*No-one could ever prove anything but I think there was something in the rumours. It's not nice to say it but the older players used to say that when he first came down here he hadn't two ha'pennies to rub together. There was all that kind of talk going about. I think that's what set off all the rumours as he was doing so well. He'd never let anybody take over.*"

Elsie Yates said, "*He was awkward with the girls you know, but I was alright so I didn't bother about him. All the money was given to him and we just got our bare expenses, what we lost through not being at work, but he was always there*

135

with his money bags. Sometimes it was hard work getting money from him."

Alice Woods' son said his father, who acted in an official capacity with the team in the early 1920's, was of the opinion that things were *'not always as they should have been'.* He said his father had stated that Mr Frankland would never let anyone else take over, *"He had to be running the whole show,"* he said.

Whether or not there is any substance in these comments, and whatever his ethics might have been, the fact remains that he did an enormous amount for women's football and without him they would probably not have had the opportunity to play the game. Which might explain why no one said anything at the time.

In 1926 they played another match at night. The game took place at Burnley and they used the same kind of lighting technique that was used at Deepdale some six years earlier. It was said that the ground was so well illuminated that a *Lancashire Daily Post* reporter could actually read a newspaper in the centre of the field! But with matches being less frequent than before, some of the original members of the team only turned out for them if they were really needed. New players who joined the team in 1926 and became household names in the second generation of the club were, Edith Hutton and Polly Scott. They were regular members of the team for ten years or more.

Team picture, post 1926
Back row: GK Maggie Shaw, Lydia Ackers, Lily Parr
Front row: 3rd left Eva Gardner, 2nd right Lily Buxton, Hilda Parkinson

The majority of the ladies who played in the early years who experienced at first hand the full force of prejudice from the FA and indeed some quarters of the medical profession, proved the establishment wrong in the best possible way. Many of them lived a long and healthy life.

Alice Kell played in goal for a short time and became the trainer for a while before leaving the team when she married master baker, Albert Cook. Their only son Reg was born in 1930. She was a keen Preston North End supporter, a season ticket holder and a big fan of Tom Finney. In later life she developed arthritis and died in 1990 not long after falling and breaking her hip.

Florrie Redford spent some time between Preston and Paris before emigrating to Canada in 1930 to pursue her career as a nurse. She made a brief return to the team in 1938, but subsequently moved to Coventry. In later life she developed a heart complaint and died in the late 1960's or early 1970's.

Jennie Harris left the team and lived in Bradford where she played for the Heys team for a while. She returned to Preston and continued playing into the 1930's. Her family said she was a very kind person and always brought them souvenirs from wherever she played. She returned to her home town of Lancaster to live out the rest of her days.

Lily Parr went on to become probably one of the games greatest players of all time.

Jessie Walmsley sadly passed away in 1934 when still only in her late 30's. She is buried in her home town of Lancaster.

Alice Mills made a new life in America and despite the myth of football harming a woman's fertility, she gave birth to six healthy girls and lived a long and prosperous life.

Lily Lee left the team for a while sometime during the 1920's to play for a team in Ireland. According to family members she would travel to Dublin on a Saturday and come back to Preston on Sunday after the match. Born in 1898 and one of 13 children, Lily began her working life in the cotton mills at the tender age of twelve. In 1929 her mother died and she was forced to retire from the game to take care of her father. She stayed with him until his death in 1940. She died in 1985.

Lily Jones, who became Mrs Martin when she was married in London during the team's return from the French tour, died in Sheffield at the age of 91.

Annie Crozier married Percy Darlington. He worked at a glassworks in Preston and was later transferred to Pilkingtons in St Helens. They had one daughter, Olive. Annie is buried in St Helens.

Alice Woods married Harold Stanley, whom she had met while playing for the team. Some sixty years later she would find new fame as Mrs Alice Stanley when she became famous all over again as the thirst for the history of women's football came to the fore. In the 1980s, TV documentaries were eager to chart the beginnings of the women's game and in particular, the world famous Dick, Kerr Ladies. Alice was taken back to Goodison Park, where she played in the record breaking match against St Helens. There must have been some wonderful memories for her as she re-lived those far off days when Dick, Kerr Ladies were the best in the land. It was thanks to Channel 4's coverage of women's football that Alice was also the guest of honour at several Women's FA Cup finals in the new era of the women's game and she loved every minute of it. Alice won a gold medal while playing for the Dick, Kerr Ladies in the 1920's, a medal she treasured and her son Bert said she wore it around her neck every day for the rest of her life. She died peacefully at her home in Manchester in 1991. She was 92 years old.

Alice Norris married Robert Barlow at St Andrews church in Preston in 1927. They had two children, Lenna and Doreen. Alice was taken ill in November of 1994 and unable to attend the launch of the first edition of 'In a League of Their Own!'. Alice was delighted that a book had been written about her old team and she enjoyed hearing the story unfold as her daughter Doreen read her a chapter every day when she visited her in hospital. She passed away peacefully on Boxing Day, but not until Doreen had read her the last chapter. She was 89 years old.

Elsie Yates, born in 1902, and played right half for the team said, *"I don't think there is a place in England where we didn't play. I enjoyed all the travelling and the good times we had. We always had big crowds wherever we played. They were good days, I really did enjoy myself."* Elsie worked at Dick, Kerr's for a time before returning to her home town of Fleetwood where she worked in the fish industry. *"I used to get time off work as easy as anything when I was playing football,"* she said. In later life, Elsie lived in a residential home for the elderly until her death in 1995. She was 92 years old.

Lydia Ackers, a nippy little midfield player, said her fondest memories were, *"The travelling and staying in the different hotels. When we went to London we would stay where all the business people stayed and we were always very well treated."* And of the players in the team she said, *"Well you see, I was so young. They were famous and everybody made such a fuss of them. I really had this feeling of inferiority about the likes of Florrie Redford, and her being centre forward in this great team."* And of Lily Parr she said, *"I have never seen any woman, nor many a man, kick a ball like she could. Everybody was amazed when they saw her power, you would never believe it."* Lydia passed away in 1993. She was 90 years old.

Bull & Royal Hotel courtyard

Back row: Annie Crozier, Lily Martin, Lily Lee, Florrie Redford, Lizzy Ashcroft, Lily Parr

Front: Maggie Shaw, Polly Scott, Lily Buxton, Jennie Harris, Lydia Ackers, Hilda Parkinson, Jenny Lancaster

Throughout this transitional period for the Dick, Kerr team, the public were always willing spectators at their matches, and to dispel the 'novelty' myth which has followed the women's game since its inception, it was interesting to hear the opinion of William Crook from Preston. Mr Crook saw the Dick, Kerr Ladies play on several occasions just before the General Strike of 1926. When asked why he went to watch them play he said that like many other people, he went along because he enjoyed watching a good game of football. *"The Dick, Kerr Ladies had some brilliant players,"* he said.

Their extremely high standards were still very firmly set, but could their phenomenal success story continue despite all the obstacles that had been placed before them? Could their reputation as being the best in the world remain intact in their new guise as Preston Ladies? Could anyone else take away their crown?

CHAPTER EIGHT

PRESTON LADIES (THE WORLD FAMOUS DICK, KERR'S)

Although they had now adopted the new name of Preston Ladies, the team would continue to be known as the World Famous Dick, Kerr Ladies for the remainder of their existence and to present day. The players *always* regarded themselves as the Dick, Kerr Ladies and were fiercely proud of the clubs history and retained the name in brackets on letter headings and programmes.

By 1927 the team were still rated the best and on 8 Sept 1927, in a match played at Leicester against Blackpool Ladies, the Preston side notched up a convincing 11-2 victory. The headline in the *Leicester Mercury* was: **"WOMEN CAN PLAY FOOTBALL"** The article went on to say: *"Everyone who went to the game came away with one big impression. And that was that they had seen an outside-left (Lily Parr) who if she had been a man would have gained international honours. She really was extra-ordinarily good and she scored five of her sides eleven goals. She made wing play look absurdly simple and there is no doubt that this girl has a natural ability for the game. The Dick, Kerr eleven were far too good for the Blackpool girls and whoever has coached them has done his work well, for they displayed a knowledge of the game and revealed skill that was surprising. The girls were not afraid to use their heads either and the length of their kicks was as good as many men who are in the game."* The Dick, Kerr team was: J Frankland, Polly Scott, Lizzy Ashcroft, E Buxton, Florrie Redford, E Latham, Hilda Parkinson, Jennie Harris, Lily Buxton, H Shaw, Lily Parr. Goals were scored by: Lily Parr (5), Lily Buxton (3), H Shaw (2), Jennie Harris (1).

Alfred Frankland was a strict disciplinarian. He was a stickler for punctuality and very particular about the girls appearance. He would only ever allow them to wear trousers on the bus while travelling and they had to change into something more suitable before getting off and meeting officials of other teams. He was just as particular about their football kit too which had to be immaculate. He was after all a gentleman from the Victorian era and this was reflected in his values. The girls however did like to let their hair down when travelling to away matches and would often try to get the better of him.

Team photo circa 1927-28

*Back row players: Sue Chorley, Hilda Parkinson, GK unknown, Lizzy Ashcroft,
unknown.*

*Front row: Annie Yates, Lucy Hoyle, Jennie Harris, Lily Parr, Edith Hutton,
Lily Buxton*

Eva Gardner recalled: *We played a match in Derbyshire and we stayed in a hotel just outside the town. We had the time of our lives that night, oh we did have a good time. Mr Frankland gave his usual list of rules and said to us, 'Now girls, I don't want you drinking any alcohol tonight. There's to be no beer, do you understand? No beer! I want you all to get to bed early.' He was strict with us, well he tried to be, but we didn't take any notice of him. We asked the porter to get some beer for us and he brought quite a few bottles up to the room. It wasn't long before we were singing and having a really good time, we were well away. Then Frankland came up and caught us: 'What's going on here?" he said, and when he saw all the bottles, we could see the look on his face and we thought, Oh bloody hell, now we're for it! He demanded the porter remove them immediately. 'Get those bottles out of here now! I told them there was no beer allowed'. The porter said in his defence as he was removing all the empty bottles, 'It's not my fault mister, they asked me to bring them', and he scurried out of the room.* The result of the match isn't available, but let's hope they managed to complete the game without too many headaches from their high spirits the night before!

The French Ladies regular visit to play a series of charity matches had evolved into a tour solely with the Dick, Kerr team. The players would arrange to take their two weeks summer holiday for the tour, and both teams would travel up and down the country raising money for charity.

The right to vote was finally given to women over twenty-one in 1928. The General Election of 1929 was known as the Flapper Election and women's votes greatly outnumbered that of the men as they made use of their newly acquired 'privilege'. The Labour Party took office for the second time with Ramsay McDonald as Prime Minister. Margaret Bondfield was appointed Minister of Labour to become the first woman to hold a Cabinet position. The Wall Street Crash of 1929, saw millions of dollars wiped off the New York Stock Exchange and the effects of this were a contributing factor to the world-wide depression of the 1930s, which was to last for the greater part of the decade. In 1931 the depression deepened and the great financial crisis began to take hold as the bank rate fell. There was a serious weakening in sterling and in British funds. By the end of the year it was announced by the government that owing to the prevailing depression and the need for economy, work on the Cunard ship '534' would have to be suspended. It would be two years before work would be resumed on the 534 which when launched, was christened, *Queen Mary*. (in fact, it was only with re-armament in the period leading up to the outbreak of World War 2 that the worst of the Depression could be said to be over)

Other world events at the start of the new decade saw Amy Johnson make her solo flight to Australia in just under three weeks, and the world was shocked by the wreck of the Airship R101 during a storm at Beauvais in France. Built in 1929, the R101 was the largest of British Airships. It struck a hillside, exploded and burst into flames. Only six out of a total of fifty-four crew and passengers were saved. This disaster resulted in the abandonment of all airship construction by Great Britain. Germany's Graff Zeppelin held supreme place as the world's most successful airship and made a remarkable successful round the world flight.

In November of 1930, the *Daily Dispatch* reported that Mr Frankland had received a letter from Prague inviting him to send out two teams to play a series of exhibition games in Czechoslovakia. He replied to the invitation and suggested that the French team should make up the opposition. Sufficient funds to finance the trip were not forthcoming and it never came to fruition.

Sixteen-year-old Edna Clayton joined the team in 1930 and another major signing in 1931 was that of Margaret Thornborough. Her brother Eli played half back (midfield) for Bolton Wanderers and Preston North End and the team were able to take advantage of some valuable coaching from him during the 1930's. Margaret would in later years become the assistant manager of Preston Ladies with Alfred Frankland.

The team was still in great demand for its fund raising efforts and they were glad to be of service in times of crisis to those in need. Although the charities and the public still had enormous respect for their efforts, the Football Association continued with their dictatorial attitude at every available opportunity. A game had been arranged for 8 June 1932 on behalf of the Stafford Infirmary and all the plans and publicity had been completed by the organising committee. However, a week prior to the match, the FA refused permission for the game to go ahead on any ground under their jurisdiction. They didn't personally inform the promoters of their actions, instead they were left to gather the information from a press announcement. Thankfully, the Stafford County Police came to the rescue when Chief Constable H P Hunter OBE, allowed the use of their ground for the match. Quoted in the press regarding the *Autocratic ruling of the FA*, Mr Frankland said: *One is reminded of Shakespeare's lines: "Oh, it is excellent to have a giants strength, but it is tyrannous to use it like a giant."*

THE FAMOUS PRESTON LADIES' F.C. Late DICK KERR LADIES' F.C.
THE UNDISPUTED WORLD'S CHAMPIONS WHO HAVE TOURED EXTENSIVELY ABROAD
WINNERS OF 8 SILVER CUPS AND 4 SETS OF GOLD MEDALS

Team Postcard 1932

Back row: Lizzy Ashcroft, Ms Hodgkinson, Elsie Yates, Maggie Shaw, Lily Buxton, Ms Knowles, Edna Clayton

Middle row: Annie Yates, Lydia Ackers, Jennie Harris, Mr Frankland, Lily Parr, Sue Chorley, Edith Hutton

Front row: Hilda Parkinson, Margaret Thornborough

Royal Lancashire Show 1932
Lizzy Ashcroft going for goal v French

Training on Moor Park 1932
Edna Clayton left, Lily Parr heading the ball

In December of 1932 the team were invited to play a game against Lovell's Ladies at Newport, South Wales, in aid of the Mayor's Christmas Distress Fund. The Lovell's team were all under 17 years of age and were a relatively inexperienced side but were unbeaten in their matches before their duel with Preston Ladies. The match was to be played at night under floodlights and the venue was Newport Athletic Rugby Ground. In those days football by floodlight was still a novelty and it is quite probable that this game was the first of its kind to be played by women. It was in fact, only the second time that a floodlit match had been played in Newport.

The Preston team were met at the Queens Hotel after a long overnight journey and soon seemed quite refreshed after polishing off a full English breakfast. They were later officially welcomed at the town hall to a civic reception held for them by the Mayor, Councillor Mr W.J. Wall who expressed his sincere gratitude for their help in raising money for his distress fund during these very difficult times. A crowd of 7,000 came along to Newport Athletic Rugby ground on 8 December, to see history in the making as women's football reached another landmark by playing at night under floodlights.

But what a difference in stature there was between the two teams. For the most part Lovells looked like schoolgirls in comparison to their opponents, who recorded a convincing 5-0 victory. The pick of the goals came from Lily Parr who cut in from the left and scored on the volley *"with a magnificent oblique shot of the approved text book style"*. Edith Hutton was carried off in the second half with a 'dead leg', but even with only ten 'men', the Lovells girls still couldn't break through the Preston defence. The *Daily Dispatch* quoted Lovell's captain Violet Iveson, conceding that, *"Dick, Kerr's were a bit too good for us"*, and Lily Parr attributed her team's victory to the lack of experience of their opponents and said, *"I would have liked them to have scored a goal"*. Lovells team: Violet Rowlands, Winnie Slatters, Maggie Way, Gwen Williams, Lily Hillman, Mary Fitzgerald, Olive Price, May Yendall, Violet Iveson, Winnie Hook, Doreen Watkins. Preston: Annie Derbyshire, Edna Clayton, Lizzy Ashcroft, Lily Buxton, Edith Hutton, Polly Scott, Lydia Ackers, Margaret Thornborough, Sue Chorley, Hilda Parkinson, Lily Parr. Goalscorers: Lily Buxton, Lily Parr, Edith Hutton, Margaret Thornborough, Sue Chorley.

Towards the end of 1933, Mr Frankland received a letter from Belgian side, Atalante Ladies from Brussels. The Belgian team had heard of the Dick, Kerr success story and of their claim to be *Champions*. But they felt that their playing record justified their claim in being called *Champions*. They were unbeaten over the previous three years having played against some of the best teams on the continent. The manager and president of the Brussels club wrote: "*We distinctly challenge you for the right to use this title, and will come over to England with the determined intention of proving that it is we who are the champions. We have never been beaten for three years. We play frequently in Belgium and are members of a big Women's Athletic Federation*". Naturally they accepted the challenge and a series of matches were arranged during August of 1934 and it was hoped that a reciprocal tour would take in games at Brussels, Antwerp and Liege. Mr Frankland was quoted in the press saying, "*I am confident that our team will prove superior to the Belgian girls. We gladly accept this challenge. Our record speaks for itself. We have played 373, won 352, drawn 16, and lost 5. We have scored 1823 goals, with only 157 against.*

(A point to note from Mr Franklands figures is that their fifth defeat actually took place when they lost to the French Ladies at Stamford Bridge in 1920 when at that time the team had played approximately 50 games. The manager now claims that they had not lost a game since then. There could be those who will contradict his calculations, but if we accept him as correct this would mean they had played around 323 games without defeat! Wouldn't that make this a world record?)

INTERNATIONAL WOMEN FOOTBALLERS *who will welcome the Belgian team when they arrive for the championship of the World match against the women of Preston.* Miss E. A. Ashcroft, Miss M. A. Thornborough and Mlle. Carmen Pomies and Mlle. Andre Gauckler.

Championship Line up

Lizzy Ashcroft, Margaret Thornborough, Carmen Pomies, Andre Gaukler

Atalanta Ladies

The Belgian girls did actually cause something of a sensation when they defeated the Preston team during a freak weather storm at Bolton. However, they were subsequently thrashed in every other match during the tour and the Lancashire lassies felt that their claim of being *Champions* was still very much intact. A return trip to Belgium was never to come to fruition.

British tennis had a good year in 1934 when for the first time ever Great Britain scored two remarkable successes at Wimbledon. Dorothy Round won the women's singles and Fred Perry won the first of his three successive singles titles. It was also the year that saw the opening of the Mersey Tunnel by King George V.

Plans were on the table for another tour to France and the Dick, Kerr Ladies crossed the channel in April of 1935 for a welcome return to play a series of matches. The Mayor of Preston gave each of them a sprig of white heather for luck before their departure. It was their first visit to France since 1920 and this would turn out to be their last trip abroad. The evening ferry crossing to Calais was a smooth one and thankfully on this occasion no one was affected by sea sickness. The Band of the Scots Guards, who were en-route to an engagement in Montpellier, were on board and they entertained the passengers with a selection of tunes from their programme.

Unfortunately this tour wasn't quite as successful as their previous one and they had one or two disappointments during their match in Paris. They had to play without three of their regular first team players and also had to play in red jerseys for the first time because of a colour clash. They wore the white heather on their shirts given them by the Mayor of Preston, but there was no luck going their way in this game. In the 12th minute the first goal of the match scored by Edith Hutton, was disallowed. The disappointment was evident in the play of a very tired team. The French girls scored three goals in quick succession in a big effort which showed them to be the fitter side on this occasion and they won the match by 5-2. It was a big shock to lose to the French Ladies and this was their first defeat by them since the match at Stamford Bridge back in 1920. Perhaps the absence of Lily Parr was a significant factor and Bessie Cunliffe, who was making her debut in goal, found the occasion a little too daunting in front of the large crowd. The team was: Bessie Cunliffe, Edna Clayton, Lizzy Ashcroft, Miss Donoghue, Lily Buxton, Polly Scott, Sue Chorley, Margaret Thornborough, Edith Hutton, Hilda Parkinson, Annie Lynch.

The French team were back in Preston again in July and a series of nine matches were arranged to be played from 28 July–11 August. The regularity of their visits proves that there was a place for women's football and these women were able to do it despite an FA ban. It also confirms that women's football was still thriving. This year also saw another new player arrive at the club. Daphne Coupe travelled from Derby to Preston for a trial with the team without telling her parents. Her uncle was a player at Derby County and she supported them all her life. Her own football career ended when she joined the ATS in 1939. A keen football supporter for the remainder of her life, Daphne died in 2007 while actually on her way to watch a match. She was 92 years old.

King George V died on 20 January 1936 and his son Edward ascended to the throne as King Edward VIII. However his reign was to be short

Daphne Coupe

lived and the country was rocked by his abdication on 10 December 1936, in favour of the woman he loved, the American divorcee Mrs Wallis Simpson. Also this year, English Electric needed finance for the manufacture of Hampden Bombers and so the Ashton Park site was sold to Preston Borough Council for £27,500 to assist in their production. Locally, work was in progress to build the Royal Ordnance Factory at Euxton, and Courtaulds was being built to produce rayon for parachutes and barrage balloons. The opening of these two factories was to considerably ease unemployment problems in Preston.

March of 1937 saw the signing of fifteen-year-old local girl Joan Whalley to the Dick, Kerr team. She was to become a significant member of the club for many years and she made her debut on Coronation Day, 12 May 1937 against a Welsh representative side at Roundhay Park, Leeds.

It was customary at the women's games to have a famous celebrity or a civic dignitary to kick-off the match. This would most likely have been instigated by the promoters in order to attract a big a crowd to boost the funds for their charity. The French visit in August of 1937 saw world renowned comedian and film star George Formby and his wife Beryl, invited along to start the match for the international game at Bolton. George was a huge star and this was a great coup for the match organisers. Gracie Fields was among other big name celebrities who kicked off for them during this period. By comparison, this would be on a par with having Robbie Williams or Lady Gaga putting in an appearance today.

JOURNAL AND GUARDIAN, FRIDAY, AUGUST 13, 1937

GEORGE FORMBY KICKS OFF

George Formby Kicks off with his wife Beryl

The club had now been in existence for 20 years and throughout that time had proved over and over again that they were the best women's football team in the world. They had always maintained their very high standards with each new generation of the team and consistently produced a fine blend of talented and skilful players. Many girls from all over the country still dreamed of playing for the Dick, Kerr Ladies. They were extremely proud of their impressive playing record and because they had defeated representative sides from other European countries, they felt justified in claiming to be World Champions. There were others however, who had different opinions.

One such team was Edinburgh Ladies and they became the second club to challenge the Dick, Kerr Ladies right to assume the mantle of Champions. Secretary of the Scottish side, Mrs Proctor, had seen the official letter headed paper of the Preston team which had printed on it in bold black letters, "**CHAMPIONS OF THE WORLD**". The girls from Edinburgh disputed their right of claiming to be champions when they hadn't played them, the best team in Scotland. The challenge was promptly accepted by the Preston club and the match was arranged to take place at the Squires Gate Stadium, South Shore, Blackpool.

Talking tactics

Although they felt confident that no other women's team in the world were their equals, Mr Frankland said the team would be undergoing intensive training in preparation for the game. The press were quick to pick up the story and a sizeable number of them hailed the game as the championship of the world match. *The Daily Mail, Daily Herald, Daily Sketch, Lancashire Daily Post, Daily Mirror, Daily Express* and *the Daily Dispatch* were all keen to photograph the Preston team in training.

In the build up to the match, Mr Frankland said in the *Daily Mail*, *"We are told that the Scottish lasses have beaten two mens teams and consider their craft will overcome the speed of the English team. But we have no fear on that score. Never since Preston began its brilliant history in women's football have they come across a team in Great Britain, France, Belgium, or America whom we have not beaten. We are going out for a big victory. I believe that the present Preston forward line is the best ever seen in women's football, and I am certain that we shall win. I admit there has never actually been a world championship, but when you consider all the foreign teams we have defeated, I think we are entitled to call ourselves World Champions."*

Legs Up!

The Preston side had a better record than their opponents. They had already won all of their 26 matches in that year, while the Edinburgh girls had won 18, drawn one and lost one. They were the first Scottish girls team to cross the border. The Lancashire lasses started the match as favourites and Mr Frankland was confident of a Preston victory: *"I'll eat my hat if we don't win"* he said. And as he wore an outsize in hats, his confidence had to be admired. *"Everybody says we are the world champions, except Edinburgh that is. But they will acknowledge it after the game".* Daphne Coupe, centre half for Preston said: *"The match will be a big test for us,"* and May Helme the goalkeeper added, *"We are regarding this as our biggest match. Our season is nearly over now as we play largely in the summer, but we are always ready to take up a challenge."* The night before the match, the team gathered at the home of Mr Frankland, (now referred to as 'Pop' by the girls) to discuss tactics and plan their strategy for the game. The girls were taking the match more seriously than any other.

151

On Wednesday, 8 September 1937, Preston Ladies played Edinburgh Ladies for the Championship of Great Britain and the World. The teams were: Preston: May Helme, Margaret Thornborough, Lucy Hoyle, Hilda Parkinson, Daphne Coupe, Sue Chorley, Joan Whalley, Irene Phillips, Edith Hutton,(capt) Annie Lynch, Lily Parr. 1st reserve: Stella Briggs. Edinburgh: Misses, Scott, Bain, Robertson, Owenson, Saunders, Ralph, Clements, Kerr, Anderson, McDonald, Russell. Reserves: Leslie, Dickinson.

Preston's Soccer Girls Retain World Title

Mrs. Fanny McDonald, the Edinburgh captain (left) watching Miss Edith Hutton, Preston's captain, tossing-up before the women's football match at Blackpool yesterday. Preston retained their world title with a 5-1 win.

Frances McDonald left with Edith Hutton who wins the toss

Edith Hutton in action

Action from the game

Both sides had been used to crowds averaging 5,000, but a disappointing turnout of only one thousand spectators came to watch the match at Squires Gate. They saw a hard fought contest resulting in a 5-1 victory for the Preston girls. All the Preston goals were scored in the first half as the home side took full advantage of the weather conditions. Having won the toss, they decided to play with a strong breeze at their backs. A hat-trick was scored by centre forward Edith 'Ginger' Hutton with the other goals coming from Lily Parr and Joan Whalley, who at 15-years-old was the youngest player on the field. It was said again that had Lily Parr been a male football player she would almost certainly have been an international. She was very prominent for the Preston team and her strength of shot was always a problem for the Scottish side. Frances Macdonald was the scorer of a fine individual goal for Edinburgh. After the match she said, *"We were well beaten, but it was a good game and we shall play Preston again."* Joan Whalley had taken the day off school to play the most important match in her first season with the club. Another favourite pastime for Joan was playing the harmonica and after the game she couldn't resist playing some of her favourite tunes as both teams joined in with the post match celebrations.

To celebrate their victory and the 20th anniversary of the club's formation, a World Championship Victory Dinner was held at Booths Cafe in Preston on 24 November 1937. In its day Booths Cafe was one of the more sought after venues in the town for such occasions. On the menu was a mouthwatering choice of tomato cocktail or grapefruit starters, celery soup, lemon sole & tartar sauce, roast chicken and sausage, baked and boiled potatoes, sprouts and peas, followed by plum pudding & sauce or apple tart and cream, and coffee to finish off. The tables were decorated in the clubs colours of black and white and prominently displayed were pennants representing the names of other countries of teams they had played against. America, France, Canada and Belgium.

Among the many dignitaries present at the dinner, given by Sir Meyrick Hollins, were Captain Cobb, MP for Preston, and Alderman Mrs A.M. Pimblett. Patricia Moores, of the famous Moores family from Liverpool, and President of the English Ladies Hockey Association, presented gold medals to the winners. Guest of honour for the team was Mrs Alice Cook, formerly Alice Kell, and first ever captain of the famous Dick, Kerr team in the inaugural 1917 season. She expressed her opinion to the press before the dinner, that the team she played in was as good as the present team which was maintaining the standards established by the older brigade. The original captain modestly said nothing about her own part but she herself had few equals as a full back.

Team captain Edith Hutton, a team member for eleven years, naturally

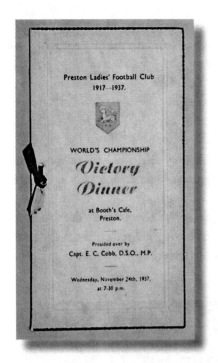
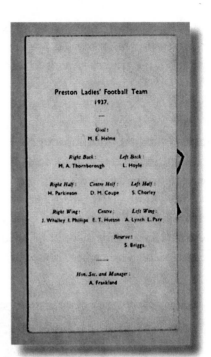

Victory Dinner Menu Card

disagreed and thought that the current side was the finest the world had seen. *"I don't deny the brilliance of some of the former players"* she said, *"but we now have a superior balance and blend."* Both captains did agree that they had never known any women to suffer harmful effects from playing football.

Captain Cobb presided over the dinner and paid compliments to the girls by saying, *"I had heard of this wonderful football team who had defeated all of their rivals, but I had always imagined that ladies who played football were probably pretty tough guys".* This was met with laughter from the audience as he went on to say, *"I am very glad to have that illusion removed. I now realise that ladies can play a man's game without losing any of their attractive femininity. The most striking thing about the club in spite of its great achievements on the field of play, was its raising of tens of thousands of pounds for charitable purposes, which is something that must make a very strong appeal to everybody".* Capt Cobb proposed a toast to the team and wished them continued success.

In reply, Mr Frankland said that since 1917 the women footballers had raised over £100,000 for various hospitals, ex soldiers, poor children and even football and cricket clubs without a penny for personal gain. He said that they had received many offers to go about 'stunting' for private gain but had always turned a deaf ear to them. He stated, *"Since our inception we have played 437 matches, won 414, drawn 16, lost 7, scored 2863 goals and had only 207 scored against. We have raised over £100,000 in this country and in foreign lands for charity. We have won 14 silver cups, 5 of them outright, and hold a trophy awarded for the most meritorious assistance given to ex servicemen".* Speeches in reply for the players were made by team captain Edith Hutton and vice captain Margaret Thornborough.

When presenting the medals, Mrs Moores said she had always admired the team from afar for the help they had given to deserving causes. Alderman Mrs A.M. Pimblett, recalled that when she was mayor she had the privilege of welcoming the Belgian and Preston teams at the Town Hall. She thought the Preston girl footballers could be proud of having helped to make the town of Preston better known in various parts of the world.

Cheers!

Stella Briggs, Mary Bowles, Lily Parr, Joan Whalley, Bessie Cunliffe

Celebration Dinner 1937

Mr Frankland, Margaret Thornborough, May Helme

Celebration Dinner - holding the ball autographed by President Harding in USA 1922

Lucy Hoyle, Edith Hutton, Margaret Thornborough, May Helme, Lily Parr, Alice Kell, Joan Whalley

And the Press said!

A glittering and most memorable night held in the team's honour came to a close. This must surely have been the pinnacle of their career. There was no doubt that they were the toast of the town. Proud Preston had paid a fitting tribute to the Dick, Kerr Ladies. Were there any new horizons left for them to conquer?

Fifty four years later the Women's World Championship for the M&Ms Cup was staged by FIFA in China. In 1991, women's football teams from Europe, Asia, USA, Africa, South America and Oceania competed in qualifying tournaments for a place in this competition which was also known as the first Women's World Cup. Twelve countries went on to compete in the final rounds in this modern day historic event. They were: China, Norway, Denmark, New Zealand, USA, Sweden, Brazil, Japan, Germany, Italy, Taiwan and Nigeria. The competition was played in three groups of four with China, Germany and the USA all winning their groups to reach the quarter finals, along with Sweden, Denmark and Taiwan.

The emergence of the United States women's national team on to the world stage since its formation in 1985, came as no surprise to their coach, Anson Dorance. It was his belief that there are four parts to the game of football. Technical, tactical, physical and psychological and he taught his players about all of them. A thrilling semi-final saw the USA defeat Germany by 5-2, proving that they could more than hold their own with the best footballing nations in the world. In the other semi-final, Norway defeated Sweden 4-1.

The final was staged at Canton, China on 30 November 1991 and the USA defeated Norway 2-1 to become world champions as winners of the first Women's World Cup.

In the opinion of Anson Dorrance, the most dominating woman player in the world at that time was Michele Akers. The then 26-year-old striker from Oviedo, Florida had averaged more than a goal a game for the national side since 1988, after being switched from midfield to forward by Dorrance.

Lily Parr, when playing in the World Championship match in 1937, was described by manager, Alfred Frankland as, *"The best outside left playing in the world today,"* and Bobby Walker, a famous Scottish footballer said she was, *"The best natural timer of a football I have ever seen."* The US press said of her in 1922 that she was *"the most brilliant female player in the world."* We can only wonder how Michele Akers would have compared to some of those wonderful ladies who had played on the world stage all those years ago. How would she have coped with the ability of such defenders as Alice Kell or Jessie Walmsley's calibre? Admittedly the level of training received in the United States is of a very high standard but if we could have given the same opportunities to the likes of Alice Kell, Florrie Redford, Jennie Harris and Lily Parr, one might suspect that English women's football would have been in a much healthier position than it was in the early 1990's.

Joan Whalley, herself one of Dick, Kerr Ladies all time greats said of Lily Parr, *"She had a kick like a mule. She was the only person I knew who could lift a dead ball, the old heavy leather ball, from the left wing over to me on the right and nearly knock me out with the force of the shot. Those old balls used to retain the wet, and the longer the game went on when it was raining, the heavier the ball became, but it never bothered Parr. When she took a left corner kick, it came over like a bullet and if you ever hit one of those with your head, you knew about it! I only ever did it once and the laces on the ball left their impression on my forehead and cut it open. I thought, never again, not from one of Parr's crosses."*

The ladies taking the world stage in 1991 were probably unaware of those who had gone before them, perhaps they may not have even cared. But whatever happens in women's football, in all probability, it was the Dick, Kerr Ladies who did it first.

MATCH FACTS 1937

DATE	VENUE	TEAMS	RESULT
April	Paris	French v DK	5-2
12 May	Leeds	DK v Welsh	
?	Middlesborough	DK v Scotland	3-0

Scorers: Gladys Lunn 2, Lily Parr 1

?	Blackpool	DK v Spondon	13-3

Scorers: Lily Parr 5, Joan Whalley 4, Margaret Thornborough 4

28 July	Birmingham	DK v French	13-0
29 July	Nuneaton	DK v French	12-3
30 July	Wilmslow	DK v French	7-0
2 Aug	Wakefield	DK v French	8-1
3 Aug	Rochdale	DK v French	7-0

Scorers: Edith Hutton 3, Lily Parr 3, Joan Whalley 1

4 Aug	Haslingden	DK v French	6-0
7 Aug	Bolton	DK v French	5-2

Scorers: Edith Hutton 2, Joan Whalley 2, Hilda Parkinson 1

8 Aug	Pontypridd	DK v French	4-2
11 Aug	Blackpool	DK v French	10-2
8 Sept	Blackpool	DK v Edinburgh	5-1

Scorers: Edith Hutton 3, Joan Whalley 1, Lily Parr 1

N.B. All known games are listed.

CHAPTER NINE

ANOTHER WORLD WAR

The 1938 season began on 17 June with the French Ladies returning for another tour playing a series of nine matches with the Dick, Kerr Ladies. Carmen Pomies was still a prominent player with the French side being captain of the team and a regular goal scorer. August was a busy month too with the girls taking in matches with Spondon Ladies from Derbyshire and Darlington Quaker Ladies, before going on another tour of the North West playing four games against a team from Edinburgh.

In November, Mr Frankland received a letter from Florrie Redford. She had emigrated to Canada in 1930 and was returning home to visit family and friends. She was hoping her old team might have need of her services during her stay. Speaking in the *Daily Mirror,* he said, *"If ever there was a natural woman footballer it was Miss Redford. She was a wonderful dribbler of a ball and had a powerful shot. She helped to make the team what it is today and I shall give her a try out. If she is anything like she was she will be given her place again."* Florrie was quoted in the *Lancashire Daily Post,* saying, *"I am looking forward to returning to football again after my long absence and I intend to play for my old team as often as I can."*

NOVEMBER 17, 1938

Miss Florrie Redford

Florrie Redford

During her nine year playing career with the Dick, Kerr Ladies she was a prolific goal scorer and became one of the most famous women footballers of her generation before seeking pastures new. She didn't give up football completely. We are told that while in Canada she kept herself fit and whenever she had the chance she took part in practice games with men's teams. She made her comeback for the Dick, Kerr Ladies at the age of 36, playing in her former position of centre forward against Whitehaven Ladies. The result of the match is not available but Florrie couldn't recapture the form of her younger days and sadly her comeback was shortlived.

The public face of opposition to women's football came to the fore once again in December of 1938 and this particular incident further illustrates the hypocrisy surrounding the game. Reported in the *Daily Mirror*, Mr Ted Robbins, secretary of the Welsh FA banned a ladies charity match from taking place in Wales. *"It's a mans game and women don't look well playing it,"* was Mr Robbins firm statement on the matter. Mr Frankland replied saying, *"I would very much like Mr Robbins to recall 1919 when the recently formed Dick, Kerr Ladies played St Helens on the Wrexham racecourse ground and the gates had to be closed owing to the big crowd. Mr Robbins was there with the rest of the Welsh FA and they gave the Dick, Kerr team the Welsh dragon to wear on their jerseys. All the officials were delighted with the game and afterwards Mr Robbins and others handed out bouquets to the women for their fine display. It is a nonsense to suggest that football is not a women's game. At that match at Wrexham in 1919, the verdict was unanimous in favour of women's football so long as women played women. Women's football has been justified and has raised thousands of pounds for charity, but apparently what was acceptable nearly twenty years ago is just the opposite today. I cannot understand the complete changeover."*

The Belgian team returned for another tour in 1939. The tour took in eleven matches but the visitors were unable to emulate their famous victory of 1934 and failed to win any of their games. Joe Loss, a well known band leader was among the celebrities who came along to 'kick-off' at one of the matches. During the tour members of both teams placed floral tributes on the grave of the late president of the FA, Mr Charles Sutcliffe, who had done much to promote football for women.

The Belgian team

Belgian team at Blackpool Baths

At the time of the Belgian tour, Nancy Thomson, an Edinburgh City player, was staying in Preston at the home of Joan Whalley. Mr Frankland was very keen for Nancy to join the Dick, Kerr set up as she was a very good player and had played extremely well against them. Nancy became an immediate regular in the team playing at either centre forward or centre half and she soon earned the nickname *"Cannonball"* from her team mates.

Nancy Thomson in action v Belgian team

Nancy says, "*I was invited to be a guest player for Preston against the Belgian side and ended up staying for fifteen years! Both my parents were dead and I was living with my married sister, so I had no strong ties. She had a fit when I sent for my clothes. Joan's family were absolutely marvellous to me, they adopted me like one of their own, especially her mum. My mother had died when I was seven years old and believe me I adored Joan's mother, she was wonderful. Mr Frankland had contacted me several times about playing for the team. He said a job would be found for me and also a place to live. He had a lot of influence at Whittingham Hospital. Margaret Thornborough, Lily Parr and other girls were already working there and he got me a job without any form to sign, no introduction, not even an interview. So I started working at Whittingham on the Friday before war broke out. The hospital were very keen on sport and they welcomed me with open arms. I finished up playing hockey, cricket and badminton for the hospital teams whilst other poor devils were making beds! At that time, Whittingham and indeed every other psychiatric hospital, were all enclosed, they all had locked doors. That meant that we had to supply the entertainment for the patients from the inside, so we had staff hockey, cricket and badminton teams. We had a very extensive sports programme and once a year some jewellers in Preston would donate prizes such as cigarette lighters and watches etc. It was a very big hospital with each division having its own Matron and we all competed against each other. For the patients entertainment, a nurse from each ward would take out those who were able, to watch us playing cricket or hockey or whatever it was. There would be hundreds of patients all around and they even had a 'bookie' on the races.*"

NURSES AS FOOTBALL STARS.—Four nurses at a Whittingham Hospital who are members of the Preston team of women footballers which will oppose a Scottish team at Edinburgh today. They are (left to right) the Misses Briggs, Lynch, Parr, and Thornborough.

Nurses at Whittingham Hospital

Stella Briggs, Annie Lynch, Lily Parr, Margaret Thornborough

After spending fifteen years nursing at Whittingham, Nancy joined the Colonial Nursing Service and was posted to St Josephs Hospital in Gibraltar as 'Sister Thomson'. But whilst on holiday in Spain she hit the headlines for something very different than playing football. She was on the beach at Algerciras on the south coast of Spain with her friend Sister McEvilly, when they heard cries for help. Her friend was in a bathing suit and immediately dived in and swam towards a drifting dinghy with a young mother and her two children on board. After reaching the dinghy she was too exhausted to push them towards the beach. It was then that Nancy, who was still fully clothed, swam out to complete the rescue and brought them all safely back to the shore.

It was during the Belgian visit of 1939 that Alfred Frankland claimed to have received a telegram from the War Office asking him to ensure all the Belgian players went home after their last match. War was declared just over a week later on 3 September. Joan Whalley said, "*They didn't want to go back because they were afraid. My friend, Arlene said, 'I don't want to go back, can I stay with you and your family until the war is over?' They had to go back of course but after the war we heard that some German soldiers had gone into one of the girls' homes and tried to rape her. She struggled and fought for her life but they shot her. It was heartbreaking to hear these stories.*"

The Second World War saw the disappearance from shops of all but necessities and the rationing of food and clothing became extensive. In order to deal with the extreme shortages the Ministry of Food introduced a system whereby each person was only allowed a certain amount of basic foods. They had to register with their local shops and they were provided with a *ration book* which contained coupons. On 8 January 1940, bacon, butter and sugar were rationed. This was soon followed by meat, cheese, eggs, milk, breakfast cereals, jam, biscuits and canned fruit. Fish and chips however, were not on the list! Rationing was to continue for some time after the war and certain items were rationed until 1954 when the system finally ended.

The team played only a handful of games after the outbreak of the war and there were obvious travel difficulties during this period. Petrol was rationed and there were frequent air raids. As a consequence Mr Frankland put the football team on hold until after the hostilities and the games with Bolton were the last until the war was over. They were one of the few teams at that time who were almost at the same level as Preston Ladies and their games were always skilful and competitive encounters. A famous centre forward with Bolton was Nellie Halstead, an Olympic sprinter who won a bronze medal in the 4x100 relay team at the 1932 Olympics in Los Angeles. Nellie was running last and the team were lying in fifth position when she took the baton. Nellie said, *"I ran like hell, I must have run the race of my life!"*

Nellie Halstead

In 1941 Ernest Hunt, the manager of Bolton Ladies, organised a trip to Wales for the Bolton and Preston teams, where they played a series of five games. Another game arranged by him, and possibly the last before the end of the fighting, was played at Horwich on Saturday, 25 October 1941. There was no love lost between messers Hunt and Frankland and there was an obvious rivalry between the two managers. Judging by the tone of a letter to the parents of one of the Preston players from Mr Hunt, and an interesting reference to travel expenses, it seems that everything in the garden may not have been quite as rosy as they appeared. Perhaps a little munity may have been on the cards. Mr Hunt says: *"At the request of the members of the Preston team some months ago, I took over the management of their club, and I shall run it on similar lines as to that of the Bolton club, that is complete understanding between parent, player and management. I shall also guarantee no matter where the games may be played, the players shall have travelling expenses paid on all occasions."* It may be that the girls had wanted to continue playing as long as possible despite the restrictions brought about by the war, but in the long term Mr Hunt did not become manager of the Dick, Kerr Ladies.

Joan Burke (Tich) aged 14

Even through those dreadful times of the Second World War there was still some kind of humour to be found. Joan Whalley tells us: *"There were blackouts and allsorts happening and we had to take gas masks with us wherever we went. There were always three of us went around together, myself, Joan Burke (Tich), and Stella Briggs. We had gone to bed one night and Tich said, "I can smell gas". No one else could smell anything but Tich insisted, "Well I can smell gas and I'm not taking any chances", and she got her gas mask out and put it on in bed! She was laying there trying to talk to us with this muffled voice, but we couldn't tell a word she was saying. It was so funny, we were all falling about laughing. But we finally realised that the gas mantle on the wall was leaking so we sent for the hotel manager to get it fixed. It's a good job we did because I had visions of us all being dead the morning after! Tich, was right after all."*

Tich joined the Army in 1942 and served with the anti-aircraft battery for four years and was demobbed in 1946. She said, *"I did my basic training in Lancaster and from there I went to Oswestry where our battalion, 544 Anti-Aircraft Battery, was formed. We went to Bude in Cornwall for three months training in firing the guns out to sea. My first posting was Newcastle upon Tyne where I was on a height finder. They were mixed heavy ack-ack batteries and the men were on the guns. There was three of us looking out for the aircraft. One would be the spotter, one the height finder and the other would be following the flight path of the plane, plotting it with the radar. I only served in England so I still managed to play for the team whenever I got home on leave."*

Mr Frankland acted as an ARP Warden (Air Raid Precautions) for the duration of the war. This involved escorting people safely to the air raid shelters when the sirens went off and ensuring that no lights were visible during the blackout. In May of 1943 it was reported that he was repeatedly having requests from different parts of the country for the team to play matches for charity, and girls in the services and war factories were writing to him asking to be given trials for the team. But to all requests Mr Frankland answered, *"Nothing doing at present. Try again after the war."* Although he said he could have raised a first class team he felt it was not the right time to revive the club, mainly because of travel difficulties and food rationing.

When the Allied Forces liberated Paris in 1944, Carmen Pomies, former player with the French team, wrote to tell Mr Frankland of the *"delirious joy of deliverance"*, at her country's liberation and of being able to speak of football again because, she said, *"the Germans had stopped us from playing."* Carmen was a heroine of the French Resistance and said, *"Of course I was FFI, (French Forces of the Interior) and I did it with all my heart and strength. I went on*

NEWS CHRONICLE. Friday, Oct. 5, 1945

MDLLE. CARMEN POMIES (right) is here seen with Mr. Alfred Frankland, manager, and Mrs. Farnworth (Margaret Thornborough), assistant manager of the Preston Ladies team.

Carmen returns to Preston

Margaret Thornborough, Alfred Frankland, Carmen Pomies

the barricades and fought my part." She worked in an office where a German officer signed passports. It was here that she put her own life at risk working undercover for the Resistance by securing passports to help those wanted by the Gestapo to escape. Carmen was also secretary to Renee Saint Cyr, a French film star.

The War ended on 8 May 1945 and it was in October that Carmen returned to Preston where she stayed at the home of her friend, Florrie Redford. Interviewed by the press she said, *"English troops in Paris were always asking me when I was coming to England again. I have longed so much for this moment, I have been coming to Preston since 1920 when I was a schoolgirl."*

It was with the approval of the French Ministry of Sport and Education that she came to explore means of organising women's international events again between France and England. She said, *"Our sport suffered terribly during the occupation. Football for women was stopped completely but we kept on playing even though it had to be in secret. I did all I could to keep my team together. Even though the Germans stopped us playing football we played secretly. In a men's section of a tennis club, there was a field which the men, rather fearfully, allowed us to use. And so we played but not very often."* When it was suggested to her that keeping a football match secret must have been a tricky business, she laughed and said, *"Ah, but those Germans, they were slow. We played on the men's ground when they weren't looking. They would have thrown us in jail if they had caught us."* She had retained her membership of the Cercle Athletique de Montrouge Club in Paris, which had tried to keep sport alive during the war and German girls used to go to the club to play hockey and tennis. It was a favourite trick for them to steal their clothes in their absence, leaving the frauleins to wander around in an undressed state! Both teams planned to resume training in October of 1945 and if transport was sufficiently relaxed they hoped to begin playing again in the summer of 1946.

Margaret Thornborough, now Mrs Farnworth, had been appointed assistant manager. Like many of the other players, Margaret had also been a nurse at Whittingham hospital and that was where I found her. She was 82 years old, suffering from dementia and ironically now receiving the same care she had given to so many. I had been warned by those who knew Margaret that a visit would be fruitless as she was unable to remember anything. But nothing ventured, nothing gained, I thought it was worth a try. I had been given an old photograph album by Tony Frankland, passed down from his grandfather. It contained quite a number of pictures of Margaret and I was hoping that a spark from the past would help re-kindle something in her mind that might just hold the key to unlocking some of the lost memories of her days with the Dick, Kerr Ladies.

When I arrived at the hospital, Margaret was by chance walking in the corridor and the ward sister told her I had come to talk to her about her time with Dick, Kerr Ladies. She took my right arm and we walked together to the day room. It was as if she knew me, as though we were old friends and to me, this was no frail old woman, this was Margaret Thornborough, a living legend from the Dick, Kerr Ladies. I was actually touching history! It was an incredibly moving experience and I was totally in awe of her, yet desperately sad as she approached the final chapter of her life. We arrived at the day room to find it full of other ladies in the same predicament who had little or no idea of who, or where they were. I showed Margaret the photographs of herself, as a young lass playing football, tennis and bowls and the

Margaret Thornborough

old team pictures of the Dick, Kerr Ladies, but sadly, there was nothing. She just sat there staring into space. She wasn't really seeing the photographs at all. But I had hoped that as she sat gazing at them, perhaps there might just be a familiar scene that would trigger a memory and she would remember something from those far off days when she was a young woman in her prime. For a brief moment, it looked as though she was flicking through her mind like seeing an old black and white movie, searching through her memories desperately trying to recall something in the photographs. Unfortunately it was not to be. Margaret's memories remained locked away for ever. I was so very sad for her. Sad for her lost memories and sad for the way she was living out the end of her days. There was a tragic irony knowing that having cared for so many people at Whittingham Hospital in days gone by, Margaret was now receiving that same nursing care. She was later transferred to Ribbleton Hospital in Preston, where she died after suffering a massive stroke in 1994.

MATCH FACTS 1938

DATE	VENUE	TEAMS	RESULT
17 June	Slough	DK v French	3-1

Scorers: Lily Parr 2, Daphne Coupe 1

| 18 June | Kettering | DK v French | 4-2 |

Scorers: Lily Parr 2, Joan Whalley 1, Daphne Coupe 1

22 June	York	DK v French	?
23 June	Darwen	DK v French	?
25 June	Cheltenham	DK v French	5-1
27 June	Fleetwood	DK V French	7-1

Scorers: Annie Lynch 4, Lily Parr 2, Edith Hutton 1

28 June	Workington	DK v French	?
29 June	Macclesfield	DK v French	?
1 Aug	Burton on Trent	DK v Spondon	3-2

Scorers: May Helme 2, Joan Whalley 1

| 3 Aug | Blackpool | DK v Darlington | 5-2 |

Scorers: Margaret Thornborough 2, Lily Parr 1, Joan Whalley 1, Annie Lynch 1

| 10 Aug | Blackpool | DK v Edinburgh | 5-2 |

Scorers: Margaret Thornborough 3, Lily Parr 2

| 11 Aug | Garstang | DK v Edinburgh | 8-2 |

Scorers: Margaret Thornborough 3, Lily Parr 2, Annie Lynch 1, Joan Whalley 1

| 12 Aug | Great Harwood | DK v Edinburgh | 4-0 |

Scorers: Joan Whalley 2, Annie Lynch 2

| 13 Aug | Nelson | DK v Edinburgh | 4-2 |

Scorers: Annie Lynch 4

| 3 Sept | Bentham | DK v Grimsargh/Longridge | 14-0 |

Scorers: Annie Lynch 8, Miss Thomas 3, May Helme 2, Joan Whalley 1

| 7 Sept | Ripley | DK v Spondon | 4-2 |

Scorers: Joan Whalley 3, May Helme 1

| 14 Sept | Shrewsbury | DK v Parwich | 16-2 |

Scorers; Annie Lynch 6, Lily Parr 6, Joan Whalley 3, May Helme 1

| 19 Sept | Grantham | DK v Spondon | 8-0 |

Scorers: Margaret Thornborough 3, Joan Whalley 2, Miss Thomas 1, Stella Briggs 1

| 21 Sept | Blackpool | DK v Spondon | 12-3 |

Scorers: Lily Parr 6, Margaret Thornborough 4, Joan Whalley 2

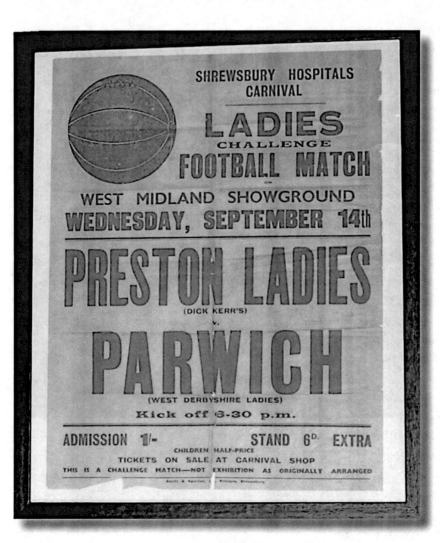

Match Poster 1938

DATE	VENUE	TEAMS	RESULT
May	Tour of Scotland	?	
June	Tour of North Wales	?	
7 Aug	Burton on Trent	DK v Macclesfield	7-5

Scorers: Lily Parr 5, Nancy Thomson 2

10 Aug	Birmingham	DK v Belgian	5-2

Scorers: Nancy Thomson 3, Lily Parr 1, Margaret Thornborough 1

12 Aug	Chorley	DK v Belgian	6-0

Scorers: Nancy Thomson 4, Lily Parr 2

14 Aug	Bradford	DK v Belgian	6-0

Scorers: Nancy Thomson 3, Lily Parr 2, Joan Whalley 1

15 Aug	Keighley	DK v Belgian	5-1

Scorers: Nancy Thomson 2, Joan Whalley 2, Lily Parr 1

16 Aug	Manchester	DK v Belgian	7-0

Scorers: Annie Lynch 4, Nancy Thomson 2, Lily Parr 1

17 Aug	Garstang	DK v Belgian	8-2

Scorers: Joan Whalley 3, Nancy Thomson 2, Lily Parr 1, Joan Burke 1, Annie Lynch 1

21 Aug	Crewe	DK v Belgian	6-2

Scorers: Nancy Thomson 3, Joan Whalley 2, Annie Lynch 1

22 Aug	Nelson	DK v Belgian	5-1

Scorers: Nancy Thomson 3, Joan Whalley 1, Annie Lynch 1

23 Aug	Bolton	DK v Belgian	3-2

Scorers: Nancy Thomson, Sue Chorley, Annie Lynch

24 Aug	Northampton	DK v Belgian	3-0

Scorers: Nancy Thomson, Annie Lynch, Margaret Thornborough

18 Nov	St Helens	DK v Bolton	9-4

Scorers: Nancy Thomson 4, Lily Parr 3, Annie Lynch 2

25 Nov	Leeds	DK v Bolton	3-3

Scorers: Nancy Thomson 2, Margaret Thornborough 1

MATCH FACTS 1940

DATE	VENUE	TEAMS	RESULT
6 Jan	Bolton	DK v Bolton	3-2

Scorers: Annie Lynch, Lily Parr, Margaret Thornborough

| 16 Mar | Hindsford | DK v Bolton | 3-3 |

Scorers: Annie Lynch, Nancy Thomson, Joan Whalley

MATCH FACTS 1941

DATE	VENUE	TEAMS	RESULT
	Wales	DK v Bolton	?
25 Oct	Horwich	DK v Bolton	?

Programme 1941

CHAPTER TEN

THE POST WAR YEARS

After the war there were lots of girls eager to become would be football stars and Mr Frankland received a sackful of letters from young ladies who aspired to play for the Preston team. Quoted in a magazine article he said: "*All the promising girls are tested on the field and I have recruited about twenty. They will be trained and weeded out until I have selected the players who are, in my opinion, potential football stars.*" The girls aged between thirteen and forty came from towns as far as twenty miles away from Preston. The club has no funds available so they practice on the local park. They soon had enough players on the books to field two teams and were regularly seen training on Waverley Park where they were frequently photographed by the press as they prepared for their first post war fixtures. Mr Frankland said, "*Altogether we have thirty three girls in our club and we only have so many because there are such a lot of excellent players to choose from and I felt I just couldn't turn them away on account of exceeding my normal maximum of twenty-five. When we tour there are just fifteen of us, including myself and the manager Margaret Thornborough, but we always keep a good number of reserves in case of work or sickness.*"

Training on Waverley Park 1946

Marion Barker, Marjorie Foulkes, Frances Appleby, Lottie Worrall, Sally Kendal, Margaret Thornborough, Joan Wilkinson, Doreen Norris at rear

Ready for action.

*Margaret Thornborough, Jean Moizer, Marion Barker, Florence Coles,
Doreen Norris, Frances Appleby, Lottie Worrall, Marjorie Foulkes, Joan Whalley,
Alma Hopkins, Joan Wilkinson, Dorothy Whalley, Sally Kendal*

There was still a great deal of interest in the club and many charities would no doubt have had great expectations at the teams re-formation particularly as they claimed to have raised around £120,000 for charity since their inception. The *Daily Mirror* reported that British troops in Germany had made a request for women footballers to go out and play some exhibition matches. One soldier who wrote to Mr Frankland said, *"The frauleins seem to think British girls shrink from anything with hard knocks, so it's up to the bonnie girls from Lancashire to knock the notion out of their heads."* A nice sentiment from the 'lads', but the Dick, Kerr Ladies didn't make the trip. Mr Frankland was quoted saying, *"It's a question of money. We don't want to make anything out of it. All we want is our fares guaranteed. We should love to entertain the troops, we did it in 1917 and we can do it again. We're only waiting for someone to give us the chance."*

Their first post-war fixture was arranged to be played on Good Friday 1946, at Glossop FC in Derbyshire, in aid of the Mayor's Welcome Home Fund and the organising committee hoped to reach a target of £100. The Preston club provided both teams for the game, the opposition being Lancashire County

Ladies, who were in fact Dick, Kerr's 2nd team. Lily Parr was becoming quite a legend as she reached yet another milestone in her illustrious career. Since joining the team in 1920 she had missed only five games and according to Mr Franklands calculations, she had scored an amazing number of 967 goals since joining the Preston team. Missing from the squad though, was twenty-year-old goalkeeping star, Dorothy Whalley which is probably what gave the young Brenda Keen an opportunity for the dream debut she thought would never happen. Dorothy was retiring from the game due to her forthcoming marriage to Alan Nightingale. He had recently been demobbed after serving six-and-a-half years in the RAF where he had seen active service in France, Belgium and Germany. Dorothy said, *"It wouldn't do to get hurt just for the sake of having one more game, but I am sorry to leave the team. Alan has never put a ban on my playing football, but I know he isn't keen. I shall have enough to do looking after him when we are married."*

Mr Franklands pre-match publicity quoted that to date, the team had played 489, won 465, drawn 17, lost 7, scored 3022 goals with only 259 scored against. However, for reasons unknown, a match against Edinburgh City Girls in June of 1939 appears to have been omitted. It resulted in a 5-2 defeat for the Preston side. Nancy Thomson did recall this match and mentioned it in interviews and it has now been verified. (In an effort to create as accurate an account as possible the total games lost therefore is eight matches and probably played 490)

Tickets for the Glossop game were selling quickly and the organisers were expecting a crowd of around 3000. The local press reported: '*Glossop hit the headlines with the best holiday event in the north, attracting a huge crowd from the Manchester, Stockport, Ashton and Hyde districts. People poured into the town throughout Friday morning to see the game and the trek continued all day. Some would-be spectators even had to walk to the ground because they could not get on buses.*'

After having lunch with the officials of Glossop FC, both teams were given a warm welcome as they were driven up to the venue in their private coach headed by the town's military band. Glossop Football Club had their biggest crowd in over thirty years when 5,000 people came to watch Dick, Kerr Ladies play Lancashire County Ladies. They roared with approval as both teams took to the field, and the band played, '*She's a lassie from Lancashire.*' The Dick, Kerr team got their new campaign off to a flying start when they defeated their opponents by 5-0. The goalscorers were: Nancy Thomson (3), Lily Parr (1), Annie Lynch (1) The first post war team was: Brenda Keen, Jean Moizer, Hilda Parkinson, Sally Kendal, Margaret Thornborough, Stella

Briggs, Joan Whalley, Joan Burke, Nancy Thomson, Annie Lynch, Lily Parr.

After the match the teams were entertained at a civic reception where the Mayor thanked all concerned in helping to raise over £150 for his Welcome Home Fund, which had far exceeded their expectations. Mr Goldthorpe, President of Glossop Football Club, said, *"It has been a wonderful holiday event. I cannot recall a ladies football team coming to Glossop before and this has been a unique occasion in the history of the town."*

This picture shows part of the crowd watching a goalmouth tussle.

Glossop 1946

The Dick, Kerr show was back on the road at last, and the 4th June saw a vintage performance from Lily Parr as she scored four of her teams goals in a 7-4 victory against Lancashire County Ladies at Hyde in front of 5000 spectators. Next stop on their travels was a three day tour of Weymouth where they won the Jack Pitman Challenge Cup and Shield, after defeating Weymouth by 8-2. After the match, Mr Pitman hosted a dinner for the teams and the trophies were presented to Lily Parr, who had played a magnificent game.

Nancy Thomson said, *"Mr Frankland demanded nothing but the best for us, the absolute best. But he expected the best from us in return. We weren't allowed to wear trousers anywhere in public, it wasn't done in those days. We could do what we liked when travelling on the bus, but we had to change into our skirts or dresses before meeting any of the officials, - that was a must."* Joan Burke recalled, *"Pop was easy-going. We always used to sing when we were on the coach, and we used to sing a song called 'Swanee' for him. He liked that, we were always singing it for him. Whenever I hear it now I always think of him."*

PRESTON LADIES' (DICK KERRS) F.C., 1946

Winners of the Pitman Cup
June 12th 1946

Pitman Cup Winners

Back row players: Annie Lynch, Margaret Thornborough, Sally Kendal,
Daphne Coupe, Stella Briggs, Joan Whalley, Jean Moizer

Front row: Hilda Parkinson, Nancy Thomson, Lily Parr, Joan Wilkinson, Jean Gollin

Born in 1882, Alfred Frankland was typically Victorian in his values. He always wore a three piece suit and walked with a silver topped cane and he always tipped his hat to the ladies. He had the habit of frequently taking a fob watch from his waistcoat pocket to look at the time. The post war Alfred was perhaps a little more mellow than in his younger days and was now referred to as *'Father'* or *'Pop'* by the girls. Unlike their predecessors, they could often get the better of him when staying longer than he would wish at 'watering holes' on return journeys from away matches. At his home in

Alfred Frankland

Preston he had a wooden chest full of football boots and any new player who didn't have her own could look through them to find a suitable pair. He was still as strict in his organisation of the football team being very meticulous and planning everything down to the finest detail. An example of the standards he expected are shown in extracts from this letter to one of the players: *"Please be most particular to have all your football gear in very clean condition, boots and laces etc. Most important to all players is to have their football studs examined; already in our practice games, damage has been done by nails protruding below leather of studs. I shall most probably go round and examine all boots for any defects. A few more points for our post-war programme: (i) Be punctual in your appointments (ii) Always conduct yourself in such a manner that will bring credit to the famous club you belong to, both on and off the field."*

A new star was born in 1946 when fifteen-year-old Edna Broughton, from Crewe made her debut for the Preston team on 12 August against Weymouth at Portland. Standing only five feet tall and playing in the centre forward position, she was always seen in the thick of the action and although she didn't score, she played some beautiful football.

In October, Mr Ernest Hunt, the Bolton Ladies manager was organising an International match at Salford Rugby ground between England and Scotland, and he invited three of the Preston players to play in the game. Jean Moizer, Daphne Coupe and Joan Whalley were selected to play for the England team. In a letter written to each of the players Mr Hunt said, *"This may not meet with the approval of your manager, but if he objects to any of your players taking part, I am afraid he is not showing the sporting spirit which is necessary. No matter what little differences we may have, I can assure you it is not with you the players, for I hold every one of you in the highest esteem and I know my players do likewise."*

Mr Frankland rejected the invitation for the girls to play in the match, because he said it was against their principle to play football on a Sunday. He stated that, *"We have never played on Sunday, and we do not intend to do so, but we do of course recognise the very worthy object of the game."* Perhaps it was a little churlish on his part but it does show another example of the rivalry between the two men.

Their last match of the 1946 season was played at Lancaster in support of the Invalid Childrens Aid Association. Comedian Duggie Wakefield kicked off the match which was refereed by former Everton and PNE full back, Jasper Kerr. The local press reported that this game marked the 160th Civic reception attended by the Preston team. Others included those given by Lord Mayor's of London, York, Manchester, Liverpool, Sheffield, Birmingham, Belfast and Glasgow.

DATE	VENUE	TEAMS	RESULT
19 Apr	Glossop	DK v Lancs County	5-0

Scorers: Nancy Thomson 3, Lily Parr 1, Annie Lynch 1

4 June	Hyde	DK v Lancs County	7-4

Scorers: Lily Parr 4, Nancy Thomson 2, Jean Gollin 1

10 June	Weymouth	DK v Kent	0-3
11 June	Weymouth	DK v Weymouth	8-2

Scorers: Nancy Thomson 3, Joan Whalley 2, Lily Parr 2, Jean Gollin 1

27 June	Stretford	DK v Lancs County	8-1

Scorers: Lily Parr 5, Joan Whalley 2, Jean Gollin 1

12 Aug	Portland	DK v Weymouth	11-2

Scorers: Jean Gollin 5, Joan Whalley 3, Lily Parr 2, Miss Duxbury 1

24 Aug	Lancaster	DK v Lancs County	2-0

Scorers: Edna Broughton 1, Jean Gollin 1

28 Aug	Lancaster	DK v Lancs County	11-3

Scorers: Jean Gollin 4, Joan Whalley 3, Edna Broughton 3, Nancy Thomson 1

The French team returned to Preston in June of 1947 to play a series of matches with the Dick, Kerr team. It was their first visit in ten years. Mr Frankland and Margaret Thornborough commented in the Preston match programme that they didn't feel the team was quite up to their pre-war standard but were confident that with patient re-building they would more than hold their own with any other ladies team. The match, played at Fulwood Barracks, saw Joan Whalley celebrating her 10th anniversary with the club and she was made captain to mark the occasion. She even managed to score one of the goals in the teams 8-3 victory.

In 1947 the FA once again showed their pompous bigotry when referee, Mr E. Turner, was suspended by the Kent County FA because he refused to end his association as manager/trainer with Kent Ladies FC. The Kent County Football Association were of the opinion that, *"Women's football brings the game into disrepute."* The newspaper report in Joan Whalley's scrap book said that, Mr Turner, an ex RAF Corporal, intends to stay with the club and stated: *"All these girls are doing is what in war times would have been classed as a man's job. Where would the country be now if the powers that be had said, that is a man's job and girl's must not do it - they might bring the country into disrepute?"*

In the same year, the FA came in for some sharp criticism from the Mayor of Stalybridge after Dick, Kerr's had played Bolton Ladies in aid of the War

Memorial Fund. Commenting on the "*Arrogant and old fashioned outlook of the FA,*" he said how much he appreciated their coming and playing in Stalybridge, and added, "*I hope you will go ahead and fight the FA which is a narrow bigotted authority. From one who has been involved in the game for thirty years, I personally resent it. Anything I can do to help you break down the barrier, I will do so.*" The Bolton team were captained by Nellie Halstead, the Olympic Sprinter, but the game resulted in a close fought win for the Preston side by 3-2.

At Stalybridge 1947

Back row: Lily Parr, Joan Burke, Nancy Thomson, E Glover, Lottie Worrall, Stella Briggs

Front row: Joan Whalley, Jean Gollin, Margaret Thornborough, Miss Duxbury, Edna Broughton

At this time there were just seventeen ladies teams throughout the country. The team were playing regularly in the late 1940s and still winning most of their matches. Alice Hargreaves from Blackpool and Jean Dent from Preston, were notable signings for them. But just as before the war, Bolton Ladies, particularly with the speed of Nellie Halstead, were proving tough opposition and were the victors in some of their meetings.

Mr Frankland often referred to Edna Broughton as *"his little star"*, and in a letter to Edna's parents in September of 1947, he said: *"I wish with all my heart to say thank you for Edna. She had a great promise when she came to us. But do you agree she is 100 percent better and she will make one of the loveliest players the ladies' game has ever seen? She had Bolton on toast in spite of their fouls on her. One foul against her in the first ten minutes should have seen the Bolton right half sent off the field. I love to watch her bewilder players."*

MATCH FACTS 1947

DATE	VENUE	TEAMS	RESULT
23 June	Preston	DK v French	8-3

Scorers: Nancy Thomson 2, Jean Gollin 2, Joan Burke 2, Edna Broughton 1, Joan Whalley 1

25 June	Hyde	DK v French	6-3

Scorers: Jean Gollin 2, Joan Whalley 2, Edna Broughton 1, Nancy Thomson 1

26 June	Stretford	DK v French	5-1

Scorers: Jean Gollin 2, Joan Whalley 2, Lily Parr 1

4 Aug	Presall	DK v Manchester	9-0

Scorers: Joan Whalley 4, Jean Gollin 3, Joan Burke 2

18 Aug	Burnley	DK v Bolton	1-3

Scorer: Joan Whalley

4 Sept	Bamber Bridge	DK v Rest of Lancs	10-2

Scorers: Jean Gollin 2, Edna Broughton 2, Joan Burke 2, Joan Whalley 2, Lily Parr 1

11 Sept	West Hoghton	DK v Bolton	1-0
15 Sept	Stalybridge	DK v Bolton	3-2
4 Oct	Much Hoole	DK v Wythenshawe	9-1

Scorers: Jean Gollin 3, Edna Broughton 2, Margaret Thornborough 1, Lily Parr 1, Joan Burke 1, Nancy Thomson 1

6 Oct	Morecambe	DK v Wythenshawe/Barnsley	5-1

Scorers: Jean Gollin 2, Joan Whalley 2, Edna Broughton 1

26 Dec	Stoke	DK v Stoke	16-0

Scorers: Alice Hargreaves 5, Margaret Thornborough 3, Jean Gollin 3, Joan Whalley 2, Edna Broughton 2, Nancy Thomson 1

The 1948 season got off to a bad start when the Preston team suffered a rare defeat at the hands of Bolton Ladies. In May, Mr Frankland challenged the Secretary of the Welsh FA to a public debate on women's football. Speaking at the reception following the game between Preston and Wythenshawe at Eirias Park, Colwyn Bay, he was criticising the attitude of both the English and Welsh FA's towards women's football following the comments of Mr R Williams-Jones surrounding the difficulties encountered by the organisers. The proceeds of the match were in support of the Mochdre Village Centre Fund and they had intended to stage the game on the Mochdre ground which was owned by the Council and used by Colwyn Bay FC. However even though the Welsh FA had no real jurisdiction over the ground they still stepped in with threats saying that if the match took place on that ground the Colwyn Bay club would not be allowed to play there. Eventually permission was obtained to play the game at the local Grammar School ground and in spite of the interference from the FA, 4000 spectators still turned out to watch the match and support the Village Centre Fund.

The French tour which began in June and took in six matches in various parts of the country, raised over £2000 for local charities.

Preston and French teams at Kent, 1948

Margaret Thornborough and French Goalkeeper

Lancs County capt, Stan Mortensen (referee), Joan Burke, 1948

MATCH FACTS 1948

DATE	VENUE	TEAMS	RESULT
29 Mar	Southport	DK v Bolton	2-4

Scorers: Margaret Thornborough 1, Edna Broughton 1

10 Apr	Much Hoole	DK v Bolton	1-1

Scorer: Margaret Thornborough

17 May	Colwyn Bay	DK v Wythenshawe	2-0

Scorers: Joan Whalley 1, Joan Burke 1

22 May	Clitheroe	DK v Wythenshawe	16-2

Scorers: Alice Hargreaves 6, Joan Whalley 4, Edna Broughton 3,
Lottie Worrall 2, Joan Burke 1

19 June	Preston	DK v French	8-0

Scorers: Alice Hargreaves 4, Edna Broughton 2, Joan Whalley 2

21 June	Hyde	DK v French	5-1

Scorers: Edna Broughton 2, Alice Hargreaves 2, Joan Whalley 1

22 June	Nelson	DK v French	5-2

Scorers: Edna Broughton 2, Alice Hargreaves 2, Joan Whalley 1

23 June	Hull	DK v French	4-1

Scorers: Margaret Thornborough, Edna Broughton 2, Joan Whalley 1

24 June	Stretford	DK v French	7-2

Scorers: Alice Hargreaves 3, Edna Broughton 2, Jean Dent 1, Joan Whalley 1

28 June	Gillingham	DK v French	4-1

Scorers: E Sorrell 2, Joan Whalley 1, Alice Hargreaves 1

29 July	Blackpool	DK v Wythenshawe	6-1

Scorers: Edna Broughton 2, Alice Hargreaves 2, Joan Whalley 2

30 July	Ormskirk	DK v Wythenshawe	9-2

Scorers: Alice Hargreaves 4, Joan Whalley 2, Lottie Worrall 1,
Edna Broughton 1, G Lyons 1

18 Aug	Blackpool	DK v Barnsley	8-1

Scorers: Edna Broughton 4, Alice Hargreaves 3, Joan Whalley 1

19 Aug	Bamber Bridge	DK v Wythenshawe	3-2

Scorers: Joan Whalley 2, Alice Hargreaves 1

?	?	DK v Bolton	0-6

Dick, Kerr's v French at Nelson

Both Lily Parr and Margaret Thornborough were still playing and scoring goals, and Lily would even play in goal if she was needed. As Margaret had the role of assistant manager, she now preferred to play only in an emergency. Irene Swift, the daughter of England and Manchester City goalkeeper Frank Swift, signed for the Preston club in 1949. She followed in her father's footsteps and played in goal although she didn't stay with the team for very long.

In June of 1949 they played Blackpool Ladies at Freckleton in aid of the Village School Fund. It was the first competitive

Irene Swift

match for the Blackpool team and although they tried hard, the result was a convincing 8-1 victory for the Preston club. The game raised in excess of £45 for the school. As a former resident of Freckleton and an old boy of the school, Mr Frankland helped organise the event with the Vicar, Reverend J W Broadbent to commemorate the 5th anniversary of the Freckleton Air Disaster. Part of the school was destroyed during a thunder storm in August of 1944, when an American Liberator bomber crashed on to it and thirty-eight school children, 2 teachers, and 7 civilians lost their lives. Before the game the team laid a wreath of 38 red roses on the memorial grave at a simple ceremony in the church yard. Relatives of the children gathered round as two members of the WRAF, both players with the Preston team, stood in Salute, one at each side of the grave.

Mary Carter & Doreen Richards salute at the 5th Anniversary as Alfred Frankland places flowers

The French team returned in 1949 for another tour. They were never as good as the pre-war team and were regularly defeated by Dick, Kerr's, but the crowds still turned up in their thousands to watch them play. For these international matches the Preston team were feted as England, just as they had been throughout their history. The match played at Derby on 14 July was recorded as being the Dick, Kerr Ladies 600th game. The last match of the tour was played in

Match day Poster

Blackpool at the Co-operative Society employees sports ground. Before the game the teams were taken on a whistle stop tour of the town, visiting the pleasure beach, central pier, open air baths and to the top of the tower itself. They attended a Civic reception in the afternoon and danced at the tower ballroom in the evening. Acting interpreter Madame Allane, told the *Evening Gazette* that the French girls do enjoy the English breakfast and are very fond of fish and chips but they don't like the way our peas (mushy peas) are cooked! They didn't much care for English coffee either but she said, *"this coffee in Blackpool is as good as ours at home."*

MATCH FACTS 1949

DATE	VENUE	TEAMS	RESULT
28 Apr	Leigh	DK v Corinthians	0-0
10 May	Nelson	DK v Bolton	4-0

Scorers: Doreen Richards 2, Margaret Thornborough 1, Joan Whalley 1

18 May	Blackpool	DK v Bolton	3-1

Scorers: Margaret Thornborough 2, Joan Whalley 1

25 May	Clitheroe	DK v Corinthians	3-2

Scorers: Lily Parr 1, Doreen Richards 1, Joan Whalley 1

28 May	Salford	DK v Corinthians	2-3

Scorers: Doreen Richards 1, Joan Whalley 1

6 Jun	Colwyn Bay	DK v Wythenshawe	7-1

Scorers: Doreen Richards 4, Alice Hargreaves 3

11 Jun	Litherland	DK v Wythenshawe	9-1

Scorers: Joan Whalley 4, Doreen Richards 3, Mary Carter 2

20 Jun	Freckleton	DK v Blackpool	8-1

Scorers: Doreen Richards 5, Joan Whalley 2, Alice Hargreaves 1

11 Jul	Ormskirk	DK v French	7-0

Scorers: Joan Whalley 4, Doreen Richards 3

13 Jul	Hull	DK v French	5-1

Scorers: Joan Whalley 4, Doreen Richards 1

14 Jul	Derby	DK v French	6-0

Scorers: Joan Whalley 2, Doreen Richards 2, Alice Hargreaves 1, Edna Broughton 1

16 Jul	Colwyn Bay	DK v French	6-1

Scorers: Joan Whalley 2, Doreen Richards 2, Alice Hargreaves 2

18 Jul	Blackpool	DK v French	6-1

Scorers: Joan Whalley 3, Doreen Richards 2, Edna Broughton 1

23 Jul	Bootle	DK v Wythenshawe	6-0

Scorers: Joan Whalley 3, Alice Hargreaves 2, Doreen Richards 1

3 Aug	Blackpool	DK v Blackpool	4-0

Scorers: Edna Broughton 2, Alice Hargreaves 1, Joan Whalley 1

20 Sept	Padiham	DK v Corinthians	3-2

Scorers: Joan Whalley 3

24 Sept	Stalybridge	DK v Corinthians	5-3

Scorers: Joan Whalley 2, Edna Broughton 1, Doreen Richards 1, Margaret Thornborough 1

By 1950, after a career spanning some thirty years, Lily Parr was playing at left back and still getting good reviews in the press. In a 1-1 draw with Manchester Ladies at Belle Vue, an article in Joan Whalley's scrap book said, *'Lily Parr was dominant at left full back. But for her long experience and positional play, Manchester might have won comfortably.'* The Preston side were not out-played but the Manchester team did have an advantage over their opponents - they practiced regularly. The Preston players all now lived in various parts of Lancashire and seldom had the same opportunity to train together as they had in days gone by.

Capt Lily Parr introducing the team, Stretford 1950

Nineteen-fifty was the first time the Preston side had been forced to advertise for players and unless more new talent could be introduced their impressive playing record would begin to have some blemishes upon it. Fortunately, major signings this year were that of 15-year-old Jean Lane from Wigan, June Gregson and Muriel Heaney from Preston, Yvonne Hamer from Crewe and Kath Latham. Kath soon became involved with all the clerical work for the team. She was a competent shorthand typist and 'Pop' asked if she would take over some of the secretarial duties. She gradually did more and more of the paperwork and as 'Pop's' health began to fail, Kath stopped playing and became his assistant.

Dressing room banter!

Edna Broughton, Margaret Thornborough, Nancy Thomson, Betty Sharples, Stella Briggs, Lily Parr, Joan Whalley, Sally Kendal, Joan Burke

1950's Line up

Jean Dent, June Gregson, Muriel Heaney, Audrey Coupe, Margaret Groom, Jean Lane, Dorothy Saycell, Joan Pomfrett

During the French tour of 1950, both teams travelled to Northern Ireland to play a series of matches in aid of the War Memorial Fund. The highlight of their visit was a chance meeting with the Queen (later, Queen Elizabeth, the Queen Mother) during her tour of Northern Ireland. The local press said of the Royal visit: *During all of yesterday's tour her Majesty never failed to give the impression of a real and sincere interest in everyone she met and everything she saw. At a relatively isolated spot on the route, just outside Dunmurry, the Queen noticed a group of girls displaying an outsize French tricolour. On her order the car, which had been gathering speed on an empty road, slowed down while she bestowed an extra special smile on the excitedly delighted group of girls.* June Gregson recalled their royal encounter: "I remember seeing her car coming along the same road as us and I remember being so excited to see her. Our coach was decorated with the French tricolour and our Union Jack and we all got off the coach and lined up on the side of the road. We were all waving and I was so excited, the Queen was actually going to pass us in her Royal car. As it got nearer to us it slowed down, and we all saw her in her favourite colour of powder blue and she waved to us all with such a nice smile on her face. I remember telling my Mum when I got home and I think she told the whole street that I'd met the Queen! She was very proud of me playing football but my father was never interested." The press reported that the English girls played some sparkling football at Shamrock Park, Portadown having taken part in two games in one day. But it was Joan Whalley, playing on the right wing who stole the show. They compared her style of play to that of Tom Finney, the Preston North End winger, saying, *'her footwork and positioning, together with her team spirit, brought bursts of applause from the thousands of spectators.'*

Margaret Thornborough was to score her last goal for the Dick, Kerr Ladies in a 3-1 victory against the French team at Bolton on 22 July 1950. The last match of the French tour was played at Kirkham, just outside Preston. The game was kicked off by Tom Finney and a crowd of 7000 spectators helped raise £300 for the Wesham Village Hall Fund. Lily Parr's last goal for club and country was against Scotland at Carlisle on 12 August. She scored from the penalty spot in an 11-1 victory over the Scots.

Throughout the following years, they would always attract crowds numbered in their thousands. Calculating their playing record to the end of the 1950 season by combining Mr Frankland and Joan Whalley's accounts, their record to date was, Played 647, Won 607, Drawn 27 and lost only 13 since 1917. He also claimed that the team had raised £140,000 for charity. They ended the 1950 season unbeaten, having won all their games except the 1-1 draw with Manchester, and Joan Burke (Tich) was the leading goalscorer with 22 goals.

Joan Whalley introduces the Lord Mayor of Leeds to the team, 1950

MATCH FACTS 1950

DATE	VENUE	TEAMS	RESULT
17 May	Belle Vue	DK v Wythenshawe	1-1

Scorer: Joan Whalley

| 29 May | York | DK v Wythenshawe | 2-1 |

Scorers: Doreen Richards 2

| 31 May | Blackpool | DK v Wythenshawe | 4-2 |

Scorers: Alice Hargreaves 2, Jean Lane 1, Joan Whalley 1

| 10 Jun | Liverpool | DK v Chester | 14-0 |

Scorers: Jean Lane 6, Joan Burke 3, Alice Hargreaves 3, Edna Broughton 1, Nancy Thomson 1

| 14 Jun | Nelson | DK v Wythenshawe | 3-1 |

Scorers: Alice Hargreaves 2, Edna Broughton 1

| 23 Jun | Stretford | DK v Lancs XI | 4-1 |

Scorers: Jean Lane, Edna Broughton, Joan Burke, Nancy Thomson

| 28 Jun | Blackpool | DK v Corinthians | 4-1 |

Scorers: Joan Burke 2, Jean Lane 1, Edna Broughton 1

| 8 Jul | Bootle | DK v Blackpool | 5-1 |

Scorers: Joan Burke 2, Alice Hargreaves 1, Jean Lane 1

| 8 Jul | Prescot | DK v Blackpool | 5-0 |

Scorers: Alice Hargreaves 2, Joan Burke 1, Joan Whalley 1, Jean Dent 1

| 17 Jul | Portadown | DK v French | 3-1 |

Scorers: Joan Burke 1, Jean Lane 1, Joan Whalley 1

| 17 Jul | Portadown | DK v Portadown | 10-0 |

Scorers: Margaret Thornborough 5, Edna Broughton 2, Joan Burke 1, Jean Lane 1, Joan Whalley 1

| 18 Jul | Belfast | DK v French | 4-1 |

Scorers: Joan Burke 3, Margaret Thornborough 1

| 19 Jul | Ormskirk | DK v French | 5-1 |

Scorers: Alice Hargreaves 3, Stella Briggs 1, Joan Whalley 1

| 20 Jul | Leeds | DK v French | 7-2 |

Scorers: Joan Burke 3, Alice Hargreaves 1, Edna Broughton 1, Jean Lane 1, Joan Whalley 1

| 22 Jul | Bolton | DK v French | 4-0 |

Scorers: Edna Broughton, Margaret Thornborough, Jean Lane, French o.g.

| 24 Jul | Kirkham | DK v French | 4-1 |

Scorers: Alice Hargreaves 3, Joan Whalley 1

| 12 Aug | Carlisle | DK v Scottish XI | 12.0 |

Scorers: Joan Burke 4, Edna Broughton 3, Alice Hargreaves 3,
Lily Parr 1 (pen), Jean Lane 1

| 4 Sept | Wigan | DK v Manchester | 6-2 |

Scorers: Joan Whalley 2, Edna Broughton 2, Alice Hargreavs 2

| 12 Sept | Wigan | DK v Manchester | 5-0 |

Scorers: Edna Broughton 2, Jean Lane 1, Joan Burke1, Joan Whalley 1

| 30 Sept | Wigan | DK v Manchester | 8-0 |

Scorers: Yvonne Hamer 5, Joan Whalley 3

At Manchester Belle Vue, 1950

*Margaret Thornborough, Betty Sharples, Lily Parr, Joan Burke, Sheila Pinder,
Nancy Thomson, Stella Briggs, Alfred Frankland*

Doreen Richards, Jean Lane, Joan Whalley, Alice Hargreaves, Barbara Gilbert

By 1951 there were now 26 women's football teams in the country. Edna Broughton left the Dick, Kerr Ladies in a shock transfer to Manchester Corinthians, and this was also to be Lily Parr's final season with the Preston team. Her last match was played during the French tour on 24 July at Windsor Park, Belfast. Playing at full back in a 5-0 victory she was still praise-worthy in a press report which described her as '*a cool, reliable back.*' In recognition of her long and distinguished playing career, she was made an honorary life member of the club. Only Alice Kell and Margaret Thornborough had previously received this honour. Mr Frankland placed an advert in *the Lancashire Daily Post* for new players. The last few years had seen the loss of some of the longest serving members of the team and they would prove difficult, if not impossible to replace.

Lily Parr in particular was such a big part of the

Lily Parr

history of the club. It must have been a very sad day for her and the whole team when she finally hung up her boots. She was the last playing link from the glory days of women's football when they were welcome at any stadium in the country. And what an incredible journey she had undertaken since joining the team as a scrawny teenager back in 1920. From leaving the rougher end of St Helens with relatively no prospects far behind, to rubbing shoulders with Lord Mayors, show business and sporting celebrities and all manor of gentry throughout the length and breadth of the land. She could never in her wildest dreams have imagined the places she would visit, the people she would meet, the friends she would make or the respect she would receive and not forgetting her nursing career at Whittingham Hospital. Her life with the Dick, Kerr Ladies was totally transformed from what she could ever have expected had she remained in her native St Helens. Even Catherine Cookson couldn't have scripted it better! Lily probably scored over 1000 goals during her football career with Dick, Kerr's and St Helens, which will make her the leading goalscorer in the club's entire history, and probably the all time leading goalscorer in women's football. She had an excellent football brain with the knack of being in the right place at the right time and when playing at full back, she always said that she didn't need to do a lot of running because she knew exactly what her opponent was going to do with the ball before she even got it! She was indeed a footballing icon and legendary status would follow our unlikely heroine in later years.

Lily Parr sharing a joke with the French girls

In June of 1951, the team visited Cheshire to play Bolton Ladies in the small village of Croft near Warrington. Although the village had a population of only 1400, the girls were able to draw a crowd of over 4000! The *Daily Mirror* reported later in the year that since their formation, the Dick, Kerr Ladies had scored 3215 goals and they had been invited to play a series of matches with the French ladies in Portugal the following year. Two Portuguese sportsmen were said to be sponsoring the scheme and Mr Frankland said, *We will go if our expenses are guaranteed.* But alas, the tour never came to fruition.

MATCH FACTS 1951

DATE	VENUE	TEAMS	RESULT
3 May	Barnsley	DK v Barnsley	2-0

Scorers: Joan Whalley 1, June Gregson 1

| 7 May | Preston | DK v Littlewoods | 4-1 |

Scorers: Joan Burke 2, Yvonne Hamer 1, Jean Lane 1

| 14 May | York | DK v Manchester | 3-2 |

Scorers: Jean Dent 1, Jean Lane 1, Peggy Sharples 1

| 16 May | Altricham | DK v Manchester | 5-0 |

Scorers: Joan Burke 3, Joan Whalley 1, Jean Lane 1

| 23 May | Pemberton | DK v Manchester | 3-3 |

Scorers: Joan Burke 1, Jean Lane 1, Joan Whalley 1

| 1 Jun | Glossop | DK v Manchester | 3-1 |

Scorers: Joan Burke 1, Jean Lane 1, Doreen Richards 1

| 5 Jun | Burnley | DK v Northenden | 16-1 |

Scorers: Yvonne Hamer 6, Joan Burke 5, Joan Whalley 3, Jean Lane 2

| 6 Jun | Litherland | DK v Liverpool | 8-2 |

Scorers: Yvonne Hamer 4, Jean Lane 2, Joan Burke 2

| 16 Jun | Croft (Warrington) | DK v Bolton | 4-2 |

Scorers: Joan Burke 2, Yvonne Hamer 1, Muriel Heaney 1

| 22 Jun | Crosby | DK v Bolton | 6-0 |

Scorers: Joan Burke 2, June Gregson 1, Joan Whalley 1, Jean Lane 1, Stella Briggs 1

| 5 Jul | Preston | DK v Manchester | 4-2 |

Scorers: Joan Burke 3, Doreen Richards 1

| 16 Jul | Hull | DK v French | 9-1 |

Scorers: Doreen Richards 2, Jean Lane 2, Yvonne Hamer 2, Joan Burke 1 Nancy Thomson 1, o.g.

| 17 Jul | Leeds | DK v French | 8-3 |

Scorers: Yvonne Hamer 3, Doreen Richards 3, Joan Burke 2

| 19 Jul | Castletown, IOM | DK v French | 4-3 |

Scorers: Joan Burke 1, Yvonne Hamer 1, Jean Lane 1

| 21 Jul | Fleetwood | DK v French | 11-2 |

Scorers: Doreen Richards 5, Jean Lane 2, Joan Burke 2, Yvonne Hamer 1 o.g.

| 23 Jul | Bangor, N.I. | DK v French | 5-2 |

Scorers: Doreen Richards 3, Yvonne Hamer 1, Jean Lane 1

| 24 Jul | Belfast | DK v French | 5-0 |

Scorers: Yvonne Hamer 2, Joan Burke 2, Jean Lane 1

| 28 Jul | Chester | DK v Littlewoods | 9-2 |

Scorers: Joan Burke 3, Yvonne Hamer 2, Jean Lane 2, Nancy Thomson 1, Joan Whalley 1

| 4 Aug | Dewsbury | DK v Barnsley | 5-0 |

Scorers: Joan Burke 3, Jean Lane 1, Nancy Thomson 1

| 6 Aug | Leyland | DK v Manchester | 4-3 |

Scorers: Doreen Richards 3, Jean Lane 1

| 15 Aug | Belle Vue | DK v Manchester | 10-3 |

Scorers: Doreen Richards 3, Joan Burke 2, Jean Lane 2

| 18 Aug | Barnsley | DK v Barnsley | 5-2 |

Scorers: Joan Whalley 2, Joan Burke 2, Jean Lane 1

Other new players in the early 1950s were Audrey Coupe from Preston, Rosette Huard from France, who was staying in Preston on a three month holiday, and Joan Clay from Liverpool. Years later Joan was to say, *"My first memory of the Dick, Kerr Ladies was when I played for Littlewoods and we offered Dick, Kerr's a challenge*

Rosette Huard signs for Preston, watched by Mr Frankland and June Gregson

thinking that we were going to be the only team ever to beat them. I was very disappointed on that occasion, we lost 15-1! It was a match of mixed emotions, disappointment at losing, but admiration for the quality of play shown to us that evening by Dick, Kerr's. I joined them not long after that and it was a truely marvellous experience playing for them."

The 1952 season saw Edna Broughton return to the fold, and the team were unbeaten for the third successive year, with Joan Burke being leading goalscorer for the third consecutive season. Earlier in the year Mr Frankland had sent out a letter to all the players outlining the arrangements for the coming season which further illustrates his role within the team. Extracts are as follows: *"At the very outset I am trying to present to you a picture of all I have in my mind at the moment. Things have been made increasingly difficult by the real mess-up of 2 prospective tours in our minds:-*

(I)   Prospective tour of Spain and Portugal, where the most frightful neglect of correspondence was most apparent in matters of vital importance which could not stand dormant. I can state very concisely that no tour can be a safe proposition with a receipt of 2 letters - one in November and one on January 15th, and if we will not allow our enthusiasm to run away with our sober judgement, such arrangements cannot succeed.

(II) I had therefore to do something very quickly and so went on at once with some very late arrangements for a French visit - even the very apparent neglect of earlier matches all of which are good for our reputation, so none of you can blame me for all this laxity of method or procedure. I can now assure you I have lost none of my keenness to keep our Club right in the front row, and our colours at top mast."

The letter goes on to say: *Once more, I remind particularly our young players when they travel - the rules are as follows: As a private party we can all have a good time and please ourselves within all reasonable limits, but when we appear as a Club, outside our coach no matter when or where, all should stand on their dignity, and never bring a friend without my permission".* He signs the letter, Yours sincerely, *A. FRANKLAND* Honorary Manager, with a P.S. that states: *This is my 35th year in that position.*

King George VI died in his sleep on 6 February 1952 and the twenty-five-year old Princess Elizabeth was proclaimed Queen Elizabeth II. At the cinema, High Noon starring Gary Cooper was a box office success, and in sport, Maureen Connolly from the USA became the Ladies singles champion at Wimbledon.

The town of Preston also celebrated its Guild this year. The unique Preston Guild celebrations which occur only once every 20 years, should have taken

Kirkham 1952

Back: Betty Sharples, Jean Dent, Nancy Thomson, Mary Goodinson, Audrey Coupe,
Muriel Heaney

Front: Joan Whalley, Joan Burke, Doreen Richards, Jean Lane, Yvonne Hamer

place in 1942 but had to be postponed until after the war. Alice Mills, (now Mrs Lambert) the young lass who made the trip with the team to the United States in 1922 and eventually settled in Seekonk, Massachusetts, returned to Preston for the Guild celebrations this year. Alice was staying in her home town for five weeks, but was heard to say that she was homesick for the USA during her visit. She saw the team win their match at Blackburn and graciously said, *"Their standard of play is comparable with that of the old team."* Lily Jones, (now Mrs Martin) was also to see her old team in action. She had travelled with them to France in 1920 and was the lady who was married in London on their return journey.

After fifteen happy years with the club, the team was rocked with the shock departure of Joan Whalley from her beloved Dick, Kerr Ladies. The team were due to go on tour with the French girls for two weeks during the summer of '52. Playing football was much more important to Joan than having a holiday, football was her life and she was eagerly looking forward to the tour arranging her annual leave accordingly. At that time, she was working as a conductress on

Alice Mills Lambert and Alfred Frankland 1952

Ribble buses doing split shifts and the day before their departure she had to work late and didn't get to bed until the early hours of the morning. After having only a few hours sleep before being up at the crack of dawn to meet everyone, that morning of all mornings, Joan overslept. She was frantic trying to get there on time but arrived at the meeting place about 20 minutes late, only to find that they had left without her. She was devastated.

Joan said, *"I thought they would still be there when I arrived but there was no sign of them. They must have gone exactly on time because old Frankland was always in and out of his pocket looking at his watch. I've known times when we waited quarter of an hour for people to arrive, yet he wouldn't wait for me. I was desperate, I knew they would be going through Ormskirk, and wondered if I should get on a bus to see if I could meet up with them, but I was so upset, I had a big lump in my throat. I'd never missed a match since I started playing for Dick, Kerr's in 1937.*

I went home and cried my eyes out. I didn't go out for the rest of that day. The next day I went to work and told them what happened. I was crying in the office as I explained to the boss that I couldn't stay at home for two weeks knowing that they were all playing football. I asked if I could cancel my holidays and come back to work. He said I could and I started work straight away. When they came back, Tich came to see me and I told her what had happened, and she said, 'He wouldn't wait Joan, we were on at him but he wouldn't wait.' I thought it was disgusting, I never really got over it, he broke my heart.

I did see him afterwards but he never apologised to me. We did speak again but only to exchange a polite greeting. Whenever I saw him I would just say 'Hello Pop.' Her years in exile were spent playing for Manchester Ladies. What made him do such a callous thing? Surely he knew the depth of her love for the game. He must have known how much his actions would have hurt her. She did not return to the Dick, Kerr team during Franklands lifetime.

French and Preston teams on tour without Joan Whalley 1952

MATCH FACTS 1952

DATE	VENUE	TEAMS	RESULT
15 May	Preston	DK v Manchester	5-2

Scorers: Joan Burke 3, Rosette Huard 1, Yvonne Hamer 1

| 2 Jun | York | DK v Manchester | 2-1 |

Scorers: Joan Burke 1, Rosette Huard 1

| 14 Jun | Litherland | DK v Manchester | 4-1 |

Scorers: Joan Burke 1, Lily Harris, 1, Joan Whalley 1, o.g. 1

| 17 Jun | Padiham | DK v Manchester | 7-0 |

Scorers: Joan Burke 3, Yvonne Hamer 3, Jean Dent 1

| 23 Jun | Hull | DK v Manchester | 4-1 |

Scorers: Yvonne Hamer 2, Joan Burke 1, Edna Broughton 1

| 3 July | Kirkham | DK v Lancs County | 6-4 |

Scorers: Joan Burke 2, Jean Lane 2, Yvonne Hamer 1, Joan Whalley 1

| 10 Jul | Kirkham | DK v French | 6-3 |

Scorers: Jean Lane 2, Joan Burke 2, Yvonne Hamer 1, Doreen Richards 1

| 13 Jul | Dewsbury | DK v French | 5-1 |

Scorers: Jean Lane 3, Joan Burke 1, June Gregson 1

| 14 Jul | Leyland | DK v French | 5-1 |

Scorers: Rose Wilson 2, Joan Burke 1, Jean Lane 1, Nancy Thomson 1

| 15 Jul | Bradford | DK v French | 4-3 |

Scorers: Rose Wilson 2, Yvonne Hamer 2

| 19 Jul | Liverpool | DK v French | 5-1 |

Scorers: Rose Wilson 2, Jean Lane 1, Yvonne Hamer 1, Edna Broughton 1

| 21 Jul | Whitley Bay | DK v French | 5-0 |

Scorers: Jean Lane 2, Yvonne Hamer 1, Joan Burke 1, Rose Wilson 1

| 22 Jul | Whitley Bay | DK v French | 4-0 |

Scorers: Yvonne Hamer 1, Joan Burke 1, Doreen Richards 1, Jean Lane 1

| ? | Carlisle | DK v French | 6-1 |

Scorers: Doreen Richards 3, Joan Burke 1, Edna Broughton 1, Muriel Heaney 1

| 4 Aug | Bridlington | DK v French | 5-2 |

Scorers: Joan Burke 3, Jean Lane 2

| 18 Aug | Blackburn | DK v French | 3-1 |

Scorers: Joan Burke 2, Yvonne Hamer 1

| 21 Aug | St Helens | DK v Manchester | 10-1 |

Scorers: Doreen Richards 4, Jean Lane 3, Edna Broughton 2, Joan Burke 1

Star Line up

Bill Eckersley, Joe McCall, Nancy Thomson, Tom Finney, Mr Frankland, Bobby Beattie, Lancs County Captain

June Gregson began her career as goalkeeper for the Dick, Kerr Ladies in 1953. She would later tell of how joining the team would prove to be a life changing experience for her. *"I had never been outside of Preston before I started playing football and I now found myself going on trips to places like Bridlington, Bradford, Whitley Bay and Blackpool. Then came the Isle of Man and Ireland. I was meeting people from all walks of life and I realised that there was a better life out there for me. The only work available in Preston at the time was either in a factory or the cotton mill. I didn't want to do either of those and chose to work as a packer in a tea and coffee business. I always arrived home from work with loads of coffee and tea dust up my nose! I finished working there after a severed finger came down the chute and I nearly packed it!! I made many new friends because of football; one in particular with the French team. We became pen pals after she had returned home following our tour. When I was eighteen-years-old she invited me over to Paris for a holiday. It was a wonderful experience and it made me even more determined to have a better lifestyle. I never dreamed that I, a girl from a working class background, living on a council estate, could actually have a holiday in Paris. I also had another holiday in Holland with a friend who played for the Dutch team. Football certainly changed my life and made me aware that there was another life to be lived. It made me more independent and gave me the desire to improve myself. When I was twenty-one-years old, I put an advert in a French newspaper, Le Paris Soir, and the New York Herald Tribune, which were sold on the streets of Paris at that time. I advertised myself as an 'au pair' and had several replies. I chose to go to a family in Bordeaux where I looked after two children in a very posh family home. They were in the Champagne business. I stayed there for six months and in that time I learned quite a lot of the language which would help me later in life. Football was my passion, and without it I would never have left Preston. My life would have been so different had I not joined the Dick, Kerr Ladies, and I will always be grateful for that opportunity."*

Blackpool won the FA cup in 1953 beating Bolton Wanderers 4-3 in what became known as the Stanley Matthews final. It was also Coronation year and on 2 June, Queen Elizabeth was crowned at Westminster Abbey in London. The ceremony was watched by millions around the world as the BBC set up their biggest outside broadcast to provide live coverage on radio and television. The Dick, Kerr Ladies celebrated the occasion with a 6-2 victory against Manchester at Leeds. During this time, the team would sing their own victory song which was:

Hurrah, Huroo, Hurrah we're here again
Hurrah, Huroo, Hurrah we're here again
We don't care who we're meeting
The Preston team will take a lot of beating.
We're here to cheer the lassies from Lancashire
To fight with might and mane
Ours is a good team ours is
Hurrah, Hurrah, Hurrah we're here again!

Prior to a match played at Liverpool on 4 July against London Ladies, 'Pop' sent out a letter to the girls regarding the arrangements for the game. In it he said: *"An important note to each of you. London are determined to defeat us and they will not if we are all fit and keen on the day. I hope you are all ready and fit for this great match in our history. Take things easy and avoid all late nights and excessive pleasures during the next week. Mr Eli Thornborough asks me to stress upon you to look after yourselves for this match. Finally, let the spirit of dear ol' Swannee be with you at Liverpool and jolly good luck to you all."* The result of the game was a 5-3 victory to the Preston team.

A thrilling game took place at Coventry on 11 July, which illustrates just how important it was to the girls not to lose *any* match. The team managed a

4-4 draw with Manchester with Jean Lane scoring a hat trick. Jean describes the game in her diary: *"They were leading 2-0, and then we made it 3-2. They scored another two to make it 4-3. We played for about fifteen minutes at that score. Then, in the last three minutes, Yvonne took the ball down the wing to the goal line, centred and I scored to make it 4-4. All our team mobbed me. Nancy put her arms round me and kissed me. Soon after, the final whistle went and June, Kath and Anne came running to me. Even in the dressing room I was mobbed again. I felt very happy and proud, but it was as much Yvonne's goal as mine."*

Later that month they played a match at Castletown in the Isle of Man. It was a landmark trip for the girls as it was the first time that they had made the journey by air. Jean Lane said, *"It was smashing flying for the first time."* But it must have been a strange and emotional occasion for Joan Whalley. She was playing for Manchester Ladies and she scored from the penalty spot against her old team.

Their last match of 1953 saw them play another match under floodlights, when they met Manchester Ladies at the vast Odsal Rugby League Stadium in Bradford. It was 33 years since they became the first women's team to play a match under artificial light. The result was a 6-2 victory for the Preston team. Statistics at the end of the 1953 season were: played 709, won 665, drawn 31 and lost only 13 games in 36 years.

MATCH FACTS 1953

DATE	VENUE	TEAMS	RESULT
9 May	Great Harwood	DK v Manchester	3-0

Scorers: Jean Lane 2, Joan Clay 1

May	Pemberton	DK v Manchester	5-1

Scorers: Joan Clay 2, Jean Lane 2, Yvonne Hamer 1

May	Leyland	DK v Manchester	3-3

Scorers: Joan Clay 1, Edna Broughton 1, Joan Burke 1

2 Jun	Leeds	DK v Manchester	6-2

Scorers: Jean Lane 2, Yvonne Hamer 1, Edna Broughton 1, o.g. 2

6 Jun	Preston	DK v Manchester	3-2

Scorers: Joan Clay 1, Yvonne Hamer 1, Jean Lane 1

13 Jun	Litherland	DK v Manchester	1-1

Scorer: Joan Clay

20 Jun	?	DK v Manchester	7-0

Scorers: Yvonne Hamer 3, Jean Lane 3, Joan Clay 1

4 Jul	Liverpool	DK v London	5-3

Scorers: Joan Burke 2, Jean Lane 2, Joan Clay 1

11 Jul	Coventry	DK v Manchester	4-4

Scorers: Jean Lane 3, Joan Burke 1

13 Jul	Preston	DK v French	3-1

Scorers: Jean Parnell 1, Joan Clay 1, Edna Broughton 1

15 Jul	Carlisle	DK v French	6-1

Scorers: Joan Burke 3, Edna Broughton 1, Hilda Nettle 1, Jean Lane 1

15 Jul	Carlisle	DK v Cumberland	1-0

Scorer: Joan Burke (10 mins each way)

16 Jul	Workington	DK v French	7-3

Scorers: Yvonne Hamer 2, Joan Burke 2, Joan Clay 1,
Edna Broughton 1, Jean Lane 1

18 Jul	Liverpool	DK v French	5-0

Scorers: Joan Burke 2, Jean Lane 2, Nancy Thomson 1

20 Jul	Hull	DK v French	1-0

Scorer: o.g.

21 Jul	Bridlington	DK v French	5-0

Scorers: Yvonne Hamer 2, Joan Clay 2, Pat Ellis 1

23 Jul	Belle Vue	DK v French	5-1

Scorers: Joan Clay 3, Yvonne Hamer 1, Jean Lane 1

30 Jul	Isle of Man	DK v Manchester	2-1

Scorers: Joan Burke 1, Jean Lane 1

11 Aug	Blackburn	DK v Manchester	5-1

Scorers: Rose Wilson 3, Yvonne Hamer 1, Edna Broughton 1

14 Aug	Warrington	DK v Manchester	3-2

Scorers: Jean Lane 1, Amy Duxbury 1, Joan Clay 1

24 Aug	Bury	DK v Manchester	3-0

Scorers: Nancy Thomson 2, Joan Burke 1

2 Sept	Oswaldtwistle	DK v Manchester	1-0

Scorer: Amy Duxbury

12 Nov	Bradford (Odsal Stdm)	DK v Manchester	6-2

Scorers: Jean Lane 3, Yvonne Hamer 2, Joan Burke 1

Mayor of Leeds signing match ball watched by Nancy Thomson (right)

A new era in music was born in 1954 as Rock 'n Roll became the latest craze with Bill Haley and the Comets bursting on to the scene with *Shake, Rattle and Roll.* A young man by the name of Elvis Presley quit his job as a truck driver when he signed his first recording contract with Sun Records. And in the world of sport Maureen (*little Mo)* Connolly won her third consecutive Wimbledon singles title. This year also saw the introduction of Match Box Cars for boys, *Burger King* arrived in the world, *Nautilus* became the first atomic powered submarine and Preston North End were beaten 3-2 by West Bromwich Albion in the FA cup final.

From 1954 onwards, football matches for the Dick, Kerr Ladies became less frequent but they were still being coached by Eli Thornborough and Kath Latham was acting as correspondence secretary. At this time the majority of their games appeared to be against Manchester Ladies and as 'Pop' was now into his seventies perhaps the administration was becoming just a little too much for him.

The occasional defeat was also beginning to creep in too. On 5 June they lost their first match since 1949 at the hands of old rivals Manchester Ladies when they were beaten 2-1 after completing their second match of the day against the Manchester team. This brought to an end an unbeaten run of 96 games. Jean Lane said, *"We were very disappointed. We thought we deserved a draw."*

MATCH FACTS 1954

DATE	VENUE	TEAMS	RESULT
29 May	Nottingham	DK v Manchester	2-1

Scorers: Jean Lane 1 o.g.1

5 Jun	Pemberton	DK v Manchester	4-2

Scorers: Joan Burke 2, Yvonne Hamer 1, Jean Lane 1

5 Jun	Pemberton	DK v Manchester	1-2

Scorer: Joan Burke

19 Jun	Atherton	DK v Manchester	3-2

Scorers: Nancy Thomson 2, Jean Lane 1

3 Jul	Staffordshire	DK v Manchester	2-3

Scorers: Nancy Thomson 1, Alice Walmsley 1

12 Jul	Blackburn	DK v French	4-0

Scorers: Nancy Thomson 1, Amy Duxbury 1, Joan Burke 1, Jean Lane 1

14 Jul	Carlisle	DK v French	4-0

Scorers: Nancy Thomson 2, Jean Lane 2

15 Jul	Newcastle	DK v French	3-1

Scorers: Joan Burke 2, Jean Lane 1

17 Jul	Manchester	DK v French	5-1

Scorers: Joan Burke 2, Alice Walmsley 1, Jean Parnell 1, o.g.1

19 Jul	Bridlington	DK v French	3-2

Scorers: Jean Lane 1, Nancy Thomson 1, Joan Burke 1

22 Jul	Castletown IOM	DK v French	3-0

Scorers: Nancy Thomson 1, Jean Lane 1, Joan Burke 1

3 Aug	Leeds	DK v Manchester	3-2

Scorers: Joan Burke 3

2 Sept	Leyland	DK v Leyland	6-2

Scorers: Jean Lane 3, Alice Walmsley 2, o.g.1

Match Poster 1954

In 1955, Anthony Eden succeeded Winston Churchill after the latter's resignation as Prime Minister. Argentina ousted Juan Perón, and Rosa Parks began her equal rights campaign when she refused to sit at the back of a bus, breaking the Alabama segregated seating law between black and white citizens. James Dean died in a car accident and the first Disneyland was opened in California.

The 1955 season got off to a bad start for the Dick, Kerr Ladies when they suffered a heavy defeat to Manchester by 6-1. They were on the losing side again only a few weeks later when they again lost to Manchester by 3-2. Jean Lane said: *"Tom Bindottie, their manager, was the referee and he gave them a penalty. I didn't think it was."* A new signing this year was Joan Hall from Stockwell, London who was also an amateur athlete and AAA champion over a mile. She was so keen to play for the team that she travelled up from London every week and it would be 4 a.m. before she would arrive back at Euston station in the early hours of Sunday morning.

Later in the year they went on tour with a team from the Netherlands. It was the first time a women's team from Holland had played in England. They played a series of seven games and the Preston team were the victors on each occasion. They scored 33 goals during the tour, and conceded only nine. The scorers were: Jean Lane (12), Edna Broughton (8), Joan Hall (7), Alice Walmsley (2), Joan Clay (2), Joan Burke (1) and Barbara Widdows (1). During the tour Jean Lane was to score her 100th goal for the team and she said of the Dutch visitors, *"They were a very sporting team. In one game we had with them, one of our girls went off injured and we were down to ten players. They immediately let one of their players leave the field so that they didn't have an advantage over us."*

MATCH FACTS 1955

DATE	VENUE	TEAMS	RESULT
11 Apr	Middlesborough	DK v Manchester	1-6

Scorer: Alice Walmsley

?	Shevington	DK v Manchester	3-2

Scorers: Alice Walmsley 2, Jean Lane 1

?	Pemberton	DK v Manchester	2-3

Scorers: Alice Walmsley 2

?	Staffordshire	DK v Manchester	3-0

Scorers: Joan Hall 2, Jean Lane 1

9 Jul	Bilston	DK v Manchester	6-0

Scorers: Joan Hall 4 others ?

21 Jul	Castletown IOM	DK v Manchester	3-2

Alice Walmsley 2, Joan Hall 1

27 Jul	Bridlington	DK v Holland	3-0

Scorers: Jean Lane 2, Alice Walmsley 1

28 Jul	Sale	DK v Holland	3-1

Scorers: Edna Broughton 2, Jean Lane 1

30 Jul	Nelson	DK v Holland	4-0

Scorers: Jean Lane 2, Joan Hall 1, Joan Clay 1

2 Aug	Leeds	DK v Holland	6-3

Scorers: Joan Hall 3, Edna Broughton 1, Jean Lane 1, o.g. 1

3 Aug	Blackburn	DK v Holland	5-2

Scorers: Edna Broughton 2, Joan Hall 2, Jean Lane 1

4 Aug:	Castletown IOM	DK v Holland	4-0

Scorers: Jean Lane 3, Joan Burke 1

6 Aug	Preston	DK v Holland	6-3

Scorers: Jean Lane 2, Joan Hall 1, Joan Clay 1, Barbara Widdows 1, Edna Broughton 1

*Back row in white: Joan Clay, Pat Preece, Barbara Widdows, Yvonne Hamer,
Stella Briggs, Joan Hall*

Front in white: Joan Burke, Edna Broughton, June Gregson (gk), Jean Lane

At the end of 1955 'Pop' was taken ill and he relied heavily on Kath Latham to organise things for the team until he improved. She had been doing most of the paperwork over the past couple of years and was the obvious choice to take on the responsibility. By February of 1956 however, 'Pop's' health had deteriorated further. A week before their first match he had a relapse and Kath was left to make all the arrangements for the start of the new season and he agreed for Kath and team captain Stella Briggs to become joint acting managers because he was no longer fit to travel, but he still regarded himself as the team's official figurehead.

MATCH FACTS 1956

DATE	VENUE	TEAMS	RESULT
12 May	Blackpool	DK v Manchester	4-1

Scorers: Joan Hall 1, Edna Broughton 1, Joan Burke 1, Alice Walmsley 1

| 26 May | Shevington | DK v Manchester | 6-3 |

Scorers: Jean Lane 3, Joan Burke 1, Yvonne Hamer 1, an other 1

| 3 Jun | Hesketh Bank | DK v Manchester | 4-2 |

Scorers: Jean Lane 3, Joan Hall 1

| 9 Jun | St Helens | DK v Manchester | 4-1 |

Scorers: Alice Walmsley 2, Edna Broughton 1, Yvonne Hamer 1

| 16 Jun | Bilston (Staffs) | DK v Manchester | 1-0 |

Scorer: Joan Hall

| 16 Jun | Bilston | DK v Midland Ladies | 4-0 |

Scorers: Joan Burke 2, Yvonne Hamer 1, Doreen Gibbons 1

| 21 Jun | Leyland | DK v Manchester | 3-1 |

Scorers: Joan Burke 1, Joan Billington 1, Alice Walmsley 1

| 24 Jul | Nelson | DK v Manchester | 3-1 |

Scorers: Alice Walmsley 2, Joan Eckton 1

| 26 Jul | Castletown IOM | DK v Manchester | 4-4 |

Scorers: Joan Hall 3, Joan Burke 1

| 7 Aug | Bridlington | DK v Manchester | 4-2 |

Scorers: Jean Lane 2, Edna Broughton 1, Joan Burke 1

| 9 Aug | Castletown IOM | DK v ? | 3-1 |

Scorers: Yvonne Hamer 1, Alice Walmsley 1, Jean Lane 1

An article in the *Reveille* in 1956 claimed that there were 15 women's soccer teams in the country. For the match against Manchester Ladies played at Hesketh Bank, Kath invited Alice Cook, formerly Alice Kell, the first ever captain of the Dick, Kerr Ladies, to kick-off the game. The Preston team were the winners by 4-2.

In 1957, Althea Gibson became the first black player to win Wimbledon. Russia launched the first satellite, Sputnik 1, and four months later the space race began when the USA launched a smaller satellite. Elvis Presley starred in his first motion picture, Love Me Tender and Jean Lane became leading goal scorer for the Preston team for the fifth consecutive season.

Although 'Pop' was now seriously ill, he had heard that Edna Broughton was considering leaving the club again and he was most concerned at the prospect of losing her. He wrote to Edna on 26 February 1957 saying: *"I have really had another shock, and believe me I have had a few this last twelve months, one on top of the other. But I ask you Edna, while I live, you will carry on. You know what I think of you and you all know I have had a very serious illness that has taken all the starch out of me. Since November last, I never went out at all. Actually the Doctor would have liked me to pack up everything. I have not been able to look after my own business, never mind the football for a very long time. Mrs Frankland has had to look after me and on top of it all we both had the flu together. I wondered when it was all going to end. I have not conducted my business until last Friday, when I wrote Kathleen a list of our arrangements to date to send out to you all. I further owe you five shillings which I am sending to you now. Now Edna, forget about leaving us, while I am head you stay. But if one is ordered by a specialist and a Doctor to take an absolute and complete rest, what could I do? I just had to lay there in bed for over 3 weeks, and then get up and sit around, a most miserable thing for me as you will know. I enclose a postal order for 5 shillings which I have owed you far too long, and remember Edna, just this, I love my football and you know that as long as I am the manager I want my little star to stop with me, I cannot say more. It is to me a very good job I had arranged so much before I went to bed. No one has got even decent attention from me, reason was I was far too ill to reply to many questions from Italy, Sweden and Germany, they had to wait. There was nothing I could do to help. But take this as final I could not release you from my club. That is my regard for you."*

Alfred Frankland died on Wednesday, 9 October 1957. He was 75 years old. He had been taken ill again earlier in the year and his health was adversely affected by the sudden death of his wife in July, as it was she who had been nursing him at home. He was cremated at Carleton, near Blackpool. Whatever our conclusions about the man might be, there is no doubt that he was a wonderful advocate of women's football. He instilled a great sense of pride into his team and continually maintained their extremely high standards. His contribution to the success of the Dick, Kerr Ladies should never be underestimated. Without him they would not have achieved their iconic status. During his forty-year association with the Dick, Kerr Ladies, they had played 753 games of football. They won 703, drew 33 and lost only 17 games. They had also raised in excess of £150,000 for charity.

MATCH FACTS 1957

DATE	VENUE	TEAMS	RESULT
18 May	Shevington	DK v Manchester	2-1

Scorers: Jean Lane 1, Stella Briggs 1

1 Jun	Preston	DK v Manchester	4-3

Scorers: Joan Eckton 1, Jean Lane 1, Edna Broughton 1, Yvonne Hamer 1

25 Jul	Castletown IOM	DK v Manchester	3-1

Scorers: Jean Lane 1, Anne Lymath 1, Alice Walmsley 1

30 Jul	Bridlington	DK v Manchester	2-0

Scorers: Alice Walmsley 1, Edna Broughton 1

8 Aug	Castletown IOM	DK v Manchester	1-1

Scorer: Joan Hall

31 Aug	Chipping	DK v Manchester	6-1

Scorers: Joan Eckton 2, Jean Lane 2, Edna Broughton 1, Joan Burke 1

6 Sept	Belle Vue	DK v Manchester	1-0

Scorer: Joan Eckton

CHAPTER ELEVEN
THE FINAL WHISTLE

Kath Latham said that following the death of Alfred Frankland, his son Ron expected the team to fold. *"Of course we all objected to this, we wanted to carry on with the team and the girls called a meeting. As I had been doing quite a lot of the secretarial work for 'Pop', they asked me to take over officially as the new manager."* Kath willingly agreed to take on the new role and was initially helped by Doreen Gibbon who acted as assistant manager for several years. The job entailed a multitude of duties: dealing with all the correspondence, arranging matches, estimating and paying the team's expenses, contacting the widely scattered team members, and making sure they all arrived at the venue. Laundering the kit was a big job too, but was willingly tackled by Jean Lane's mother. In spite of all these administrative duties, Kath still found time to fulfil her role as organist and treasurer for the Church of England Chapel in her home town of Crawford. She began playing at the church when she was nine-years-old and had become an accomplished player and was a staunch member of the church all her life.

Kath went on to say, *"I don't know how 'Pop' used to run it because there were no books handed over to us. When I took over, there was nothing except for an old scrapbook and some photographs, and we even had to pinch those because Ron had destroyed everything. There was no correspondence, no address book, no record books, nothing, absolutely nothing. We didn't even know who the organisers of the matches were. We had to start from scratch. We had to rely on someone having some old programmes which had some information, then find a telephone directory for that area and hope they were listed. That's how I had to start because there was nothing left."*

Undeterred by the lack of information available, Kath and Doreen took on their new task in earnest. The search through all the old programmes proved successful and the 1958 season got underway at Shevington on 24 May against Manchester with the prodigal Joan Whalley returning to her beloved Dick, Kerr Ladies. The result was a 1-1 draw. The first team to play under their new Manageress was: Barbara Widdows, Ann Lymath, Pat Preece, Pauline Rimmer, Yvonne Hamer, Stella Briggs, Joan Whalley, Joan Burke, Jean Lane, Edna Broughton, Alice Walmsley

Yvonne Hamer played her last match for the team at the end of the season. Jean Lane said, *"We will all miss her, she is a great centre half."*

MATCH FACTS 1958

DATE	VENUE	TEAMS	RESULT
24 May	Shevington	DK v Manchester	1-1

Scorer: Edna Broughton

| 10 June | Accrington | DK v Accrington | 4-0 |

Scorers: Jean Lane 2, Edna Broughton 2

| 24 July | Castletown IOM | DK v Oldham | 0-4 |
| 30 July | Bridlington | DK v Accrington | 8-3 |

Scorers: Joan Whalley 3, Joan Hall 2, Edna Broughton 1, Jean Lane 1, o.g. 1

| 7 Aug | Castletown IOM | DK v Manchester | 1-1 |

Scorer: Joan Hall

| 9 Aug | Middleton | DK v Oldham | 2-4 |

Scorers: Edna Broughton 1, Pauline Rimmer 1

| 13 Aug | Clayton le Moors | DK v Accrington | 3-3 |

Scorers: Joan Whalley 2, Jean Lane 1

| 30 Aug | Chipping | DK v Manchester | 3-0 |

Scorer: Joan Hall 3

| 4 Sept | Manchester | DK v Manchester | 7-0 |

Scorers: Joan Hall 3, Joan Whalley 2, Jean Lane 1, Edna Broughton 1

The Manageress! Castletown, Isle of Man 1958

Back row: Barbara Prescott, Barbara Widdows, Ann Lymath, Pauline Rimmer, Pat Preece, Kath Latham

Front row: Joan Whalley, Irene Lydiate, Jean Lane, Edna Broughton, Doreen Espley, Joan Euxton

They had quite a number of games with Accrington Ladies until they folded and several of the Accrington players then came to join the Preston team. Kath recalled, *"They had tried to arrange some fixtures with us while 'Pop' was still alive, but for some reason he wouldn't let us play against them."* One of the players they inherited from Accrington was 16-year-old Val Walsh who was a very skilful player. Val's first love though was hockey and after a couple of seasons with them she returned to her hockey roots and went on to represent England and Great Britain 149 times and was later awarded an OBE. She was also twice winner of BBC televisions Superstars competition. Kath says, *"Matt Busby came to see one of our matches at Blackpool. He sat in the stands and remarked to the people sitting around him that Val was the best player he had ever seen in his life and if she had been a man, he would have signed her up there and then, to play for Manchester United! She was absolutely marvellous. After the match we were chatting to him and he asked how we went about obtaining our footballs. We told him we had to beg, borrow or steal them and just hope somebody would let us have one. The following week one arrived through the post. Matt Busby actually sent us a football! It had only been used once by the Manchester United players and we were all thrilled to bits because there was no way could we afford to buy our own. As I said, there was nothing handed over after 'Pop' died. I don't know how he ran things but I tried to get enough from the expenses to put a little bit to one side. We only had one football strip but eventually, over a couple of years, we managed to raise enough money to buy a second one. You couldn't ask the girls to pay for it although they had previously provided their own shirts and things and washed them themselves. The problem with that was if somebody didn't turn up to a match, you were a strip short, so after a while we kept all the kit and did the laundry to avoid that sort of thing happening."*

Under Kath Latham's guidance they played from May through to September. Kath said, *"We played at more places than 'Pop' did towards the end. Naturally he was getting older and he tended only to play Manchester and Littlewoods Ladies, unless on tour with the French team. When I was running things we would play Fodens from Cheshire and Handy Angles from the Midlands, as well as the other local fixtures. The Isle of Man was an annual fixture which was played during the French tour. They used to go by boat from Fleetwood on a Thursday morning, play the match on Thursday night, stay over, and come back on Friday. I suggested to the charity organisers in the Isle of Man that it might be cheaper if we flew from Blackpool in the morning, play the fixture and then fly back at night as it would save them the expense of overnight accommodation for two teams. We contacted Blackpool airport who said we could have a day flight but the departure time from Ronaldsway airport was 6 p.m., but that was the* same time we were due to kick-off so it was no good for us. But as Castletown was only five minutes from the airport, they eventually agreed to delay the flight until 9 p.m. The pilot used to come to the match so we always knew that the plane wouldn't go without us! It saved a lot of money in expenses and by doing it that way, the charity we were playing for asked us to play two games for them, one in July and one in August, so we got an extra fixture out of it. It was a mad rush though because Blackpool airport closed at 10 p.m."

Making her debut in the opening match of the new season was 14-year-old Freda Garth from Preston. She scored both goals in the team's 2-2 draw with Accrington Ladies. In July, Jean Lane tore some fibres in her side during the first minute of a match in the Isle of Man and was carried on to the plane on a stretcher for the journey home. She was fully recovered and back playing again in August. Nat Lofthouse kicked-off for them in their last match of the season.

MATCH FACTS 1959

DATE	VENUE	TEAMS	RESULT
9 June	Accrington	DK v Accrington	2-2

Scorer: Freda Garth

DATE	VENUE	TEAMS	RESULT
13 June	Preston	DK v Accrington	8-2

Scorers: Joan Hall 5, Jean Eckton 1, Joan Burke 1, an other 1

| 23 July | Castletown IOM | DK v Manchester | 4-0 |

Scorers: Jean Lane 2, Joan Whalley 1, Freda Garth 1

| 30 July | Castletown IOM | DK v Accrington | 3-0 |

Scorers: ?

| 3 Aug | Southport | DK v Benfica | 3-2 |

Scorers: Joan Burke 2, Glenis Cocker 1

| 6 Aug | Castletown IOM | DK v Manchester | 2-2 |

Scorers: Freda Garth 1, Val Walsh 1

| 12 Aug | Bridlington | DK v Lancashire | 5-1 |

Scorers: Joan Hall 3, Jean Lane 2

| 19 Aug | Bridlington | DK v Benfica | 4-2 |

Scorers: Joan Hall 1, Joan Whalley 1, Jean Lane 1, Freda Garth 1

| 25 Aug | Oswaldtwistle | DK v Accrington | 7-2 |

Scorers: Freda Garth 2, Joan Burke 2, Jean Lane 2, Mavis Glover 1

| 3 Sept | St Helens | DK v Manchester | 5-0 |

Scorers: Joan Hall 4, Joan Burke 1

| 10 Sept | Orrell | DK v Accrington | 3-0 |

Scorers: Joan Hall 2, Jean Lane 1

N.B Benfica Ladies were from the Manchester area.

In their new kit 1959

Back row: Kath Latham, Pat Preece, Irene Lydiate, Ann Lymath, Jean Gibson, Pauline Rimmer, Glennis Cocker, Doreen Espley

Front row: Joan Whalley, Joan Hall, Jean Lane, Freda Garth, Mavis Glover

"*We could still pull in the crowds*", said Kath, "*we would usually have three or four thousand spectators, probably more in the Isle of Man. There was one time when we played there we couldn't get to the ground because of the queue's of traffic. We had been at a function at the Marine Hall in Douglas and we couldn't get through. They said every coach on the island had been booked, they were all going to watch our game and we just couldn't get through. Then a policeman came up on a motorcycle and radioed somewhere and they just had to clear the road. We daren't delay the kick-off because of having to fly back, so we had a police escort to the match with the sirens going. We thought it was great.*

On many occasions though when we went somewhere new, you would get a lot of men turning up and there would be a lot of hilarity and a lot of remarks passed until we kicked-off. But they all changed their tune after a few minutes into the match. They would soon be shouting for one team or another, applauding the moves and everything. They would come to you at half time and admit that they had come for a laugh: they thought it was a huge joke. They didn't expect women to be able to play like that, but when you had Joan Whalley scoring from a corner and Jean Lane diving in and heading a ball from about a foot off the ground; give them their due, they did come and say afterwards how much they had enjoyed it. Then when we went back to places you would get the same people coming up to you saying, 'Oh we are glad to see you again, we wondered if you were coming back', and that was great for us to get that kind of recognition.

I always made sure there was somewhere we could call and have a drink after the game. It was something 'Pop' was always very much against until later on, just before he died. But we put our foot down and said we are stopping somewhere, we've given up our free time at weekends and we are entitled to enjoy ourselves. He always lost out on it because we would tell him we wouldn't come to the next match if he didn't let us stop.

I arranged quite a lot of matches for cancer research. In each case it was for a local committee and the proceeds went direct to that particular area. We went to Buckley in Flintshire, it was our first fixture there and it was a great success. After the game we were asked if we would play again the following year. It wasn't a very big place and after the match we went to this pub and the locals were all sat there with long faces, but the pub had a piano. Of course that was it, if there was a piano anywhere I just had to play it. I immediately went over and started playing and within half an hour the pub was full, it was absolutely packed, you couldn't move in there. You see, everybody used to sing, and my older sister Edi used to come with us, she had a marvellous voice and she would get them all singing. And of course the drinks were flowing and we all had a great night. So when we went back to play the match the following year, we called at the same pub after the game, and it was packed out. They were all there waiting for us! That's what used to happen. We would have a drink somewhere, and in those days there was nearly always a piano in the big room in a pub and we would have a good old sing song and draw the crowds, and it was just the same afterwards on the coach on the way home."

Jean Lane remembered fondly the after match singing sessions, and said, "We would all be singing and Kath would be playing the piano. She was a marvellous player, she could make a piano talk could Kath. We always used to sing a song called 'How can I leave you', and whenever I hear it now, it brings back so many happy memories."

How can I leave you though I know it's time to go
How can I leave you when I love you so
Eventide is falling, I must be on my way
All the world is calling, but my heart says stay
Faithful forever, my love will be a star
Shinning forever, everywhere you are.

Doreen Gibbon resigned as assistant manager after a disagreement with Kath Latham over team selection for the match at Bridlington on 20 July

1960. Margaret Empgrave filled the vacancy following her departure. Joan Hall married her boyfriend to become Mrs Joan Briggs.

MATCH FACTS 1960

DATE	VENUE	TEAMS	RESULT
4 June	Blackburn	DK v Accrington	8-4

Scorers: Joan Hall 6, Joan Burke 1, Freda Garth 1

| 23 June | Rainford | DK v Accrington | 9-3 |

Scorers: Joan Hall 5, Joan Burke 1, Freda Garth 1, Jean Lane 1, Ann Lymath 1

| 20 July | Bridlington | DK v Accrington | 8-2 |

Scorers: Joan Hall 4, Jean Lane 3, Freda Garth 1

| 28 July | Castletown IOM | DK v Accrington | 7-1 |

Scorers: Joan Hall 4, Pat Preece 1, Freda Garth 1, Jean Lane 1

| 1 Aug | Southport | DK v Benfica | 5-8 |

Scorers: Freda Garth 2, Val Walsh 1, Jean Lane 1, Joan Hall 1

| 3 Aug | Bridlington | DK v Accrington | 3-2 |

Scorers: Jean Lane 2, Freda Garth 1

| 6 Aug | Blackburn | DK v Accrington | 5-8 |

Scorers: Ann Lymath 2, Pat Preece 1, Lesley Caldwell 1, Mavis Glover 1

| 11 Aug | Castletown IOM | DK v Accrington | 5-0 |

Scorers: Jean Lane 3, Joan Hall 2

| 17 Aug | Bolton | DK v Benfica | 5-2 |

Scorers: Joan Briggs 4, Jean Lane 1

Sheila Porter scored two goals in her debut for the team on 10 June 1961. As Mrs Sheila Parker, she went on to become captain of England in the first recognised international match against Scotland in 1972. She won thirty two caps for her country and practically every other honour possible in women's football. Sheila continued to play football in the North West Women's Regional Football League up to the mid 1990s. She also qualified as a referee and officiated in both men's and women's matches in the North West of England. In 2013 Sheila was inducted into the Nation Football Museum Hall of Fame and received her award from Sue Lopez MBE.

Sheila Parker, Freda Garth and Lorraine Mckenna

MATCH FACTS 1961

DATE	*VENUE*	*TEAMS*	*RESULT*
21 Apr	*Oldham*	*DK v Oldham*	*1-1*

Scorer: Betty from Accrington

10 June	*Cleveleys*	*DK v Oldham*	*6-2*

Scorers: Sheila Porter 2, Joan Briggs 2, Sheila Whiteoak 1, Jean Lane 1

6 July	*St Helens*	*DK v Oldham*	*1-1*

Scorer: o.g.

14 July	*Rainford*	*DK v Oldham*	*3-1*

Scorers: Joan Briggs 1, Lesley Caldwell 1, Sheila Porter 1

7 Aug	*Blackpool*	*DK v Oldham*	*4-2*

Scorers: Freda Garth 2, Jean Lane 1, Joan Briggs 1

26 Aug	*Buckley*	*DK v Oldham*	*2-1*

Scorers: Freda Garth 1, Sheila Porter 1

A crowd of 5000 watched the match at Blackpool on 6 August 1962. Kicked off by The Kaye Sisters and refereed by Blackpool and England player, Jimmy Armfield, £300 was raised for charity. Alice Walmsley returned to the team that day and scored a goal to mark her comeback. At four months pregnant, Joan Briggs played her last game for the team at Bridlington on 9 August. Billy Bingham of Everton and Ireland was the referee for the game at Liverpool on 30 August.

Also in this year, the dinosaurs at the FA were to show the full extent of their opposition to the women's game when they stopped two games between Dick, Kerr's and Oldham Ladies from going ahead. The Welsh FA banned a game from taking place in Rhyl, with prospects of a 10,000 'gate of the year' at Rhyl's football ground. *The Daily Mail* reported that the idea of staging a female soccer 'derby' on a Welsh ground came from Mr Ken Hughes, vice-chairman of the Flintshire Fire Services Benevolent Fund. He was sure it would be a real winner with Whit Monday as the day chosen for the charity match. But when Mr Hughes wrote to the headquarters of the Welsh FA in Wrexham, he was told: *"Ladies Soccer: Nothing Doing."* Herbert Powell, the Secretary of the Welsh FA said, *"Rule 34 in our rule book prohibits ladies football on any ground affiliated to the association. We think that football is a man's game and that there is no place for lady players. It makes no difference that the game is out of the soccer season".* In the opinion of Mr Hughes, he felt that the Welsh FA, which had 30,000 male footballers on its books, *"ought to move with the times and give women players a chance to shine".* He said, *"I feel sure the ladies brand of soccer would be an eye-opener to the men. These girls are really talented".*

In Lancashire too, it was the same story. The LFA stopped the match from taking place at the British Legion ground, at Newton, near Wigan, also between Dick, Kerr's and Oldham Ladies, in aid of the Wigan Society for the Blind. The ground was also used by Wigan Rovers AFC who played in the Lancashire Combination League and they were told by the FA they would be in serious trouble, and even face suspension, if they allowed the game to go ahead. Despite the fact that the tickets had been printed and posters had been put up advertising the game, the FA refused to give way on the matter and the game was re-arranged to be played at Christopher Park, Wigan. A spokesman for the Blind Society was quoted in the *Manchester Evening News* saying: *"The reason given by the FA for their decision is that women are not allowed to play on any FA ground. In fairness, it should be understood that the Legion ground is only rented to Wigan Rovers, and in the opinion of the Newton British Legion, the FA have no jurisdiction whatsoever over the match."* He added, *"The LFA's* decision is archaic. It is a Victorian hangover." In their defence, Kath Latham wrote a letter to the press saying: "We are not interested what the FA said in 1921. This is 1962. The latest excuse is that women are the wrong shape to play football. Women who play cricket, hockey, tennis, bowls, golf and netball and take part in international swimming, are, as far as we know, the same shape as women who play football, so we contend this as a ridiculous excuse."

In spite of the FA's action, they attracted a crowd of several thousand, and after the match handed over a large cheque to the charity. Kath said, "Pat Phoenix (Elsie Tanner in Coronation Street) kicked-off the match and I think we probably had double the crowd because of all the controversy."

After the last match of the 1962 season, Kath presented trophies to five of the players. Freda Garth and Val Walsh for outstanding players of the season: Ann Lymath, leading goal scorer, Sheila Porter young player of the year, and Jean Lane as captain.

MATCH FACTS 1962

DATE	VENUE	TEAMS	RESULT
7 Apr	Sandbach	DK v Fodens	2-2

Scorers: Sheila Porter 1, Jean Lane 1

14 May	Rainford	DK v Oldham	6-3

Scorers: Ann Lymath 3, Joan Briggs 1, Sheila Porter 1, Jean Lane 1

11 June	Prescott	DK v Oldham	4-1

Scorers: Joan Briggs 1, Mavis Glover 1, Val Walsh 1, Carol Barber 1

24 June	Cleveleys	DK v Oldham	4-2

Scorers: Jean Lane 3, Ann Lymath 1

7 July	Colwyn Bay	DK v Oldham	8-4

Scorers: Ann Lymath 3, Sheila Porter 2, Jean Lane 2, Carol Barber 1

15 July	Oldham	DK v Oldham	0-1
21 July	Rainford	DK v Fodens	5-3

Scorers: Sheila Porter 2, Jean Lane 2, Margaret Scratchley 1

2 Aug	Bridlington	DK v Oldham	3-0

Scorers: Ann Lymath 2, Sheila Porter 1

6 Aug	Blackpool	DK v Oldham	4-1

Scorers: Jean Lane 1, Sheila Porter 1, Carol Barber 1, Alice Walmlsey 1

9 Aug	Bridlington	DK v Oldham	3-2

Scorers: Alice Walmsley 2, Sheila Porter 1

18 Aug	Buckley	DK v Oldham	8-4

Scorers: Sheila Porter 3, Ann Lymath 2, Val Walsh 2, Jean Lane 1

| 25 Aug | St Helens | DK v Oldham | 3-3 |

Scorers: Val Walsh 1, Ann Lymath 1, Jean Lane 1

| 30 Aug | Liverpool | DK v Oldham | 1-2 |

Scorer: Freda Garth

| 7 Sept | Wigan | DK v Oldham | 2-1 |

Scorers: Carol Barber 1, Jean Lane 1

By 1963 the tide was beginning to turn for the club. In their first match of the season, Fodens had in their line up no less than four former members of the Preston side; Joan Briggs, Edna Broughton, Alice Walmsley and Yvonne Hamer. They were beaten 3-1 at home. In the return match played at York, they only managed a 0-0 draw. At the end of the season, they once more had to advertise for new players, but it was becoming increasingly more difficult to recruit young blood to replace the older experienced players who had come to the end of their career with the team. Doreen (Taffy) Richards did return after an absence of over 10 years.

They were to suffer probably the biggest defeat of their entire history when they went down 7-0 to Manchester Corinthians. The next match saw some drastic changes in the team when Kath swapped everyone around. Kath said, *"They needed a shake-up but we didn't say anything. In the dressing room I started handing out the kit. Of course they never looked at their shirts, they just put them on. Then suddenly, Freda Garth said to May Newton, "You've got the wrong shirt on, you've got my shirt". So then they started looking at one another and the penny dropped. I said to them, right girls, big-shake up today. Nobody played in their own positions. There was Taffy who was in goal and we put all the forwards to defence and all the defence to attack. They thought it was a huge joke, so much so that they had a photograph taken with their backs to the camera! Fodens were laughing too, but we wiped the floor with them; our girls were queuing up to score. They played the best football they had played in years. They just went out and played a blinder. Fodens didn't know what had hit them."* The tactics worked wonders as they trounced Fodens by 6-1.

Preston Ladies 1963

Back row: Brenda Keen, Brenda Nicholson, Doreen Nield, Sheila Porter, Margaret Empgrave, Diane Gant, Lorraine Mckenna, Kath Latham

Front row: Margaret Penberthy, Joan Burke, Freda Garth, May Newton, Margery Giles

MATCH FACTS 1963

DATE	VENUE	TEAMS	RESULT
24 May	?	DK v Fodens	1-3

Scorer: Butch?

8 June	Barrow	DK v Fodens	1-1

Scorer: May Newton

15 June	Cleveleys	DK v Burnley	7-0

Scorers: Sheila Porter 2, Barbara Large 2, May Newton 1, Butch 1, Jean Lane 1

19 June	Liverpool	DK v Fodens	2-2

Scorer: Butch

29 June	York	DK v Fodens	0-0
13 July	Buckley	DK v Fodens	5-2

Scorers: May Newton 3, Barbara Large 1, Jean Lane 1

20 July	Rainford	DK v Ripley	5-0

Scorers: May Newton 1, Sheila Porter 1, Barbara Large 1, Jean Lane 2

4 Aug	Blackpool	DK v Fodens	2-1

Scorers: May Newton 1, Taffy Richards 1

| 10 Aug | Astley | DK v Accrington/Burnley | 12-3 |

Scorers: Jean Lane 5, May Newton 4, Barbara Large 1, Sheila Porter 1

| 14 Aug | Rainford | DK v Corinthians | 2-3 |

Scorers: Jean Lane 1, Dot Barnett 1

| 17 Aug | Wolverhampton | DK v Handy Angles | 7-6 |

Scorers: May Newton 2, Doreen 1, Di 1, Dot Barnett 1, Sheila Porter 1, Ann Lymath 1

| 31 Aug | Crawford | DK v Fodens | 3-2 |

Scorers: Doreen 2, Barbara Large 1

| 8 Sept | Manchester | DK v Corinthians | 0-7 |
| 14 Sept | Sandbach | DK v Fodens | 6-1 |

Scorers: Val Walsh 2, Barbara Large 2, Freda Garth 1, Dot Barnett 1

| Sept | Ripley | DK v Ripley | ? |
| 20 Oct | Crawford | DK v Homestead | 8-1 |

Scorers: Dot Barnett 2, May Newton 2, Barbara Large 2, Butch 1, Carol Barber 1

(There is no result documented for the September match with Ripley, but according to Jean Lane's diary, the seasons tally was: Played 16 Won 10 drawn 3 and lost 3, consequently this match can be considered a win)

In 1964 they played only 12 games but there was talk of making plans for the 50th anniversary of the club in 1967. It was a struggle for Kath to keep things going and in spite of advertising in the press, it was virtually impossible to find new players. The ones they did have all lived in different areas. The girls came from Preston, Wigan, Chorley, Southport and Manchester and Kath was never really sure if and when any of them would fail to turn up for a match. They could never get together for a training session and, in fact, the only time some of them met up was when they arrived in the changing room for the game. Yvonne Hamer, now Mrs Cooper, made a welcome return to the team for the match at Chesterfield on 22 August.

MATCH FACTS 1964

DATE	VENUE	TEAMS	RESULT
9 May	Crawford	DK v Fodens	6-0

Scorers: Val Walsh 3, May Newton 2, Butch 1

| 18 May | Litherland | DK v Fodens | 2-3 |

Scorers: Val Walsh 1, Freda Garth 1

| 23 May | Sheffield | DK v Fodens | 7-4 |

Scorers: Jean Lane 2, May Newton 2, Anne Lord 1, Di ? 1

| 3 June | Liverpool | DK v Fodens | 5-0 |

Scorers: May Newton 2, June ? 2, Dot Barnett 1

| 24 June | Preston | DK v Fodens | 2-0 |

Scorers: Jean Lane 2

| 11 July | Wolverhampton | DK v Handy Angles | 2-5 |

Scorers: May Newton 1, Jean Lane 1

| 18 July | Buckley | DK v Fodens | 3-1 |

Scorers: May Newton 1, Jean Lane 2

| 26 July | Blackpool | DK v Fodens | 6-0 |

Scorers: May Newton 4, Babs Large 1, Joan Spavin 1

| 2 Aug | Bridlington | DK v Fodens | 2-0 |

Scorers: Val Walsh 1, Freda Garth 1

| 8 Aug | Colwyn Bay | DK v Fodens | 3-2 |

Scorers: Babs Large 1, Freda Garth 1, Dot Barnett 1

| 22 Aug | Chesterfield | DK v Handy Angles | 9-0 |

Scorers: Joan Tench 3, May Newton 2, Alice Walmlsey 1, Babs Large 1, Yvonne Cooper 1, o.g.1

| 19 Sept | Sandbach | DK v Fodens | 8-3 |

Scorers: May Newton 4, Jean Lane 2, Val Walsh 1, Joan Spavin 1

In 1965 they had only three fixtures arranged, all of which were against Handy Angles from the Midlands. The first game they drew 4-4. In their second match they only had nine players during the first half, but finished the game with ten players. They still won by 5-1. The last match of the 1965 season was on 21 August. Did fate play a hand in what turned out to be the last ever game in this famous club's history? The first score line in those far off days of 1917 was a 4-0 victory and fittingly, they ended in the way they had begun. They won their final game by 4-0.

MATCH FACTS 1965

DATE	VENUE	TEAMS	RESULT
29 May	Crawford	DK v Handy Angles	4-4

Scorers: Jean ? 2, Jean Lane 1, Joan Spavin 1

| 8 Aug | Blackpool | DK v Handy Angles | 5-2 |

Scorers: Pat Catterall 1, Doreen ? 1, Babs Large 1, Kath Lear 1, Joan Spavin 1

| 21 Aug | Chesterfield | DK v Handy Angles | 4-0 |

Scorers: Jean ? 1, Pat Catterall 3

No-one knew at this stage that this was to be their last match. Jean Lane wrote in her diary: *After the match, our last one this season, Kath told me that next year I shall be vice captain to Taffy and the year after, captain in the 50th year of the team's existence.* But later in the year all the players received a letter from Kath saying that the club was to fold owing to the lack of players. Jean Lane said in her diary: *At the end of the year, 1965, Preston Ladies FC (late Dick, Kerr's), ceased to be owing to the shortage of players. It was felt by the manager to bring this about after 48 years, so that the name of Preston Ladies would be remembered as one of the top women's teams in the world, and one which kept all appointments and fielded a full team each match. This is the end of a chapter in my life and the end of a great ladies team. I now have very happy memories to look back on often.*

Kath said, "We really wanted to carry on until 1967 so that the team would have been in existence for 50 years, but it was becoming increasingly impossible to find new players. The players we did have were scattered so far apart and some of them could be unreliable. We never knew if someone would fail to turn up. We were frightened of arriving somewhere and not having 11 players. It took all the enjoyment out of it and it wasn't fair to the organisers of the charities after all the time and effort they had put in to stage the matches. If the players had been more reliable, we would probably have carried on for years."

There must have been a great sadness among them all, especially the older members of the team who would never have the opportunity to play again. The support from the public had never waned and it was a very difficult decision for Kath to make. "I was very upset about it," she said, "but if I take anything on, it has to be run properly, and I tried to be fair to everybody and make a good job of it. I felt responsible. If we were booked to play a particular match with a particular organisation, it was our responsibility to turn up with a full team and it just wasn't happening any more. We advertised, we had all sorts of publicity, and a few girls came along but they would never have made footballers if they had played till they were 90! So we didn't really have any alternative."

So that was it. The end of an era, and a huge chapter in the history of this truly remarkable team came to an inevitable close. After all the glory, all the cheers, the euphoria and the fame, the end came rather quietly and a giant was laid to rest. Throughout their incredible history, they received over 160 civic receptions, and the official record now states that they raised somewhere in the region of £180,000 for charity. But by today's value's, that figure has been estimated to be worth around £10 million!

Their playing record reads: **Played 833, won 759, drawn 46, lost 28.** They scored over **3,500** goals and had **less than 500** scored against them. Yet somehow, in spite of all this, they still appear to be football's best kept secret.

However, here are some of the many achievements, they can lay claim to being the first to ever do. They were the first organised women's club side to, wear shorts (1917). Transfer a player to their club (Molly Walker 1918). Play an international match (1920) Travel to Europe to take part in a soccer tour (1920). Play a match at night under artificial light (1920). Play with a white football (1920). Play in front of 53,000 spectators (1920). Complete a run of at least 74 straight victories and total at least 107 matches unbeaten (1922). Cross the Atlantic for another soccer tour (1922). Have the President of the United States kick off a match (1922). Complete a remarkable run of well over 300 games without defeat before losing to the Belgian team (1934). Play for the championship of the world (1937). Have in Lily Parr probably the all time leading goal scorer with around a 1000 goals to her tally. Have a female manager (1957) and raise more money for charity than any other football team in the world.

Jean Lane emotionally recalled her years with the team saying, *"It was a privilege to play for them. They talk today about what it means to put on an England shirt, but it's no more a privilege for them than it was for us to wear a Dick, Kerr shirt, they were a great team."*

In 1966 England won the world cup and football mania swept the country. Suddenly *everyone* wanted to play football and there was no shortage of girls wanting to take up the game too. But it was just a little too late for the Dick, Kerr Ladies. Everything has a life and they had had theirs, their time was now over. However, progress was slowly being made and the Women's Football Association was formed in 1969. The FA finally gave way to public opinion and eventually recognised women's football in 1971. It had taken fifty very long years to reach this turning point and the WFA was granted County status. The WFA administered all its own affairs until 1993 when it was disbanded and the FA took over responsibility for the development of women's football.

But it would be many years before any significant progress would be seen to be made. An underlying negative attitude toward women playing football has been woven into British society since the injustice of the FA ban in 1921 and in many respects it is still with us today. The FA only seem to be interested in the years since they have administered the game, they seldom acknowledge its past. Despite that, we have a glittering legacy to cling on to and a history so very rich that it deserves to live on forever. An immense debt of gratitude is owed to all those wonderful women who fought so courageously against all adversity, to play the beautiful game of football for its own sake. They really were 'In a League of Their Own!'

CHAPTER TWELVE

JOAN WHALLEY

I first met Joan Whalley at her home in Carnforth on a wet summer evening in July 1992. She told me she wasn't used to talking much anymore as she had become something of a hermit during her years living alone and apologised if her voice became '*a bit croaky*'. I didn't quite know what to expect, but once we started chatting she shared with me such a wealth of fascinating tales that had been hidden away in her memory for so long that I actually ran out of tape!

Joan played for the Dick, Kerr Ladies for almost 20 years. She signed for them when she was just fifteen-years-old and she said that following her joining the team there were reporters at the front door every time she came home from school.

Joan Whalley

"*I was the only girl round where I lived who played football,* said Joan. "*I had heard of the Dick, Kerr Ladies and I used to wonder how you got to play for them. Then, one day I went to visit an Aunt who lived in Fulwood and she asked me to go to the fruit shop round the corner to get some apples. When I got there I didn't realise it was Frankland who was serving me, but somehow we got talking about football. I said I really wanted to join this Dick, Kerr Ladies team because I played football but didn't know how to get in touch with them. 'Well,' he said 'you've come to the right place, my name is Alfred Frankland, I am the manager of the Dick, Kerr Ladies team.' After I met him I went dashing home of course and rushed into the house shouting, 'Mother, Mother, I've met Mr Frankland, Dick, Kerr's manager and I might be going to play for them.'*

Training on Moor Park 1937

Joan Whalley, Edith Hutton & May Helme

Joan realised her dream and made her debut for the Dick, Kerr Ladies at Roundhay Park, Leeds, on Coronation day, 12 May 1937. She said, "*There was a big celebration to commemorate the coronation of King George VI and there was a large crowd there. It was fantastic. I was at the end of the line when we all marched out on to the field. They played the national anthem and all the crowd were cheering. It was wonderful: it was out of this world. I think I scored that day, I'm not sure, but I know I was a very happy person.*"

Joan Whalley was born in Preston on 18 December 1921 and was probably one of the best women footballer's of her generation. She was always a bit of a tomboy and loved to be out playing football with the lads any time she could. Joan said that even before she was born, her Dad was convinced she was going to be a footballer. '*He used to put his hands on my mum's tummy to feel me kicking and he'd say*', "*With all the kicking going on in there, this one must be a footballer.*" He bought her first pair of football boots for her when she was just five-years-old.

She went to Deepdale Modern School at the same time as young lad named Tom Finney. They were good friends and would often play football together on Waverley Park. Joan recalled, *"There was one time when I had a septic finger and my mum dressed it with a hot poultice and put my arm in a sling. Tom had broken his arm and he had a sling as well. One day he called for me and said, 'Shall we go for a kick around Joan?' "Yes," I said, "come on lets go." So off we went to the park, both of us with our arms in a sling, kicking a ball about, we must have looked a right pair. We must have only been twelve or thirteen at the time. I used to go to birthday parties at his house when we were kids and I would say to him, "what do you want to do most Tom?" "I want to play for North End" he said. I told him I wanted to play for the Dick, Kerr Ladies. Well eventually I did get to play for Dick, Kerr's and he got to play for North End so we both got what we wanted. But of course, as we grew up our lives took different paths and we didn't see one another again until years later at one of our matches played in Kirkham. We always had a famous person to kick-off or referee at our games and they invited Tom to be our guest celebrity for the day. They were taking him down the line, introducing him to all the players and officials. When they reached me, I put out my hand to shake hands with my old friend and I said with a big smile, "Hiya champ". He smiled back at me and said, "Hiya Champ". It was a lovely moment. It was the first time I'd seen him since he began playing for North End and I started playing for Dick, Kerr's. I always admired Tom because he never got big headed about his success. His head always stayed the same size, so it meant he kept his feet right. I always said that if your head gets too big, your feet will get out of proportion. You should never get big headed about football."*

Joan and Tom both played on the wing and it was said at the time that England could boast the best two right-wingers in the country, male and female. Joan was an excellent player and was dubbed Preston's other great winger, but in keeping with her own philosophy, she too always kept her feet in proportion.

Their football lives were something of a parallel. They both achieved their dream of playing for their chosen team at the same age, they both played on the wing and were very good at their craft, but their personal lifestyle and rewards from their careers could not be further apart. He joined Preston North End as a fifteen-year-old amateur in 1937 and was to receive all the recognition that a successful professional footballer could achieve and his status in the city is legendary. For almost a quarter of a century and over 600 games for club and country, (76 appearances for England) Tom Finney was never booked. As well as being a top class footballer he also ran his own successful plumbing business in Preston. Long after his retirement from the game, his legacy at

237

Preston North End lived on and he was President of the club. A statue based on the famous 'Splash' photograph has been dedicated to him and erected outside the ground. The main road outside Deepdale has been re-named Sir Tom Finney Way in his honour and a stand inside the stadium also bears his name. He even has the distinction of having a public house named after him too! In 1961 he was awarded the OBE, in 1992 the CBE, and in 1998 he joined that elite band of footballers when he finally received what many believed to be a long overdue knighthood.

By contrast, and like many of her team mates, Joan worked as a nurse at Whittingham Hospital for ten years and during some of that time, she lived at Grimsargh and there was many a Sunday morning when the team could be seen playing football on the village green. She started work as a conductress (*clippie*) for Ribble buses in 1950 and was a familiar figure in and around Preston during this period. Her love of football was almost tangible and she was eager to share her memories and relive her days with the Dick, Kerr Ladies.

'In my early days with the team, Annie Lynch played inside left and she was a marvellous player. She was dazzling. She used to dribble round people like you've never seen anybody do and with Lily Parr at outside left, they were a marvellous combination on the wing, nobody could beat them. They used to cross the ball over to our centre forward, Edith Hutton and she was really good with her head. It didn't matter what angle the ball came in, you knew that she could get there. Parr was crossing them over, Lynch was dribbling and passing. It was wonderful stuff! Lily Parr had a kick like a mule, and the longer the game went on in wet weather, the heavier the ball became. But it never bothered Parr, she took the left corner kicks and everything, she was a marvellous player. She reminded me a bit like Chris Waddle; a bit lazy. He used to look like a lumbering farm lad to me, like he never seemed to rush at anything; he had a lumbering gait. Well, Parr was like that. She never used to rush at things but she had a brilliant left foot.

Often when we travelled to play a game somewhere, we would be shown round a factory or a mill, or some other kind of works. There was one time we went to play a match in South Wales and while we were there the team were to be shown round a women's prison. Stella Briggs and I weren't allowed to go because we weren't old enough, you had to be eighteen. So they dropped us off at Madame Tussauds. Well what a performance that was because we got lost in there and ended up getting locked in. We couldn't get out and we were sweating bricks. We weren't scaredy types, but when you get locked in those places, they look pretty real do those waxwork dummies and they all seemed to be looking at us! Poor old Stella and I, we seemed to be locked in for ages before they came for us. 'Pop' was there with his watch in and out of his pocket, saying, "Where the hell have you been?" We said; where the hell could we go? We couldn't go anywhere because we were locked in!

Another funny story was when we went over to the Isle of Man. We used to go over by boat and the journey took something like four hours. Some of the girls were sea sick and it was a real carry on, but there would be a coach laid on to run us to our hotel. When we first went over on the boat they started putting us in these big posh hotels along the front. We were playing a game against the French team and they put us up in a big beautiful hotel called the Metropole, very posh and all that. Well, our gang were all working class girls, none of the upper classes amongst them, and they put us in this beautiful hotel. When we arrived, we had an hour or two to have a look around the shops and get some souvenirs for home then the game would kick off at 7 p.m. at Castletown on the north of the island. We'd had a good day and when we walked in our bedrooms at the Metropole, this beautiful hotel, when we turned our beds down to get in, there was a pair of manx kippers lying on everybody's pillow! One of the girls had bought a box of kippers and placed a pair on everyone's pillow in every room, and you couldn't get rid of the smell. Needless to say the management weren't very pleased and we never stayed in that hotel again. I think we shot our bolt at the Metropole!

Horse drawn tram, Isle of Man. French and Preston teams

There was a big place called the Villa Marina where they had all these outdoor shows and at the time, Ivy Benson was a famous ladies dance band leader, she had an all girl band, and they struck up quite a good rapport with the older girls in our team. Ivy and her girls used to come along and join our gang because they were such a 'rum' crowd you know, they were full of fun. You've never heard of the things they did, and Ivy would come along with all her gang and they'd have a right royal night with them all. Mr Frankland was strict and he wouldn't let us younger ones go to any of these drinking sessions. Stella and I were always packed off to bed. I never could drink though, two beers and I was under the table.

The Ivy Benson Band

We didn't play on league grounds you know, the FA would never allow it, but we would play anywhere we could. We would play on farmer's fields if we had to and even then we could get a crowd of 5000 turn up to watch us. One time, in the 1950's, we were playing at the Garstang show. They set the ropes round the pitch and the spectators were standing by but where I played down the right wing, where I had to take the corner kicks from, a cow had been there before me and there was the biggest cow pat you had ever seen in your life, right there in the corner. The crowd were cheering and I didn't know what was going on at first until I got up the top end and then I could see the thing. They were all waiting for the very first corner kick to be taken. So of course when it did come I looked at the linesman asking could I put the ball over a bit, but he said it had to go on the spot. So I had to put the ball right in the centre of the cow pat. I think they had

240

purposely led that cow there to do it! So I stepped back and I took the kick. Well naturally I was on my backside, right in the cow pat, I was covered in the stuff!! And the crowd cheered and roared, it was brilliant.

I never had a holiday. My two weeks off work every year were taken up with a football tour. It was a holiday to me of course because I loved playing football, but 'Pop' always arranged for the summer fortnight to bring the French team over. The French, Dutch and Belgian teams all came over to play these tours every year and we had a wonderful time touring, it was great. We were seeing the world and playing football too. It was a great holiday! The French teams that came over to play against us were very excitable you know. They're like that the French, aren't they? They were Oooh La La-ing all over the place. But they were brilliant, they used to draw the crowds, they were beautiful girls. Our lot came in all shapes and sizes but the French girls had lovely figures, they were like models.

French team & the tour bus, 1949.

Alfred Frankland, Margaret Thornborough and Lily Parr at rear.

When we were on the coach travelling back from a match, they used to get 'Pop' to stop at a pub. He didn't really like it, he didn't want the girls having a drink, but Lily Parr would shout, "It's time Pop, time we stopped." There were two or three of us played a mouth organ and Nancy Thomson played the accordion. All the way home we used to be playing and everybody was singing. Annie Lynch was a marvellous singer, she and her friend used to harmonise all the old songs. We had a brilliant time. One time we had been to play a match in Workington so it would be late at night when we were getting home. We always had the same driver on our bus, his name was Tommy, and whenever we wanted to stop for a drink or go to the toilet, someone would shout, "Bispham", and Tommy would always stop for us. Well, after this match in Workington someone shouted, "Bispham Tommy", and he pulled up at a pub. 'Pop' was saying: "Now girls, we'll not be stopping long." The girls of course had other ideas and all the older players stopped quite a while having a few beers. 'Pop' was trying to hurry them along and when he finally got them all out, we set off again. They were all quite tipsy and Parr was well away. I don't know how many she'd had but after we had been travelling about five miles or so, Parr shouts, "Stop this bloody bus." I always sat at the front near Tommy and I said to him, "There's something wrong, Parr's shouting to stop the bus." Tommy pulled over at the roadside and Parr said, "I'll have to get out I'm going to be sick." After a while we all got back on the bus and after travelling another five miles or so, Parr shouts again, "Stop this bloody bus, stop this bloody bus." "Not again," said Tommy. So he pulled over to the side of the road and Parr said to him, "You'll have to go back, I've left my bloody false teeth!" So, Tommy turned the bus around and he asked me if I could remember where we had stopped. I had a good idea, so off we went driving down the road looking for a pile of sick and Parr's teeth! And would you believe it but we actually found them! We wrapped them up in some paper for her and put them in her pocket. It was a while before she lived it down I can tell you!

One game that stands out in my mind is when I ended up playing a game for Wales. We were on tour with the French team and the French were to play against Wales. For some reason they said Wales could have three of our players and the French could have three. The Welsh chose me and played me at centre forward. I wore a green shirt with a big red dragon across the back. I thought the dragon was wonderful, I loved it. They told me not to speak during the game because of course I didn't have a Welsh accent. They said, "don't open your mouth, don't say anything, keep your mouth shut". That wasn't a problem for me at all because I didn't speak much when I was playing. I had a really good game that day and I scored a hat-trick for Wales. As soon as the referee blew the final whistle the crowd rushed on to the pitch, grabbed me and lifted me up on their shoulders. All these Welsh blokes were slapping me on the back saying, "Well done girl, well done, what a great game." I was just laughing and smiling, I daren't open my mouth and they took me right up to the dressing room door. I was doing nothing but grin the whole time because I had scored three goals but when I got into the dressing room I asked one of the girls to help get my shirt off. Being blonde, I had very fine skin and I daren't move because it felt like all the skin was peeling off my back. I was red raw with all the slapping and there were finger marks all down my back to my waist. When I got home my mum was asking how we had gone on. I told her all about it then asked if she would put some cold cream or something on my back. When she saw it she said, "My God, I've never seen a back like that in all my life." Now, when I watch them on television at Wembley on Cup Final day, and see them all going up the stairs to receive their medals and everyone is slapping them on their back, it makes me cringe to remember it.

There was only one team that really gave us a game in those days and that team was Bolton. They had Nellie Halstead, the Olympic runner on their side and whenever she got the ball there was nothing on this earth could catch her, never mind stop her! She couldn't half run, and she could take the ball with her too. She was a fantastic person; she was marvellous.

I remember one particular goal I scored; it was the finest shot I ever made in my life. We were back in our own half and our goalie kicked the ball out to one of our half backs, who then passed it to me. I could only have been a yard over the half way line, just where the centre spot is. Well, the ball came to me just right and I thought; marvellous. I took one look at their keeper and she was just a bit off her line and I just lifted my foot and the ball sailed right up in the air. I stood watching it and was thinking, "get in, go on, get in!" It went way over the keeper's head and dipped just under the bar in the far corner of the net. Nobody could have got it. The crowd went mad, I was thrilled to have scored from there, it was brilliant.

I was lucky when I was playing because I never really had any injuries. I put my cartilage out and odd bits like that but they just pushed those back. 'Pop' always used to tell the girls to go to his house for a soda bath. They were marvellous for getting rid of all your aches and pains. You get the bath water nice and hot and put a couple of tea cups of ordinary washing soda into the bath and have a good long soak in it. Don't rub yourself because the soda will bring your skin off, just swill the water all over and soak for about half an hour. When you've finished, pat yourself dry and when you've done that, if you have anyone who can give you a gentle massage with a bit of warm olive oil, it'll work wonders. When you get up the next day, all your aches and pains will have disappeared.

A friend in Bolton once invited me over to have what she called, 'a proper soda bath' from the trainer of Bolton Wanderers FC. She said, "He will show you how it's done, he puts the footballers through it and he is really good with it." When we got there, he ran a bath while his wife was hovering about in the background and he said, "If you are nervous keep your panties on and get in this bath but don't ever try this on your own, you must have it done with someone who is qualified to supervise the procedure." He had put 1½lbs of washing soda in the water, (2lbs for the men) and told me to just lay there. His wife was there with a stopwatch, it's as drastic as that! It was six minutes for a woman and eight minutes for a man. He was swilling the water all over my body and the sweat was stinging me, it was like being in a sauna. Next thing, his wife clicked the stopwatch and said, "Right, six minutes." He told me to get out and when I put my hands on the side of the bath to get out, I couldn't move. I told him I couldn't get up and he started laughing. He was a great big burly fella with big muscles and he just lifted me out of the bath, put me on a table and covered me with a great big bath towel. He must have used about six towels putting them on and patting me dry and the sweat was pouring off me, I was steaming hot. I thought, Dear God, what has he put in it?

When I finally dried off he dusted me all over with talcum powder, wrapped me up in a light blanket and put me into bed. His wife brought me a nice cup of hot sweet tea and said, "Drink that, then you are going to sleep for four hours." There wasn't an ounce of energy left in me and I couldn't believe it. When I woke up he asked me how I felt and I said, to put it bluntly, absolutely knackered. He told me I would feel like that for at least another five days. I couldn't believe it, but he knew we had a game the following Saturday and he had planned it so that I had five complete days before the next match. I was tired all week because of it but come the match on Saturday, nothing could stop me. Three goals no messing, it was brilliant stuff, I played a blinder. His soda bath certainly did the trick.

There was never really any rivalry at our club we all played for each other, but rightly or wrongly, I always had the feeling that Margaret Thornborough never really liked me. I've always got on with people where ever I've been but the very first time I met her she seemed quite cool and distant. I tried to shrug it off and I thought she'd be alright when she got to know me, but she never was. Even when we all worked together at Whittingham Hospital it was just the same. There was one occasion when a Saturday match came up and everyone else had managed to get the day off except me and I couldn't get a change of shift from anywhere. I had been all round the girls asking them to swap days off, I even tried to bribe them, I tried everything, but I couldn't get that day off for love nor money. The other girls in the team asked what I was going to do and I told them I was just going to take my chances and have the day off. They didn't think I should risk it and thought there would be hell to play when I went back, but I just said, to hell with it, I don't care, it'll be worth it. I'm not missing this match. I had never missed a game before and I wasn't going to miss one now. I took the day off, played the match, played a blinder in fact and scored six goals. It was one of those days when *everything went right. I went in to work the next day and I was waiting for the bombshell but nothing happened. It was a relief to learn that Matron was off for a couple of days, and I thought, brilliant, I might just get away with it.*

On the Monday, the match report was in the paper, it was quite a big article and was all about this brilliant performance by Joan Whalley scoring six goals. On Tuesday when I went in to work, the ward sister came to tell me that Matron wanted to see me in her office. I thought, oh hell she's back, this is it. When I went in to her office I was shaking from head to foot. In those days Matron's were like dragons and my stomach was turning over and over. But I thought, never mind, I don't care, at least I played football, but I did think I would lose my job. I really thought she would give me the sack. I walked in her office and stood at her desk. She pushed this newspaper cutting across to me and said, "Read that." There was a silence in the room and you could feel the tension. I pretended I hadn't seen it before and started reading it. All the time my stomach was churning over and she said, "You had a good game". My knees were knocking and I was in a terrible state, she must have been able to see I was terrified. I said, "Yes Matron". "Well", she said, "I am not going to do anything about it, I am not going to put you on suspension, I am not going to do anything at all." I couldn't believe my ears. The look on my face must have been priceless. It seems someone had put the article in an envelope and left it on her desk for her to read. "I do not like anonymous letters", she said, "and if the person concerned did not have the courage to put their name to the bottom of this, I do not wish to know anything about it." She pushed it to one side and said, "You can go". I had never been so relieved in all my life. I can never be sure exactly who it was, but whoever did put that article in her office did me a big favour. If Matron had found out any other way about me taking the day off, I dread to think what would have happened.

Away from football, Joan's other love in life was her animals and her home had become something of an animal sanctuary. She was well known for the work she did with stray animals and every night when she arrived home from work there would be some child standing on her doorstep with tears streaming down their cheeks and a tiny furry object wrapped up in a blanket. *"Please Joan, can you take it, my Dad says it has to go."* Dogs, cats, rabbits, you name it, they brought it and not only to find new homes for unwanted pets, but 7 o'clock seemed to be surgery time. Her home was just like a vet's surgery: bathing and bandaging cut legs on dogs and cats. De-lousing flea ridden pets and doctoring them up as best she knew how. All the kids came from a big housing estate where there was no money. They couldn't afford vet fees, so each week it would cost Joan a small fortune replacing ointment, bandages and worm tablets etc. Her house was full to overflowing and at one point she had nine dogs, six grown cats, seventeen kittens, one tortoise, two budgies and two rabbits that all had to be fed and cared for. She would write large notices and display them in her front windows - *"Good homes for puppies, good homes for kittens."* There was always someone standing outside her home reading her notices.

It wasn't until her football days were over that she sought a new life, on what she fondly called *'her mountain'.* It was there that Joan chose to *'drop out'* from society and live a secluded and lonely existence. Her actions were prompted after a vicious and savage attack by a cruel and mindless thug on her beloved dog Hobo. It was this despicable act that led to Joan leaving her home to seek a life of isolation. She returned home from work one day to discover Hobo, a crossbred Alsatian bitch, laying in the back yard in a pool of blood having been slashed with a knife. The yard was like a slaughterhouse. From her head to her ribs she had been cut from underneath and there was a deep gaping hole. Joan said, *'I was sure that if I had taken her to the vet she would never have survived the journey, so I decided the best thing to do was to bandage all her wounds and get her warm. She was cold and had lost a lot of blood. I tore up sheets and bound her body then I sat beside her on the rug with her head on my knee. I daren't leave her alone while I went the half a mile to the phone box to call the vet, so I just sat there, holding her and talking to her. She knew I was with her and wouldn't leave her.'* Joan kept an all night vigil comforting her faithful pal and in the early hours of the morning, Hobo finally slipped away. She was heartbroken.

After Hobo's brutal and tragic death, Joan was determined to step-up her search for an isolated farmhouse. She felt she had to get all her animals away from that house to the safety and peace of the countryside. She said, *'I wanted to find a place where I could escape from this world of cruelty.'* She wanted to be alone with only her animals for company and she advertised every week in the local papers, - *'Lady with dogs requires semi-derelict, isolated cottage or farmhouse, Prepared to do it up.*

Joan felt that life was intolerable. Each time she left the house she was sick with worry at what she might find on her return. She spent a fortune on advertising in newspapers and had just about given up any hope of escaping when her prayers were answered. She finally found the perfect place to rent in an isolated spot on top of the Belmont Moors, near Bolton. It was during the summer of 1975 that she went to live on *'her mountain'*, in a very run down cottage that had none of the things we take for granted today. There was no heating or hot running water, no bath, toilet, sink, cooker or fridge, and she had only one cold water tap which would often freeze up in the winter time.

Her only luxury was an electricity supply which consisted of two electric lights, one kettle and a black and white television. These were her only home comforts.

So Joan began her life in a remote wilderness with only her animals for companionship. She lived in a semi-derelict cottage 1500 feet above sea level. It was about a mile along an unadopted dirt track to the main road and two miles from the nearest bus stop. Living there she said, was like going back in time a hundred years. *'I had to give up a lot of what the world calls luxuries. Central heating, hot water, etc., up there it was back to nature. In winter when the snow was frozen solid, all six foot deep of it, I had to drag sledges of food, dog food, coal, calor gas and everything else I required, up the one mile dirt road. I spent hours pulling the sledge up the hill, but we all survived. I had to saw logs of wood when my calor gas didn't arrive and cook on the fire. I had to smash the ice in the water trough outside when my cold water tap was frozen, but every night after tea, when I closed the curtains, built up a big roaring fire and all the dogs and cats were sprawled out in front of it, I knew it was all worth it, for there we had peace. All my animals were safe.'* Joan named her home, OLCOTE Animal Sanctuary. OLCOTE was her abbreviation for *Our Little Corner of the Earth.*

Regrettably, and after much soul searching, Joan was forced to leave *'her mountain'* in 1988 when she was 67 years old. She had a nasty fall on the ice and suffered a serious injury to her hip which made it almost impossible to continue getting vital supplies up to her home. *'It was very difficult for me to make the decision to leave. I had to find new homes for all my animals and it broke my heart to part with them, but I took comfort in knowing they would all be well cared for. It was a sad day when I left the mountain, I feel as though that's when my life ended. I can't have animals where I live now but I'm surrounded by pictures of them. I owned my own house before I went up on the mountain and I used to earn a good wage to be able to keep everything going. I haven't got two ha'pennies to rub together now, I've spent all my lot on my animals but we've all been very happy. I'm a real pauper now you know, I've bugger all, nothing in my life.*

When you are young your life is full and you never have a minute, but when you get older and there's not so much in your life anymore, well, I drift back into the past and I relive all the happy times when I played for the Dick, Kerr Ladies. It keeps me cheerful because I never go out anymore. As I said, I'm a bit of a hermit now. But I've had a wonderful life: the games we played, the travelling and being part of a team and even though we were never allowed to play on League grounds, there were always thousands of people who turned up to watch us play. There are so many wonderful memories. We had a great time, it was a wonderful life and I don't regret one minute of it. If I had my time over I would do it all again.'

CHAPTER THIRTEEN
INTO EXTRA TIME

The Dick, Kerr Ladies story has taken me on an incredible journey of discovery and I have met some truly wonderful women who have become my own 'extended family'. However, as in all families, there are painful goodbye's to encounter as we learn to face life's inevitable conclusion. But through all of this I have witnessed the unbreakable bond that exists between these very special ladies which still keeps them all together in a unique way. In many cases it lasted for the rest of their lives.

On Saturday 24 Sept 1994, I received a telephone call from Edna Sibbert. Edna's mother Grace was the lady responsible for getting the team together in 1917. She called to tell me that Margaret Thornborough had passed away that day and as had become the norm, I then telephoned all the others to let them know. The first person I spoke to was Joan Whalley and she somehow seemed to be expecting some bad news. This is what she told me.

'On Wednesday evening I had gone to bed at my normal time and went to sleep about 11.30pm. I always left my bedroom door slightly ajar because it blows a current of air around. Sometime between 2.00 and 3.00am I woke up and my eyes were drawn towards the door which was slowly starting to open. A figure dressed in rather dark colours came through the door and around the bottom of my bed. I must have swung my feet out of the bed because the figure came towards me. As I stood up it came round the bed and a voice said, "I've come to say goodbye". I put my arms around the figure and they put their arms around me. It didn't feel like a spirit form because it felt solid, like I was hugging a human being and we just stood there hugging one another. I thought it might have been an old friend of mine who was in her 80's. It was definitely a female but there was no face. The words came but there was no mouth for them to come from, the words were just there. As we stood there, I could feel the hug on my back, I felt the response. We both gave each other a big hug and then she turned and went back round the bed. I wasn't frightened, I just wanted to know who it was because someone had come to say goodbye before they left. They must have died because they'd come to say goodbye. She didn't walk, she just glided through the door and as she went out, the door closed to where it had been before. I know I wasn't asleep when it happened because I was sitting on the edge of the bed'.

I asked Joan if she thought it was Margaret Thornborough. She said, *'She's the only one it could have been because I didn't hear of anyone else who had died'.*

After our conversation I telephoned Edna again to see if she could shed any light on what had happened leading up to Margaret's death. She told me it was actually on Wednesday that Margaret had suffered a massive stroke before finally passing away on the Saturday. It was in the early hours of Thursday morning that Joan received her 'visit'. Could it really have been Margaret coming to say goodbye? Joan certainly believed it was.

When I first set out on this journey I felt compelled to record the history of this team. It was obvious that someone had to take on this task before it was lost forever and at first I was really scared because I didn't know where or how to start. I had written a few poems before but never attempted anything so daunting. But once I began trying to piece things together, everything seemed to fall into place. It really felt as though 'someone' was guiding me. It was a strange, yet comfortable feeling and I never felt I was alone in writing this book. 'Someone' was helping put this huge jigsaw together. I would no sooner find one piece, when the next would appear and uncannily fit into place. And as I watched the old newsreel footage from the early years of the team, I found that I could recognise the players and put names to their faces. They were no longer a forgotten celluloid image, they were real people brought back to life and I felt a connection with them, as though we were old friends. Alice Kell, Florrie Redford, Jessie Walmsley, Jennie Harris etc: I *knew* these women, but I felt particularly drawn to Lily Parr. I liked her. She made me smile, and I felt that if we *had* ever met, we would have been really good friends.

Out of the blue in December of 1994, I went to see a clairvoyant as a last minute stand in for a friend who was unable to keep her appointment. It was the month after the launch of the first edition of my book and the clairvoyant knew absolutely nothing about me or my involvement with the Dick, Kerr Ladies. She was an extremely gifted lady, who was incredibly accurate with so many of the things she told me. Here is a small extract of her reading.

"Can you take Lillian or Lily? Nice lady, who is she?" I told her I wasn't sure because I wanted *her* to tell *me* who it was. She went on: *"Very strong character this person, would you understand that? Was very strong and a survivor. I feel control with her, that maybe what she wanted she would have got. She would have gone any which way she could to achieve her goal. For some reason I'm picking up cancer links around her. It feels as if she passed with cancer: A very strong lady. She's possibly saying that she's linked in with you and you won't break the link. It feels like she's attached to you, but don't worry about it. She's really with you quite strongly. There's a really strong link around her with you. She seems to be talking again here: I've got uniforms again, like nursing conditions. She seems to be saying something about wearing a nurse's uniform. There is also this feeling*

there of almost that you felt her around you. Warmth, have you had that? I'm being shown pink roses. Roses are really symbolic of love so there is obviously love coming through from this lady to you from the spirit realm. I've no doubt that you would be friends were she here now and she does seem to be saying to me that she is your friend anyway. And there's this feeling of her being really direct, that she wouldn't have kept back what she wanted to say, she'd just tell you as it was."

None of my family members have ever been in the nursing profession and I can honestly say, with hand on heart, that I know of only one person called Lily who fits the above description, and I am overwhelmed and humbled with that conclusion.

I think fate played a hand in leading me to meet Brenda Eastwood that day back in 1991 and I cannot stress enough just how important it was. But for that meeting the opportunity to compile such a comprehensive account of the Dick, Kerr Ladies history would almost certainly have slipped by. And that would indeed have been a great loss for women's football. Brenda suffered a serious heart attack in January of 1993, but made a full recovery and wanted to fit as much into life as she possibly could while still in good health. In 1994 at 70 years of age, she was awarded a bursary at the University of Central Lancashire to study for a degree in Accountancy, Business Information Systems and Physiology. The Winifred Keen Bursary was only awarded once every two years to women over the age of 60 and Brenda was chosen from six other hopeful candidates. She said, *"I decided to do something with the rest of my life after I'd had the heart attack. Being selected to receive the bursary has been a great honour for me".*

In early 1996 I was approached by the marketing department of sportswear giant, Nike. They were proposing to produce an advertising campaign that hoped to inspire and encourage women to 'get out there' and play the sport they wanted to – rather than what society expected of them. They had previously enlisted some of sports biggest stars to advertise their trendy brand name, basketball's Michael Jordan, athlete Carl Lewis, Arsenal's Ian Wright and Manchester United's Eric Cantona had all been enlisted to promote the Nike brand. And at 74 years of age, Joan Whalley joined that elite band of sporting celebrities when she became the first British female soccer player to feature in a high profile national advertising campaign in eight glossy women's magazines including Cosmopolitan and Company. Joan said, *"I did like the idea behind the advert and I thought it would be good to get young people involved in sport, especially football, so I was prepared to do it. But they wanted me to go to London to do the photo session and I didn't want to travel all that way. So I told them: If you want me, come and get me!"*

Brenda Eastwood

And that's exactly what they did! Joan lived in a small apartment at the top of a rambling country house in Yealand Conyers with her eccentric landlady Mary who occupied the lower floors of the property, which resembled something out of a Catherine Cookson novel. A mobile studio arrived and they took all the pictures in Mary's downstairs living room. I provided them with enough information to replicate a Dick, Kerr shirt and loaned them Lily Parr's boots to add a more authentic flavour to the finished shot. Joan said, *"They moved all the furniture around and filled the room with boards so that everything was white. It took more than four hours."* A spokesperson for Nike said, *"By using older women, Nike intends to avoid the stereotypical images of models in leotards and empower women to overcome the obstacles they face to participate in their chosen sport."*

The caption on the advert reads: *Boots like lead, jeering crowds and an FA Ban couldn't stop Joan playing. What chance did defenders have? Nothing could keep Joan Whalley off the football pitch. Or stop her on it. Preston Ladies star right winger scored in virtually every game she played. And she played in plenty: Hardly missing a game in twenty years. Joan believes you need three things to succeed. Commitment: Commitment and Commitment. Achieve your goals. Just do it.*

Joan Whalley Nike Ad *(©Nike)*

Joan hated that photograph and said she looked like the creature from the black lagoon! She was quoted in the press as saying, "*I'm not vain, but I don't think the picture is very nice. I can't believe they took 80 photos and chose that one! Every time I see it, I think I look like Dame Edna Everage's side kick Madge!*"

Looking back at her own playing career she said, "*I do miss playing football but I watch it on television alone in my little room, and I'm glad I am on my own because every time the ball is in a beautiful position, I'm kicking out with my feet, its brilliant. I love watching it on television but since I finished playing I have never ever gone to watch a game at a football ground because I couldn't bear it. To see those players run out on to the field would break my heart. I would want to be out there with them. It's been with me all my life has this love of football. I've never known anybody love it like I did*". When asked how she felt about being placed in the same company as Eric Cantona she said, "*Oh its brilliant isn't it, just brilliant. Cantona is a wonderful footballer and I'm very proud. You know, I never expected when I played football all those years ago, I never thought that at*

253

the end of my life, all this publicity was going to come. I never expected it at all. I thought I would just live out my retirement nice and quietly and comfortably. But no way, they've brought me out with a bang I'll tell you. I'm going to go out in a blaze of glory. When they put me in my box, I'm going out in a blaze of glory, believe me!"

Joan received a modest fee of £500 for her services to Nike and was promised a complimentary pair of trainers. She bought herself a new pair of spectacles but got the most pleasure in sharing her new found wealth among her friends and the £500 didn't last very long. To her disappointment though, the trainers never arrived.

In September of 1996, Joan was diagnosed with cancer in her mouth. When the news broke, it didn't come as a great shock to me because I had known for some time that she wasn't very well. She had already confided in me that she knew there was *'something'* growing in her stomach. We had become very close friends and I would drive up to see her as often as I could and we would talk regularly on the phone and we shared lots of secrets together. She also told me that she had previously undergone some tests for a problem in her mouth and the doctors told her that they thought she had cancer. She was adamant that if they only *thought* she had cancer, and didn't *know* she had, then she would rather be left alone. She did show me the inside of her mouth and I was shocked at what I saw. Underneath her tongue there was a large gaping hole. I was gravely concerned and frightened for her, but Joan just wanted to do things her way. All I could do was respect her wishes, admire her courage and be there for her. But I had an inkling of what was in store for her and I was heartbroken. My own precious little Mum had also suffered a similar fate with oral cancer and the surgery she endured was quite horrific. Naturally I was terrified for Joan, but she was spared the surgeon's knife and admitted to the Christie Hospital in Manchester for a course of radiotherapy. But, Joan being Joan, she didn't want a fuss and she kept quiet about just how poorly she really was. She was quite a spiritual person and did have faith in God, who she referred to as 'Big G', and she placed all her trust in Him. She was incredibly brave and gave the battle her best shot. Her illness was reported in the *Lancashire Evening Post* and as a result they contacted Nike about the missing pair of trainers. Nike was very apologetic and promised that a pair would be despatched immediately. They did arrive shortly after but to Joan's disappointment, they were too small.

Sad news was soon with us again. Following a short illness early in 1997, Brenda Eastwood passed away at the Christie Hospital, Manchester on 23 February. She was 73 years old. Brenda loved life and she loved her football with a passion. At the Lancashire Trophy that summer, as a special tribute to a very special lady, we named a trophy after her: *The Brenda Eastwood Award for the Most Sporting Team.* She would have liked that.

The tournament this year also marked the 80th anniversary of the formation of the Dick, Kerr Ladies and to celebrate this landmark occasion we turned back the clock to see the team take to the field for the first time in over 40 years. Before the final of the competition we staged an exhibition 7-a-side football match. Former members of the team with ages ranging from 60 to an amazing 82 years of age, put on their kit and football boots to honour the memory of their magnificent team. Before the game we held a minutes silence in memory of former team mate and friend, Brenda Eastwood.

Remembering Brenda

The legs may have been considerably slower but they showed they still possessed the same deft touch and skill of years gone by and they were the conquerors of Freedom Glads, a truly wonderful bunch of women from London, as they won the game by 2-0. Admittedly on this occasion the opposition and the referee were very kind, but it isn't every day that one gets the opportunity to see so much history on a football field and it was a wonderful spectacle for all those present.

I had the honour of being a guest player for the Dick, Kerr Ladies. It was a great thrill for me to be part of their team that day and I scored the first goal. Yvonne Cooper (Hamer) scored the second and it was a real cracker. Slower they may have been but their competitive spirit was still there for all to see. And the Dick, Kerr phenomenon went marching on.

Dick, Kerr Ladies and me 1997

Back: Diane Gant, Barbara Widdows, June Gregson, Yvonne Hamer, Nancy Thomson

Front: Sheila Parker, Joan Burke, Edna Broughton, Gail Newsham

Dick, Kerr Ladies and Freedom Glads

The launch of the second edition of my book at Deepdale, in October of 1997 saw Joan Whalley re-united with her childhood pal Tom Finney for the first time in almost half a century. Both soccer legends managed to catch up and chat about old times and Tom said, *"It was a great thrill to see Joan again. I haven't seen her in well over 40 years"*. And despite her recent health problems Joan said, *"I am delighted and proud to be here and it was brilliant to see Tom after all these years. He has always been my idol."*

A reporter from Woman's Hour came to record the launch and they covered it in a broadcast on Radio 4. A short time later I was contacted by Rita Tushingham, the BAFTA and Golden Globe winning actress from Liverpool who made her screen debut in the award winning British film, A Taste of Honey. Rita's love of football began when she was a young girl. She would often borrow her brother's football boots so that she could join in and have a kick about with them. She is a keen football supporter and her knowledge of the game is very extensive. When she heard of the Dick, Kerr Ladies story she said it was just the kind of thing she had been looking for. She was eager to move to the other side of the camera and wanted to direct a movie herself. Rita's passion and enthusiasm for their story was wonderful and she took the idea to her friend, impresario Bill Kenwright. He also thought it was a marvellous story and agreed to develop and produce a movie based on the team. Despite attempts to have a screenplay written his other theatre projects, and Everton Football Club took priority and the project fell by the wayside.

Only three months after the book launch, Joan Whalley was taken seriously ill and admitted to hospital for a series of tests. Her niece Gloria told me she had a large blood clot in her stomach, it was preventing the circulation getting to her legs and she was finding it extremely difficult to walk. We knew that she was gravely ill and I arranged to visit her the next day. Gloria telephoned just as I arrived home and asked me not to go that evening as Joan was exhausted from undergoing so many tests. Her voice was full of emotion, the kind of gut wrenching helplessness when you know that someone you love is coming to the end of their time. She wanted to prepare me for what lay ahead. *"She's very poorly, Gail, there's nothing they can do for her."*

On Saturday 10 January 1998, I drove to the Lancaster Royal Infirmary to see Joan and I knew I was going to say goodbye to my special pal. I arrived just after 6.p.m., but I was too late; she had passed away probably just as I had walked through the hospital doors. While I was sat in the office with the doctor waiting for the sad news, she told me that Joan had been keeping them all entertained with stories from her days with the Dick, Kerr Ladies. Even right to the end of her life, she was still fiercely proud of her contribution to this great football team. I was allowed in to see her a short while later to pay my respects. We always had such a lot to talk about and this was the first time I was able to get a word in first! I tried to console myself with the thought that true friends don't want to say goodbye and maybe that's the reason she didn't hang on. But she knew I loved her and I know she loved me too, and I am just so very grateful to have been blessed with having her in my life.

Joan Whalley passed away peacefully but she did go out in a blaze of glory, just as she had predicted. Her death made headlines in all the local newspapers and BBC Radio Lancashire reported her passing in hourly bulletins throughout the day. It was a fitting tribute to 'Preston's other great winger', and Sir Tom Finney paid a personal tribute to his old school pal when he said, "*I'm very sad and sorry to hear that she has gone.*"

Her funeral took place the following week. Everyone met at the undertakers to follow the cortege up to the crematorium. I went to see Joan in the room of repose before she was taken on her final journey. She looked very peaceful with her specs on and a packet of *Park Drive* cigarettes in her hands, it brought a smile to all our faces. I knew that 'Big G' had been good to her. She had left this life the way she had always wanted to – no fuss – no long drawn out suffering – just mercifully and peacefully. During the drive to the crematorium the cortege was passing by the Garrison public house. By chance a mounted policeman was there and as a mark of respect he stopped and saluted the hearse. I doubt he knew what precious cargo was inside but it seemed a rather fitting tribute to Joan Whalley, a football legend. The chapel at the crematorium was packed and it was lovely to see so many people there for her. It could have been so different for this very special woman who had thought that the end of her days would have been spent in isolation. The Dick, Kerr Ladies were there in force and some present day women footballers were there too. Wendy Skerritt, from Preston Rangers said, "*I just had to come and pay my respects. If it hadn't been for people like Joan, we might never have had the chance to play.*" I know it was just how she would have wanted it and one little word would sum up exactly what she would have made of it all. BRILLIANT!

Following a blaze of publicity in early 1999 about the proposed film by Bill Kenwright, I was contacted by Winnie Bourque from the USA. Her mother, Alice Mills Lambert, was the young factory girl who migrated to the States after the team toured there in 1922. She was very interested in the story of her mother's team and helped piece together more of the jigsaw through her mom's life and enabled us to catch up with Alice's story. Alice was widowed after 57 years of happily married life. By the time of her husband's death in 1981, their marriage had produced six faithful daughters, twenty-two grandchildren, twenty-six great grandchildren and two great great grandchildren.

In December of 1992 Alice suffered a stroke from which she never recovered. She was admitted to hospital and later moved to the Life Care Centre in Attleboro, where she remained until her death in 1994. Her family regarded her as an adventurer and it was her spirit for adventure, her devotion to family and her work ethic that marked her life in this world. She was a much loved lady with a down-to-earth, tell it like it is kind of attitude and she loved her family dearly. She was faithful, loyal and honest and that honesty was very much appreciated by those she loved. Her loyalty to her husband Aime was an example of how parents who love their children must work together to set rules, have standards and give encouragement. All her children were made to follow rules and were nurtured by a mother who expected them to help people less fortunate than themselves. During her final weeks of life many of her grandchildren and great grandchildren went to visit her. They went to show their love, give comfort and finally in their own personal way, say goodbye. Although Alice was unable to speak or even acknowledge those who visited her bedside, they were convinced that as she was preparing to leave this life, she knew they were there and felt their love. And the memory of that young lass from Preston, with a sense of adventure and the Dick, Kerr Ladies pioneering spirit, will continue to live on – on both sides of the Atlantic.

The Lambert Family

Back row: Winnie, Terry, Frankie, Irene

Front row: Louise, J Aime, Alice, Rose

The new Millennium was approaching and it seemed the appropriate time to bring the curtain down on the Lancashire Trophy. My Mum's death in 1998 led to the postponement of the event for a couple of years but I wanted to take that very special tournament, and the Dick, Kerr Ladies, into the 21st century for one last big finale. I wasn't sure if it would be possible to get it off the ground again after such a long layoff but it was certainly worth a try.

All the teams who had previously taken part were invited to come back for a reunion and farewell party all rolled into one. The response from everyone was nothing less than overwhelming and two teams even got together especially to be there for the weekend. Margaret McGough and Liz Deighan put together a team of veterans, calling themselves Dick, Kerr's Kids.

Dick, Kerr's Kids

Back row: Chris Slater, Lori Savona ,Joyce Mcguiggan, Angela Gallimore, Sandra Moore, Yvonne Gagen, Fiona Head, Marita Louis, ?, Margie Parsons, Liz McDonald, Julie Simmons, Liz Deighan

Front row: Louise Ryde, Viv Cutbill, Cath Tunnicliffe, Tracy Wheeldon, Gill Harrop, Karen Pugh, Ann Harkins, Jill Thomas, Margaret McGough

Their pen picture from the programme sets the scene and reads: *'Formed specifically to take part in the Millennium Lancashire Trophy, this team of veterans could not ignore the opportunity to turn back the clock and attempt to emulate the feats of their youth. Many of the team can boast of taking part in the first ever Lancashire Trophy in 1986 and some are even past winners of the competition. They've dusted the cobwebs off the old football boots and despite the extra few pounds gained over the years, are out to prove a thing or two to their younger counterparts. Like the earlier pioneers of the sport, women's football is in their blood. They may be past their prime, but they certainly won't lie down, and will be up to the challenge of competing in this year's competition. The players may have said farewell to their playing careers but for one last time they will be pulling on the jerseys and lacing the old boots, to join in the celebrations that are unique to the Lancashire Trophy.*

Maria Harper put together a team made up of Premier League players and several England internationals. Looking back now on the names of all those who took part, brings a lump to my throat and a sense of pride for what we achieved.

The G Girls

Back row: Maria Harper, Sam Brown, Karen Walker, Michelle Berry, Leanne Duffy, Louise Draper, Samantha Howarth, Sue Murphy, Claire Utley

Front row: Gayle Formston, Becky Easton, Paula Oldham, Karen Burke, Caroline Black, Gail Borman, Shireen Kempster

21st Century Girls

Back row: Rita Tushingham, Yvonne Hamer, June Gregson, Barbara Widdows, Sheila Parker, Cath O'Sullivan

Front row: Nancy Thomson, Lynn Arstall, Edna Broughton, Joan Burke, Gail Newsham

The new millennium also meant that we had all become pioneers from the last century and what better way to celebrate that milestone than with the most famous pioneers of them all? The proceedings would not have been complete without an appearance from the world famous Dick, Kerr Ladies and they did not disappoint.

We staged an exhibition match before the final but needed to recruit some 'younger legs' to the line up and Rita Tushingham showed what a good sport she was by also being a guest player. The most appropriate opposition on this occasion were the Dick, Kerr's Kids and what a spectacle it was. The BBC came along to record the game as the Dick, Kerr Ladies XI won their first, and last ever match in the 21st century. At 84 years of age, Nancy Thomson was the oldest player on the field.

Mia Carla sings

Edna Broughton, Frances Appleby, ? Yvonne Cooper, Barbara Widdows,
Pat Peterson, Nancy Thomson, June Gregson

The weekend ended in true Lancashire Trophy tradition when everyone joined in and sang the final and most appropriate football song. "*You'll never walk alone*".

It had been said for a number of years that women's football was the fastest growing sport in the country and in 2000 the FA announced that they were proposing to set up a women's professional league within the next three years. However, the lost revenue resulting from the collapse of B Sky B was the reason given for its cancellation. It would be more than a decade before a semi professional summer league, the FAWSL, would be introduced. Not quite what was promised and there is still a long way to go but great strides have been made. However, the journey for women's football is still far from complete.

The National Football Museum opened its doors in 2001 and was located within the Deepdale stadium, home of Preston North End. In 2002, they hosted an inaugural Hall of Fame event to celebrate the achievements of individuals who had not previously been afforded the recognition they deserved. Chairman of the Museum, Brian Booth, said, *"In these days of football megastars it is important that the great names of the past are not forgotten and to this end we have created the National Football Museum Hall of Fame."*

The list of inductees for the first event was indeed very impressive and included many legendary names. George Best, Sir Bobby Charlton, Sir Tom Finney, Kevin Keegan, Gordon Banks, Dennis Law, Peter Shilton, Eric Cantona, Bryan Robson, Sir Stanley Matthews, were among those chosen, and the first woman to be inducted into the Hall of Fame was Lily Parr, outside left for Dick, Kerr Ladies from 1920–1951, scorer of around a 1000 goals during her career and probably one of the greatest women footballers of all time! It was a wonderful posthumous tribute to a truly remarkable woman and I felt a deep sense of pride in having played my part in her receiving this long overdue recognition.

Words could never express how thrilled I was to be invited along to receive the award on behalf of Lily Parr and her former team mate June Gregson came with me to represent the club. It was a huge honour to be part of such a prestigious occasion and to meet so many of my heroes was a dream come true. We were sat at the same table as the great Nat Lofthouse and John Charles. Our eyes were all over the place looking out for which famous face we could spot next and we tried to curb our instincts to rush around asking for autographs. Our instincts were vindicated though when Kenny Dalglish and Bryan Robson came over to our table to ask Nat Lofthouse and John Charles for *their* autographs, so we then set off with pen in hand to capture as many as we could!

It wasn't until we were making our way to the main function room for dinner that the museum curator asked me if I would say a few words and actually present Lily Parr's award during the induction ceremony, and not receive it as he had previously said. Gobsmacked was my immediate reaction, quickly followed by terror gripping me by the throat! I hadn't prepared anything but what else could I do? Ray Stubbs was the resident compare and he introduced some archive footage of football's greatest and most exciting moments, showing exactly why these inaugural inductees had been chosen to enter the Hall of Fame. There is something rather special and unique about reliving great sporting moments. For me it brings back all the emotion felt at the time and no matter how often I see those replays, they still bring a lump to my throat. Having sat through some of George Best's finest moments, Gordon Banks making that wonderful save from Pele, Bobby Moore lifting the World Cup, Sir Stanley Matthews and Sir Tom Finney tearing defences to shreds, Sir Matt Busby and Sir Alex Ferguson lifting the European Cup, Kenny Dalglish, Denis Law, Kevin Keegan, Bryan Robson, Dixie Dean, Paul Gascoigne, Peter Doherty, Jimmy Greaves, Duncan Edwards, Johnny Haynes, Nat Lofthouse, John Charles, Billy Wright, Peter Shilton, and Dave Mackay all carving out their own place in history, along with some of the managers who helped them

Lily Parr

achieve immortality, Brian Clough, Bob Paisley, Bill Shankley and Sir Alf Ramsay. After all of that, I had to get up and tell everyone about Lily Parr. Gulp!

Gail Newsham raising a glass to Lily Parr

As I walked up to the podium and faced the audience, Sir Bobby Charlton and Sir Alex Ferguson were sat just to my left. I could see Kenny Dalglish, Denis Law and Bryan Robson in front of me and I knew that the rest of footballs finest were also in that room. I can't fully recall everything I said but I do remember saying that I could hardly believe I was actually breathing the same air as all of them! I gave a potted history of the Dick, Kerr Ladies, mentioned the 53,000 at Goodison, how few games they had lost in 48 years, told them about Lily Parr and what a great player she was, and do you know what, I could hear the silence because *they were all listening.* I heard people gasp when I told them just how many goals she had scored. It was a wonderful experience sharing that very moment when Lily Parr officially became a legend and finally received the recognition she deserved. Now the young lass from St Helens with an exceptional football talent will be remembered forever. My heart was full!

Following the success of the Hall of Fame, I approached the museum with an idea for raising awareness of the outstanding contributions that women have made, and continue to make, to our national game of football and suggested that International Women's Day, 8th March 2003 might be an ideal date for such an occasion. International Women's Day is recognised by the United Nations and celebrated the world over. Quite simply, it's the story of ordinary women as makers of history, yet embedded within the age old struggle for women to be treated as equals in society alongside that of our male counterparts. The equality battles, particularly within football still resound today and progress has been very slow. From the Premiership through every other division of the Football League, there are women executives at many football clubs who administer the sport at very high levels. Yet even here in the 21st century they too are still not given the recognition they deserve. Only by raising awareness can we hope to move forward to some kind of level playing field for all.

The Dick, Kerr Ladies *are* the history of women's football. They are the very foundation of our game and their contribution is immeasurable. But surprisingly, their glittering history has largely been buried and forgotten. Thankfully the National Football Museum recognised the need to raise awareness of this injustice and agreed to promote and host the event on International Women's Day. I loaned them a number of medals and other items along with Lily Parr's football boots to enable the first Dick, Kerr Ladies exhibition to be officially opened on the night. The event was extremely well supported and distinguished guests who attended the celebration dinner were: Rita Tushingham, Lorraine Rogers, Chairman of Tranmere Rovers, Barbara Herbert and Jean Gough, the daughters of Sir Tom Finney and Sir Stanley Matthews respectively, some members of the FA also attended along with many representatives from women's football, and of course the Dick, Kerr Ladies were there in force as were family members of some of the original pioneers from before the FA ban. But what made the occasion even more special was the arrival of all six daughters of Alice Mills Lambert. Irene, Louise, Winnie, Terry, Frankie and Rose, made their own pilgrimage across the Atlantic to visit Preston for the very first time to honour the memory of their Mom and check out their roots.

I had been in regular contact with Winnie Bourque, Alice's middle daughter, since our first telephone conversation back in 1999 and we had become firm friends. When I told her of the proposed plans for 8th March, she was keen to support the event and even made a donation to help with the finances. When Winnie first told me she wanted to come to England for

International Women's Day she said that two of her sisters would be making the trip with her. I was thrilled and could hardly sleep with excitement. But a few days later she called with even more fantastic news. All six of them were going to make the trip! My mouth fell open and my exact words were: *"Bloody hell Winnie, that's amazing!"*

The guests had an exclusive tour of the museum for the opening of the first ever official Dick, Kerr Ladies exhibition. At long last, these very ordinary working class girls from Preston had been given centre stage amongst the good and the great in a National Football Museum. It was the icing on the cake in the long struggle for recognition and hopefully the final leg of the journey in trying to achieve that aim. At the conclusion of the tour we all sat down to enjoy a superb dinner and afterwards I gave a talk on the history of the team. There was a wonderful atmosphere and everyone was full of appreciation for the remarkable achievements of this unique women's football team. But it was Alice's daughters, who had travelled so far to be with us, who really stole the show!

The Lambert Girls!
Irene, Louise, Rose, Frankie, Terry, Winnie

On 13 July 2004, we were saddened to learn of the sudden death of Kath Latham who had passed away after suffering a massive heart attack. She was

77 years old. Although Kath declined all invitations to the Dick, Kerr Ladies reunion and gatherings, her own place in the history of the team is still assured.

In June of 2005, football finally did come home. The UEFA European Women's Football Championships were staged in the North West of England. National teams from Denmark, England, Finland, France, Germany, Italy, Norway and Sweden battled it out to become The Champions of Europe, playing games at Preston, Blackpool, Blackburn, Manchester and Warrington. England's opening match of the tournament was played against Finland at the City of Manchester Stadium and attracted a crowd of over 30,000 spectators. And when I went to Blackburn to see England take on Sweden in front of a crowd of over 25,000 it brought a big lump to my throat and gave me an insight into what it must have been like for the Dick, Kerr Ladies playing in front of crowds like that week in, week out. It was wonderful to see so many people out there enjoying women's football again.

MISS LATHAM

Kath Latham

The semi-final between Germany and Finland was staged at Deepdale. The FA invited the Dick, Kerr Ladies to be their guests at the match. They were entertained to a pre match reception and buffet, just like in the good old days and people were still clamouring for their photographs and asking them to sign autographs. At half time, they were introduced to the crowd and they stood and waved in acknowledgement of the cheers and applause. Their popularity was still very much in evidence as many onlookers gathered round to talk to them once they realised just who they were. A German journalist put it very eloquently when he said, *"We do not have this kind of history in our country".* Germany may have been able to boast the best player in the world at that time in Birgit Prinz, but no other country in the world could ever boast of the illustrious history attributed to the Dick, Kerr Ladies.

As the region celebrated having the cream of Europe on its doorstep and England's finest also on display, this famous old team from Preston could still attract a great deal of attention. I couldn't help but wonder what Lily Parr, Florrie Redford, Alice Kell and the rest of the team would have made of it all. I sat in the Sir Tom Finney stand trying to imagine that very first game back in 1917, or being part of the 25,000 crowd who watched them play the first women's international against France, or that magnificent spectacle of the first game under artificial light, all played here at this famous stadium. Looking across the pitch to that very same player's tunnel where they had run out on so many occasions, I half expected to see them in the stands, smiling down on what was unfolding before us. And do you know what? I bet they probably were and still wishing that they could be out there again showing off their skills once more. Those very ordinary factory girls from Preston who carved their own unique place in history the like of which we will never see again. If only women's football had been allowed to prosper and grow.

CHAPTER 14

LOOSE ENDS AND GOODBYE'S

On 22 May 2007 we had to say a sad goodbye to Joan Burke. Affectionately known as 'Tich' she was an ever present personality at the many functions we attended since starting out on this journey back in 1992. Tich began feeling ill in November 2006 and was eventually diagnosed with stomach cancer. The following weeks saw her going back and forth for tests and we were all waiting with dread to hear what the outcome would be. She was admitted to hospital to undergo some minor exploratory surgery to try to ascertain exactly what could be done to prolong her life. However, events took a dramatic turn for the worse when complications arose from a previous operation to improve the circulation to her legs. A blockage had occurred and her left leg had been deprived of blood for over 24 hours. It was a life or death situation and the only course of action was to amputate the leg. Everyone was completely devastated but Tich was incredibly stoical and showed immense courage and dignity, and simply said, "*Well, it's happened so we'll just have to get on with it.*" One of the nurses said, "*They don't make 'em like this anymore,*" and by 'eck they certainly don't. Her courage was amazing.

True to form, the Dick, Kerr Ladies rallied round and came to give Tich their support, show their love, share some memories, have some laughs, and in their own personal way, say their goodbye's. We had twelve precious days left with her but she was very weak and hallucinating from the pain killing morphine drug she had been prescribed. She kept trying to tell us what she could 'see' and I asked her if she was afraid. She said she wasn't and still retained her sense of humour when I jokingly asked if she had *seen* Lily Parr: She shook her head and smiled when I said, "*Well if Lily does walk in, you know you're in trouble!*"

She sent for me the night before she died and I was with her just hours before she left us. Her mind was still very alert but she was so weak she could barely speak. I managed to hear her say, "*I'm gone, I'm all done.*" We both knew this was the end. I sat with her for several hours just holding her hand, trying to give some comfort and help her not be afraid. I told her how proud I was of her and that I loved her. She nodded her love for me too. Her life with the Dick, Kerr Ladies was very important to her, and I knew she was immensely proud of the part she had played in the team's history. I made her a last promise and whispered, "*I promise you Tich, I will make sure that people don't forget you".* She nodded again; she knew I would keep my word. Tich passed away just a few hours later. Everyone rallied for her funeral and I'm sure she would have been delighted with her send off. The Dick, Kerr Ladies paid their final tribute at her graveside as they sang the team song.

Hurrah huroo, hurrah we're here again
Hurrah huroo hurrah we're here again.
We don't care who we're meeting
The Preston team will take a lot of beating.
We're here to cheer the Lassies from Lancashire
To fight with might and mane
Ours is a good team ours is
Hurrah, hurrah, hurrah, we're here again.

Joan Burke and Rachel Brown (©Lancashire Evening Post)

On a much happier note, the 15th November 2007 saw Joan Whalley become only the second Dick, Kerr Ladies player to be posthumously inducted into the National Football Museum Hall of Fame. The other inductees included: Karen Walker, Alan Ball, Nobby Stiles, Peter Beardsley, Graeme Souness, Glen Hoddle, Dennis Bergkamp, Mark Hughes and Terry Venables. A glittering night in the Manchester suite at Old Trafford saw Sir Tom Finney present the award to Joan's niece Gloria Butcher. As her childhood pal Sir

Tom handed the award to Gloria, I felt sure that Joan would have been smiling down on the proceedings feeling extremely chuffed with the whole occasion. I could almost hear her say: That was BRILLIANT!

Gloria Butcher and Sir Tom Finney (© P Holme)

In July of 2008, I flew to Boston, Massachusetts as a guest of Winnie Bourque, one of the daughters of Alice Mills. I was given the trip of a lifetime by the whole family as they showed me their homeland, the house where they grew up and the good life that Alice Mills and J Aime Lambert had worked hard to provide for them. I genuinely feel as though I have another family on the other side of the pond, such is the special bond between us. Alice Mills was christened at the same church as me and we have walked the same streets. As a child attending junior school I would pass the house where she was born every day.

Joan Whalley

Winnie took me to her Mom's grave which was a very emotional visit for me as I was finally connecting with a football legend that played for the Dick, Kerr Ladies during what was probably their most successful period. It was a privilege to travel to the other side of the world to see where she had lived, worked and brought up her wonderful family, who are among the nicest and most decent people you could ever meet. Alice Mills did a damn good job. Words are inadequate to express how deeply moving it was. The house in Preston where she was born still remains and that means I still have a small piece of Alice Mills here with me.

The final resting place for Alice Mills Lambert

Sadly, it wasn't long before we were attending yet another funeral. Jean Lane passed away suddenly in March of 2009. Jean began playing for the team in 1950 and was leading goal scorer for five consecutive seasons. Her funeral took place in her home town of Hindley, near Wigan. It was a very sad occasion for everyone but a wonderful celebration of her life. Jean's three loves in life were her Faith, her family and her football. She had been a lay preacher at her local church since her youth and had many friends from all walks of life. The church was literally packed to the rafters with so many people wanting to pay their respects and say a final goodbye to a very dear friend. Her nephew shared a wonderful Eulogy and told an amusing tale from his wedding day. At the reception some of the guests were out in the grounds having a game of football. Of course, Auntie Jean couldn't resist joining in to show off her old skills. Even though she was now a respectable pensioner, Jean was running them ragged. His best man went over to him and said, *"I'm not playing with her anymore, she's too rough!!"* In paying tribute to his 'Auntie Jean', he very aptly chose to recall Jean's favourite song from her days with the Dick, Kerr Ladies:

How can I leave you though I know it's time to go?
How can I leave you when I love you so?
Eventide is falling, I must be on my way,
All the world is calling, but my heart says stay.
Faithful forever, my love will be a star,
Shining forever, everywhere you are.

Jean Lane was laid to rest in a beautiful spot beneath a large tree in a quiet corner of the church grounds. The Dick, Kerr Ladies were once again 'on parade' to sing the club song in tribute to their old team mate at her graveside. It was a moving and poignant moment for Jean's family as their voices echoed around the grave yard. The sun was shining, the birds were singing and you couldn't help but feel that Jean Lane had 'gone home'. This very gentle and much loved lady will be sadly missed but I am sure she will rest in peace.

Jean Lane

We next had to bid farewell to Nancy Thomson who sadly passed away on 22nd December 2010. She was 94 years old. I was unable to locate Nancy in time for the reunion in 1992 and a close friend of hers told me she wouldn't have been interested anyway. All I had was an old four digit telephone number for Salisbury in Wiltshire and it wasn't easy to find her but I'm so glad I didn't give up. She was delighted at having the opportunity of catching up with her old team mates again and was present at the book launch in 1994 when she said, *'Gail, you really have made us immortal'.* She said she owed her success in football to her brother Joe. He encouraged her to play the game and it's thanks to him that she went for a trial for Edinburgh City Girls and never looked back. He bought her first pair of football boots and made her stand in the bath for an hour so that the leather would mould to the shape of her feet. Speaking to the press in 2001 Nancy said her only regret was that Joe didn't live to see her at the height of her success. *"He died in a car crash in the 1940's,"* she said. *"His wallet was full of newspaper cuttings about me. If it wasn't for him none of this would ever have happened and I am so grateful."*

Nancy Thomson

More sad news followed with the passing of Edna Sibbert, daughter of Grace, the force behind the ladies first football match with the lads at the factory back in 1917. Edna was the last tangible link to the origins of the Dick, Kerr Ladies and we now have nothing but history to take us back to those days. Edna was always proud of the fact that she was born in the old Workhouse on Watling Street Road, Preston. As an

Edna Sibbert 2008
International Women's Day

illegitimate child, she was given up for adoption after her birth in 1923. Grace and Jimmy had been unable to have their own children and gave Edna the chance of a new life with them. Edna also worked as a nurse at Whittingham Hospital and was a keen supporter of the Dick, Kerr Ladies during her time there. She lived a long, happy and prosperous life and was a much loved lady by all who knew her. She died on 4th February 2011. She was 87 years old.

The football world and the city of Preston, was deeply saddened with the loss of its most famous son, Sir Tom Finney who passed away on 14 February 2014. Although regarded as one of the greatest players of all time, Sir Tom was always a man of the people. He was a true gentleman and was much loved and respected by everyone who met him. It was a great honour when he agreed to write the foreword for this book and also when he attended one of my talks about the Dick, Kerr Ladies. A memory I will always treasure.

Gail Newsham and Sir Tom Finney

CHAPTER 15

LONDON 2012 - TEAM GB

Women's football was first introduced at the Olympics in 1996 but politics had always prevented a United Kingdom team from competing on this world stage. Great Britain is made up of four separate nations, Scotland, England, Wales and Northern Ireland and each nation has a separate international team within the governing body of FIFA. The Scottish, Welsh and Northern Ireland FA's had always opposed any move to enter a unified team in case their status within FIFA was called into question. When London was selected as the host city for the 2012 Olympic Games there was pressure from the English FA, the British Olympic Committee and the then Prime Minister, Gordon Brown for the UK to enter both men's and women's teams. The PM had added his weight to the argument saying he felt the British public would find it strange if there was no British team at the Games.

Thankfully all politics were put aside and the nation waited with huge anticipation as Great Britain finally entered a women's football team into the Olympic Games. Team coach Hope Powell chose an 18 strong squad of 16 English and two Scottish players. The history making Olympians were: Karen Bardsley, Rachel Brown, Sophie Bradley, Ifeoma Dieke (Scotland), Claire Rafferty, Alex Scott, Casey Stoney, Anita Asante, Steph Houghton, Kim Little (Scotland), Jill Scott, Fara Williams, Eniola Aluko, Karen Carney, Kelly Smith, Ellen White, Rachel Williams and Rachel Yankey. Reserve players were Emma Higgins, Dunia Susi, Jessica Clarke and Jane Ross (Scotland).

Team GB opened London 2012 at the Millennium Stadium in Cardiff on 25 July when they took on New Zealand in front of a crowd of 24,445. The media were initially quite negative regarding the number of spectators at the ground reporting the stadium as being half empty. However many felt the stadium was in fact half full and Team GB got their campaign underway with a 1-0 win thanks to a fabulous goal from Steph Houghton.

The next match in their group was against Cameroon on 28 July again played at the Millennium Stadium. 31,141 spectators saw a 3-0 victory for Team GB with goals from Casey Stoney (Capt) Jill Scott and Steph Houghton grabbing her second goal of the tournament. What followed next was beyond anything we could have possibly hoped for as Wembley Stadium welcomed Team GB v Brazil with five times FIFA World Player of the Year, Marta on their team.

Only if you have ever played women's football and experienced all the struggles that went hand in hand with it, could you understand exactly how important this was. After the injustice of a fifty year ban by the FA, it had long been my dream for women's football to have an equal playing field and it's hard to put into words exactly how much pride and satisfaction I felt watching Team GB playing at the Olympic Games. I never thought that in my lifetime I would see women's football on such a big stage. In the early days of my own career I remember us getting changed in a ramshackle chicken hut with only a rusty old oil drum as a toilet. We had little or no support from the FA and administered all our own affairs but now I was watching a women's football match at our packed national stadium in front of a worldwide television audience. Kelly Smith sang our national anthem with such pride. Her emotion was almost tangible.

An incredible crowd of 70,584 came to this magnificent arena to bear witness to an unbelievable performance as Team GB pulled off a dream 1-0 victory against a very good Brazilian side. Another wonder strike from goalden girl Steph Houghton guaranteed a place in the quarter finals and their place in history was assured. Women's football finally hit the headlines on the front and back pages of every newspaper across the land as Olympic fever gripped the nation and our women's game finally had a global stage.

Team GB v Canada at Coventry 2012

Trying to get tickets for the quarter final match against Canada at Coventry was a nightmare. Twitter came to the rescue when BBC presenter Jacqui Oatley offered to help. She didn't know me from Adam but stood waiting in the rain for 90 minutes to get me a pair of tickets. God Bless her! I was very grateful.

Kelly Smith talking to Christine Sinclair of Canada

The result in Coventry was disappointing. A 2-0 defeat brought to an end an incredible few weeks for our new Olympians. But actually being there to witness a full stadium for women's football brought tears to my eyes. I thought of the Dick, Kerr Ladies who played in front of crowds like that every week and how thrilling it must have been for them. What an honour it was for women's football to kick-off The Olympic Games and I feel sure that magnificent performance at Wembley would have made the Dick, Kerr Ladies very proud.

We can but hope that with the Olympic dust now settled, women's football will continue to progress to a higher level and a Team GB in Rio will become a reality. Only when you have a sense of its glittering history can you realise just how much the women's game has lost after the events of 1921. After all we've been through, the derogatory comments, the jibes and the sneers, maybe now it really is our time to shine. The Dick, Kerr Ladies did not play on in vain after the FA Ban and London 2012 is a testament to that. They didn't just inspire a generation, they continue to inspire Every Generation!

Inspiration

DICK, KERR LADIES FOOTBALL CLUB 1917–1965

LYDIA ACKERS, FRANCES APPLEBY (FOULKES), SHEILA APPLEBY, ELSIE ARNOLD, M ASCROFT, LIZZY ASHCROFT

AUDREY BAGOT, CAROL BARBER, E BARKER, JOAN BARKER, MARION BARKER, DOROTHY BARNETT, KATH BARRINGTON, PAMELA BARRINGTON, KATH BARTLEY, JOAN BILLINGTON, E BIRKINS, LELIA BOARDMAN, MISS BOOTH, MISS BRADLEY, MISS BREAKLEY, JOAN BRIGGS (HALL) STELLA BRIGGS, E BROMAGE, EDNA BROUGHTON, JOAN BURKE, JEAN BUTCHER, D BUTTERFIELD, LILY BUXTON

LESLEY CALDWELL, JOAN CARRUTHERS, DORIS CARTER, MARY CARTER, PAT CATTERALL, SUE CHORLEY, SHEILA CLAGUE, ELSIE CLARKE, JOAN CLAY, DAISY CLAYTON, E CLAYTON, EDNA CLAYTON, GLENYS COCKER, FLORENCE COLES, VIOLET COULTON, AUDREY COUPE, DAPHNE COUPE, EDITH COX, MISS CRAWSHAW, ANNIE CROZIER, BESSIE CUNLIFFE

BETTY DAGGAR, BARBARA DANDY, LOUIE DAVIES, JEAN DENT, M DENT, ANNIE DERBYSHIRE, JACKY DEVAUX, MAY DICKENSON, JESSIE DICKINSON, CISSY DIXON, MARGARET DOLDERSON, MISS DONOGHUE, ELEANOR DOYLE, AMY DUXBURY, E DUXBURY

DOROTHY EASTWOOD, JOAN ECKTON, PAT ELLIS, MARGARET EMPGRAVE, DOREEN ESPLEY

JOAN FAIRCLOUGH, S FAIRCLOUGH, K FINNESTY, MARJORIE FOULKES, J FRANKLAND

DIANE GANT, EVA GARDNER, R.J. GARRIER, FREDA GARTH, DOREEN GIBBON, JEAN GIBSON, BARBARA GILBERT, MARGERY GILES, E GLOVER, MAVIS GLOVER, D GOLLIN, JEAN GOLLIN, MARY GOODINSON, MAY GRAHAM, JUNE GREGSON, PAM GREGSON, A GRICE, EMMA GRICE, MARGARET GROOM

YVONNE HAMER (COOPER), MARJORIE HANLEY, ALICE HARGREAVES, JENNIE HARRIS, LILY HARRIS, FLORRIE, HASLAM, ANNIE HASTIE, JEAN HAYES, MURIEL HEANEY, MAY HELME, CONNIE HILL, I HINDLEY, R HILTON, V HILTON, ANNE HODGKINSON, MISS HODGKINSON, DOROTHY HODSON, S HOLT, ALMA HOPKINS, C HOWARTH, LUCY HOYLE, MAY HOYLE, NELLIE HOYLE, ROSETTE HUARD, SALLY HULME, EDITH HUTTON, MISS HYTON

EVA JESSOP, EMILY JONES, LILY JONES

M KAY, BRENDA KEEN, ALICE KELL, SALLY KENDAL, STELLA KENDALL, K KENYON, MAY KNOWLES

JENNY LANCASTER, JEAN LANE, BARBARA LARGE, E LATHAM, KATH LATHAM, KATH LEAR, LILY LEE, ANN LORD, KATHLEEN LUKE, GLADYS LUNN, IRENE LYDIATE, ANN LYMATH, ANNIE LYNCH, G LYONS, MINNIE LYONS

MISS McAVOY, BRIDGET McCAULEY, ANN McGRATH, LORRAINE McKENNA, MISS McLEAN, MISS MARSDEN, ANNIE MARSLAND, ANNIE MARSH, F MARTIN, LILY MARTIN, PEGGY MASON, PEGGY MELLING, MARGARET MILLER, PAT MILLER, ALICE MILLS, NELLIE MITCHELL, JEAN MOIZER, M MORAN, DORIS MORLEY, HANNAH MORLEY

HILDA NETTLE, ALICE NEWSHAM, MAY NEWTON, BRENDA NICHOLSON, DOREEN NIELD, E NIXON, ALICE NORRIS, DOREEN NORRIS

Mlle OURY, SUE OWEN

SHEILA PARKER (PORTER), A PARKINSON, F PARKINSON, HILDA PARKINSON, JEAN PARNELL, LILY PARR, MISS PARTINGTON, L PARTON, MARGARET PENBERTHY, MISS PERKINS, IRENE PHILLIPS, M PICKERING, MARGARET PICKAVANT, SHEILA PINDER, JOAN POMFRET, CARMEN POMIES, MARJORIE POTTER, MISS POTTINSON, E PRAGNELL, PAT PREECE, BARBARA PRESCOTT

FLORENCE RANCE, MISS RAWSTHORNE, FLORRIE REDFORD, DOREEN RICHARDS, MISS RICHARDS, E RIEGNALL, PAULINE RIMMER, SUSAN ROBINSON, GLENYS ROSTRON, JEAN ROWLANDS

DOROTHY SAYCELL, POLLY SCOTT, MARGARET SCRATCHLEY, MINNIE SEED, C SHARPE, BETTY SHARPLES, PEGGY SHARPLES, H SHAW, MAGGIE SHAW, A SHIPPERBOTTOM, GRACE SIBBERT, CATHERINE SINGLETON, JOAN SPAVIN, ALICE STANDING, LILY STANLEY, MISS STRETTON, IRENE SWIFT

JOAN TENCH, M THOMAS, MARGARET THORNBOROUGH, NANCY THOMSON, ELSIE TIERNEY, B TRAYNOR

MISS VARLEY

DOROTHY WAINWRIGHT, MOLLY WALKER, ALICE WALMSLEY, JESSIE WALMSLEY, VAL WALSH, MISS WARING, ANNE WEBB, DOROTHY WHALLEY, JOAN WHALLEY, SHEILA WHITEOAK, ELIZABETH WHITTLE, G WHITTLE, BARBARA WIDDOWS, JOAN WILKINSON, PAT WILKINSON, ROSE WILSON, ALICE WOODS, RITA WOODS, EDITH WORRALL, LOTTIE WORRALL, MARY WORSWICK

ELSIE YATES, NELLIE YATES

Lightning Source UK Ltd.
Milton Keynes UK
UKOW05f1121011114

240955UK00001B/26/P